Boardsailing Made Easy

CHIP WINANS
with
MIMI GREENWOOD
& JOHN FURLOW

TEACHING and TECHNIQUES

First published in U.S.A. in 1984 by
Chip Winans Productions
21 Quason Lane
Harwichport, Mass. 02646

ISBN 0-9613234-0-X

ACKNOWLEDGEMENTS

Special thanks go to the many individuals whose ideas, advice and assistance helped bring this book to its successful completion

In particular, thanks to the following (in alphabetical order):

Steve Callaway
David Calvert
Karen Calvert
Tim Calvert
Henry Goodwin
Vicky Greenwood
Greg Hartley
Dave Hilmer
Dave Hopkins
Debbie Kimball
Dick Lepman
Julie Mann
Rob Nagy
Sandy Narcisso
Alan Nevins
James Nolan
Nicole Nolan
Clay Shackleton
Steve Weiss
Betsy Winans
Rob Winans

PHOTO CREDITS

Special thanks to the following photographers whose "how-to" photographs were invaluable in illustrating the techniques shown in this book.

(in alphabetical order)

Tim Calvert
Jim Farraher
Tom King
Wil Mead
Dr. Joseph Spiecker
Chip Winans

Layout, Design and Illustrations by Chip Winans

Additional Acknowledgements

Special thanks to the following companies whose products and services helped bring this project to its successful completion. (in alphabetical order):

Aitken Industries
P.O. Box 3134
Gardena, Ca., 90247
(Aitken short boards)

American Boardsailing Company
One Shore Rd.
Babylon, N.Y., 11702
(Spartan dry and wet suits)

Aqua Meter Instrument Corp.
465 Eagle Rock Ave.
Roseland, N.J., 07068
(Track-n-Tack)

Caston Products Inc.
234 Chapel St.
Lincoln, R.I., 02865
(Sailrider sailboards)

Catchit Inc.
11577 Slater Ave.
Fountain Valley, Ca., 92708
(Catchit sport and swimwear)

Fitness 1st
2234 South Pacific Ave.
San Pedro, Ca., 90731
(Wondergym)

Freedom Sails
P.O. Box 1082
Islamorada, Fla., 33036
(Freedom sails)

G.S. Sports Inc.
223 Interstate Rd.
Addison, Ill., 60101
(Wayler sailboards)

HiFly America Sports Inc.
Robin Hill Corporate Park
Rt. 22, Patterson, N.Y., 12563
(HiFly Sailboards)

Holiday Isles Resort
Islamorada, Fla., 33036

Dave Hopkins
Wayler Windsurfing School
Islamorada, Fla., 33036

O'Neill Inc.
1071 41st Ave.
Santa Cruz, Ca., 95062
(O'Neill wetsuits)

Neil Pryde Limited
P.O. Box 89379
Kowloon City, Hong Kong
(Neil Pryde sails)

Mimi Greenwood
John Furlow
Dr. Joseph Spiecker
West Chester University
Health and Physical Education Center
West Chester, Pa., 19383

Chip Winans Productions
21 Quason Lane
Harwichport, Mass. 02646

CONTENTS

CHAPTER I

PREFACE

Boardsailing is fast becoming the most popular water sport in both recreational and competitive areas in the United States today and is the latest addition to the Olympic Games. From the novice boardsailor to the international champions, the sport lends itself to excitement, enjoyment and many challenges.

Learning how to boardsail can be fun, and when the proper equipment and sailing techniques are used it is easy. Boardsailing is the purest most physical form of sailing to be found. It is a sport that allows those who have never sailed before to experience the exhilaration of moving over the water powered only by the wind.

The sport itself is an extremely safe one since the board itself is like a raft capable of supporting up to 400 pounds - a most seaworthy craft. A "free sail system" is attached to the board with a universal joint so that the minute the sailor falls and lets go of the sail system it falls down and acts as a sea anchor. If the sailor were to fall off he would have to swim less than 50 feet to recover the board and climb back onto it. A sailboard is light, easily transported and free of licenses, docking fees and expensive trailers. It can also be practiced wherever there is wind and water, be it an ocean, lake, river, puddle or pond.

ABOUT THE AUTHORS

Charles A. 'Chip' Winans, Mimi Greenwood and John Furlow have co-authored the most complete book on the sport of boardsailing that may be used as a self-teaching and informational aid for beginners, or as a textbook for boardsailing schools, camps, colleges, high schools and recreational facilities. It is called "BOARDSAILING MADE EASY".

Chip Winans is a world champion in the sport of boardsailing. He has registered more than a dozen titles in competition around the world, including several firsts in Freestyle, Racing, Slalom and Tandem Freestyle events. His feature articles and action photographs appear regularly in popular boardsailing magazines promoting the sport. He is also the Producer, Director and Cameraman of the first full-length feature film on boardsailing, entitled, "Wind Dance", which has brought the grace and beauty of the sport to the screen.

Mimi Greenwood and John Furlow are Associate Professors of Physical Education at West Chester University in West Chester, Pennsylvania. West Chester has long been a consistent leader in the field of physical education, athletics, recreation and dance. The authors, master teachers, have published textbooks, contributed to professional journals, and are popular lecturers at educational conferences. Dr. Joseph Spiecker, multi-media specialist at West Chester University, is the consultant on all visual effects in the text.

"BOARDSAILING MADE EASY" with its unique progressive lession format both in the pool and in the open water areas, is the first of its kind in the sport, which is considered to be the fastest growing watersport in the world today.

CHAPTER II

INTRODUCTION

Boardsailing, windsurfing or sailboarding - no matter what you call it, people all over the world are doing it. It's been called a safe sport, a sport for all ages, the sport of the 80's, the purest form of sailing, the fastest growing sport in the world, the latest addition to the Olympic Games, and the ultimate free ride.

Sailors are gliding across inland lakes, rivers and ponds. They're racing around buoys on the race course. They're doing hotdogging tricks off the beaches, and they're planing and surfing down ocean swells. Wherever there's water and wind, sailors are learning new skills, making new friends, and accepting the challenge to try this exciting water sport. It's fun, it's inexpensive, and it's the thing to do. Become a part of the yachting scene and beat the rising costs of owning a boat. With complete boards available at under $1,000, boardsailing offers a comparatively inexpensive sailing experience with most of the costs in the initial purchase price, and without the need to spend additional funds associated with such sports as snow skiing and traditional "big boat" sailing. The generic name of the sport is boardsailing, the sailor who practices it is called a boardsailor, and he's sailing on a sailboard. People of all ages and from all walks of life with different ability levels and with varied types of interests are finding that boardsailing supplies a wide range of satisfying and exciting activities geared more toward balance and finesse rather than sheer strength. It is practiced by people from ages 5 to 80, its devotees split equally among men and women, and it offers exciting challenges for the beginner and the seasoned pro alike.

A good school can have 90% of all beginners learning the basics of balance and sailing back and forth on a reach in 2-4 hours and have them tacking and jibing as well in under 5 hours. This entertaining exercise is all part of this unique sport with its unique appeal.

95% of the boardsailors in this country are recreational sailors. What we see and read about in the glossy sport and vacation magazines are some of the choices and continual challenges on both the competitive and non-competitive levels that are open to the talented boardsailor. The real developments of the sport are at the recreational level and it's here that the accent still remains - on the personal, the social, and the fun of it all.

For the individual who learns the basics, the sport quickly yields a satisfying reward of pure pleasurable sensations combined with a healthy amount of physical exercise. It offers a lot of special moments as one challenges the elements and tries to master the moves, while getting into the rhythm of it all without feeling the competitive pressures of speed, time, the finish line, or setting a world record. Relax, unwind and practice, and the sailboard will seem to become an extension of your body.

This book is designed to make your learning experience fun, easy and rewarding. It is possible to learn to boardsail on your own, and in the days before manuals and schools, most of us did just that. However, we believe that if you go out and rent or borrow equipment and try to teach yourself, you are potentially cheating yourself out of a fun learning experience. Your first few hours out on the board can be most frustrating if you have less than ideal conditions and no instructor. These attempts may seem to give you reason to abandon the sport...don't. Seek out a good boardsailing school and you will quickly learn how easy it is to experience the full enjoyment and exhilaration of this fascinating sport. Lessons will help to correct and avoid bad habits before they start. This book can then be used to supplement your instruction and convey to you the ultimate enjoyment of man in harmony with the wind and water.

HISTORY OF BOARDSAILING

Boardsailing or windsurfing as it was called in the early days, was the final germination of a new sailing idea developed by Southern Californians Hoyle Schweitzer, Jim Drake and Allen Parducci in 1966 and 1967. Their combined backgrounds included such skills as surfing, sailing, skiing, engineering,

9

philosophy and computers. Their idea was to design a craft that would allow them the freedom of sailing without the lengthy time spent rigging and derigging that sometimes accompanied traditional sailing, but also combine it with the excitement and "do it now" aspects of surfing without the crowds and limitations of good surf conditions.

In 1967, they had constructed a prototype vessel that offered a fascinating combination of surfing and sailing. It incorporated a free-sail system that allowed the mast, boom and sail assembly to move in all directions around a universal joint. It was initially called a "Baja Board" and it consisted of only what was essential for gathering the power of the wind and directing it efficiently.

In 1969, Hoyle Schweitzer started a family business selling these sailboards which he now called a WINDSURFER®, and began traveling around the country promoting the sport and the board. In 1971, the sport was introduced in Europe where it quickly developed into a major sport in just a few short years.

Today, refined versions of the original sailboard are being sold around the world by over 100 companies offering more than 300 models of sailboards for every type of boardsailor at every skill level. It is estimated that more than 2 million boards have been sold worldwide, and the sport is practiced in almost every country and on every ocean on the earth.

The rapid growth of this exciting new sport induced the International Olympic Committee to adopt boardsailing as the seventh Olympic Sailing event for the 1984 Olympic Games in Los Angeles. The event is garnering widespread exposure and public recognition for this young sport, as well as adding a new dimension of worldwide respect.

While boardsailing is an individual sport, it is simultaneously a family sport. Today, excellent instruction is available with techniques and fundamental principles taught in a manner that will allow those who have never sailed before to experience the thrill of moving over the water powered only by the wind. Combine this with training boards, training sails and stronger, lighter and more manageable boards and mast/boom/sail assemblies, and you have the ingredients of a safe sport for all ages; one in which women can develop equal skills as men. You become an integral functioning part of the boat; and all you have to do is know how to swim and have a little patience.

As boardsailing accelerates rapidly across the country, people in every age group and background are being drawn into something that brings them closer to one another and to themselves. Like anything else, you get as much out of the sport as you put into it.

PURPOSE OF INSTRUCTION

There are two common ways to learn how to boardsail - trial and error or lessons. In the old days trial and error was the only way to learn - there were no schools or places that offered lessons. You had seen pictures of people boardsailing in magazines and of course friends could do it and "anything they can do, we can do better". So you'd wait for a good 15 mph wind, rent a board, hop on it and fly away. Right? Wrong! First we'd head up into the wind only to get backwinded and pushed off to windward. When we did head off in the right direction, the force of the sail would pull us over to leeward. If we corrected that then the hull would hit a wave and tip too much to windward or leeward and knock us for a swim. To say the least it was a humiliating, humbling, ego-shattering and a wet experience. So where did we go wrong? The first mistake was the learning environment. Beginners should always attempt their first boardsailing lesson in a nice calm 5 mph wind on a body of water with no waves or boat wakes. Another short cut to success would have been to read a How-To-Book on Boardsailing and possibly learn some pointers from experienced boardsailors. However, the best, fastest and most efficient (and possibly a little more expensive) way to learn how to boardsail is to take a lesson. Lessons are fun. They make the learning experience more enjoyable (and a little dryer) and have you sailing better and faster than if you tried it on your own (provided you have a competent instructor. Check with some previous students). A good instructor can prevent you from picking up bad habits that you will have to unlearn or correct later. Of course you can learn to boardsail on your own but we feel you are depriving yourself of an invaluable experience which is lots of fun. Remember that boardsailing is a technique and not a brute strength sport. At a World Championship Event a few years back, a 13 year old boy weighing 87 pounds who had only been boardsailing a year and who could hardly reach the booms went on to beat 456 of the world's best boardsailors and became a World Champion. He did it by applying the proper techniques. An instructor pointing out proper technique will make what appeared to be difficult a lot easier and make you ready to enjoy the sport of boardsailing.

SAILBOARD

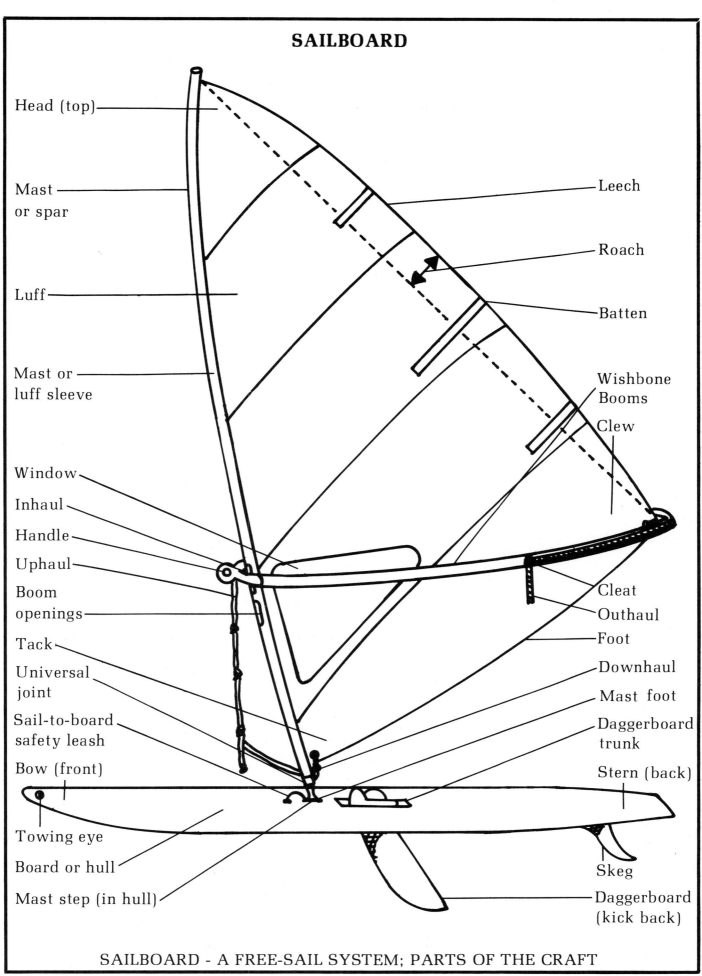

Head (top)

Mast or spar

Luff

Mast or luff sleeve

Window

Inhaul

Handle

Uphaul

Boom openings

Tack

Universal joint

Sail-to-board safety leash

Bow (front)

Towing eye

Board or hull

Mast step (in hull)

Leech

Roach

Batten

Wishbone Booms

Clew

Cleat

Outhaul

Foot

Downhaul

Mast foot

Daggerboard trunk

Stern (back)

Skeg

Daggerboard (kick back)

SAILBOARD - A FREE-SAIL SYSTEM; PARTS OF THE CRAFT

CHAPTER III

INTRODUCTION TO PARTS OF THE CRAFT

When boardsailing started back in the late 1960's one company was manufacturing one sailboard brand; it was a standard one-design sailboard. Many changes in the sport have taken place in the last 15 years causing a tremendous increase in the variety of equipment available. While some manufacturers market only one model of sailboard, others carry a line of ten models. What is the difference between Brand A and Brand B, and why should I buy one and not the other? Most boards perform well under the conditions for which they were designed. You must assess your personal needs and evaluate which of those boards fit your needs.

While it is very possible the sailboard you own, rent, borrow or take lessons on may not be one of the brands pictured, that is not to say that you have a lesser quality sailboard or one that requires different techniques to master. There are many quality sailboards on the market today. However, it would be impossible for one book to show every brand available so the authors have chosen a cross-section of brands to represent the market.

Basically, sailboards fall into three specific categories: Standard, Open Class and Funboards. Standard boards include most flat-bottom boards ranging from learning and recreational boards to one-design racers. One-design means they are produced exactly the same whether it is a learning board or a racing board. Many sailors like racing in one-design classes for that man-against-man competition rather than the equipment-against-equipment racing associated with the professional circuit. Open Class boards generally have rounder bottoms with more displacement than standard boards. They may be production made or custom prototypes, but if they plan to compete in Open Class racing they will be built within the parameters of a set of standardized rules and guidelines. Open Class boards are usually divided into two groups when it comes to racing: Division I for the flatter standard boards that may not have sufficient numbers to race one-design, and Division II for the boards with deeper displacement and rounder bottoms. These boards tend to point higher and go faster than a standard board but are generally difficult to sail off the wind in heavy air and waves. They have limited uses when not on the race course, are very fragile since they are usually hollow, and are higher priced. The last category of boards are the Funboards (which isn't to say the others aren't fun too.) They include everything from homemade custom boards to production boards. Their purpose is to have fun, go fast and expend the least amount of energy possible. These include everything from Pan Am-type racing boards and high-speed machines to wave jumping and surfing boards. Many incorporate the latest designs and technology, might be built of exotic materials, and may be characterized by footstraps, fully retractable centerboards or no centerboards at all, multiple skegs and come in lengths from 6' to 15'. While the standard sailboard will most likely remain unchanged for years to come, funboards evolve and change as each new development within the industry occurs. It is here, limited only by creativity, that new and better equipment will evolve and be made available to boardsailors all over the world.

A sailboard consists of two basic parts: the hull, similar in formation to a sailboat hull or that of a surfboard; and the rig or sail assembly, consisting of the sail, mast, boom and universal. Nautical names are given to the parts and areas of these basic elements. Together they form a compact, lightweight and easily assembled sailing craft. It is important to learn these terms and understand how the parts of the sailboard are fastened together. This will help you get the most out of participating in the sport, enabling you to understand facts and articles published in books and magazines about boardsailing.

BOARD OR HULL SHAPES

Most standard, production boards used today are generally 11 to 13 feet long, 23-30 inches wide, weigh between 32 and 50 pounds, and have a buoyancy of 7-10 cubic feet which will provide almost 400 pounds of flotation. They are virtually unsinkable and act like a large life preserver or swimming float. Hull shapes are usually broken down into three groups: Flat Bottom Boards, Semi-Displacement and Displacement Boards.

Flat Bottom Boards are generally very stable and buoyant for the beginner or recreational boardsailor yet are capable of planing and going at great speeds off the wind when it picks up. They are generally flat and wide, and do not have sharp rails.

Semi-displacement boards or all-around boards utilize a V or round bottom section in the front of the board which increases the tracking and windward pointing ability which flattens out aft of the maststep providing an effective planing hull. This combination is a compromise that gives a board that is a little more tippy and less stable than a flat bottom board, while at the same time offering better upwind performance and maintaining the planing characteristics of the flat bottom.

Displacement boards are generally round-bottomed all the way from the bow to the stern. They are exceptionally fast upwind but when sailing downwind in waves and heavy air will require perfect board control and balance due to the reduced effort on the sail while accelerating on a wave.

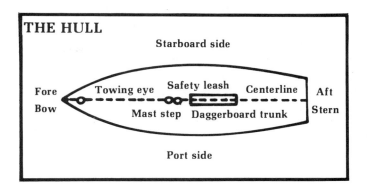

THE HULL

Starboard side

Fore / Bow — Towing eye — Safety leash — Centerline — Aft / Stern

Mast step — Daggerboard trunk

Port side

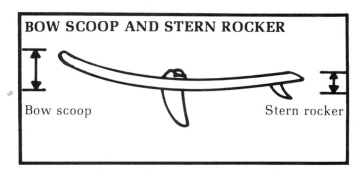

BOW SCOOP AND STERN ROCKER

Bow scoop   Stern rocker

Short Boards and Funboards come in a category of their own. They range in length from 6′ to 15′, and can weigh from 10 lbs. to 50 lbs. They can have little or no buoyancy, like a "sinker" which doesn't become effective until the wind picks up to 15-25 knots and can only be jibed. They may also be called "semi-sinkers" which provide more buoyancy and can sometimes be tacked depending on your weight and skill, or "floaters" that have enough buoyancy to support 400 lbs. and can be tacked and jibed like a standard board. Most will have footstraps, adjustable mast tracks, multiple skeg boxes, and fully retractable centerboards or none at all.

The front of the board is called the bow, the back of the board is the stern. To move toward the front of the board is to move fore, while to move toward the stern of the board is to move aft. An imaginary line called the centerline runs down the middle of the hull from bow to stern and divides the hull into two equal parts. The right side of the hull, when looking from stern to bow is the starboard side. The left side of the hull is the port side. The maststep is a well into which the universal is placed. There may be more than one maststep to allow for fore and aft adjustment in placing the mast. Generally speaking, 98% of all universals are not permanently attached to the board, and allow the sail rig to disengage from the board should you want to pull it out, or, in the situation where a sailor's foot may become entrapped between the mast and the board, it would pop out, preventing possible injury.

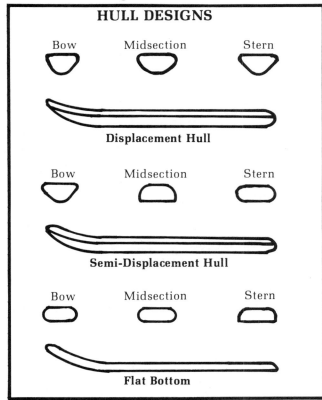

HULL DESIGNS

Bow   Midsection   Stern

Displacement Hull

Bow   Midsection   Stern

Semi-Displacement Hull

Bow   Midsection   Stern

Flat Bottom

13

Many hulls have a safety leash that attaches from the hull to the sail assembly so that in the event the universal pops out of the maststep, the two will not become separated. This is helpful in heavy winds and waves where the hull would generally drift much faster away from the rig creating a potentially dangerous sitauation. Another safety feature is a towing "eye" or towing leash cup on the bow. It may be used to tie off one end of a tether line or leash while the other end is tied to an object on shore so you can learn to boardsail without drifting out farther than your skill level allows. It is also useful when lashing your board to the roof of your car. The daggerboard well or case will hold your daggerboard. It should be strong and reinforced or be replaceable if you do not have a kick-back daggerboard or centerboard, the reason being a standard daggerboard, when run aground at high speeds, may cause damage to the daggerboard well or case. All hulls will have a skeg on them.

HiFly recreational board with footstraps

Finally, one should check the non-skid top surface of the hull. It should have an effective grip without an abrasive texture or slippery feeling. Too abrasive a surface may cause a soreness on the stomach, legs and arms, whereas, too slippery a surface may be unsafe and restrict your foot movement, causing you to fall alot. If the surface is too slippery you may try the following: Fiberglass boards may be rubbed down with emery paper and roughed up. Polyethylene boards have a soft surface and may be roughed up with a very rough sandpaper like 50 grit or a wood rasp or file. All boards may be waxed with any sort of surfboard wax, paraffin or candle wax; and, although it will improve the grip, in many cases it will mark a board and give it a discolored look. If the board is left out in the hot sun the wax may run or if it is turned

upside down onto the sand or dirt when hot, both will attach to the wax. There are also a variety of non-skid adhesives that can be glued to the surface of most boards. If your board has a smooth surface when you get it, try it first before you put wax on it because some manufacturers have a new non-skid surface that has improved traction yet is extremely comfortable and non-abrasive.

STORAGE TIPS

Never store a hull in direct sunlight. The ultraviolet rays will cause the hull to age quickly. In order to retain proper hull shape, especially in polyethylene boards, you should store the hull either standing up on end or on its side. If left lying flat, in time the bow scoop or stern rocker may flatten out. When lying flat on a flat surface, support the hull in the middle if the deck is down, or on two points at least 6' apart if you leave the deck facing up.

SAILS

After the hull, the next most important part of your sailboard is your sail. You move forward based on the total force acting on the sail. If it is poorly designed, too big or even too small, you may be pulled more sideways than forward. A sail should take on the same shape characteristics as an airplane wing. It should not have any disproportionate bulges or wrinkles in it for maximum efficiency. Technically speaking, the total force on the sail is a combination of negative surface force on the lee side of the sail (similar to pulling the boat forward) combined with the positive surface pressure on the windward side of the sail (similar to pushing the boat forward). The most important force is the negative pressure pulling the boat forward which results from an increase in the velocity of air flow over the lee side of the sail. The combination of those forces is what causes your sailboard to move forward. Sails come in many sizes, shapes, materials and colors. So for this section, the authors will try to educate you on the most common ones in use and on the market.
Like the hull, the parts of the sail are also described in nautical terms:

14

PARTS OF THE SAIL

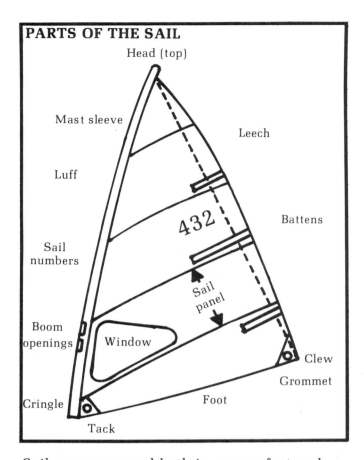

Head (top)

Mast sleeve

Leech

Luff

432

Battens

Sail numbers

Sail panel

Boom openings

Window

Cringle

Clew

Grommet

Foot

Tack

Sails are measured both in square feet and square meters, and will range in sizes from 20 square feet (1.9 square meters) to 100 square feet (9.3 square meters). The formula for converting square meters to square feet and vise-versa is square meters times 10.76 equals square feet, and square feet divided by 10.76 equals square meters. However, sails for most standard sailboards usually come in 3 sizes. These include the regatta or full-sized sail, 56-68 square feet; the marginal sail, 50-62 square feet; and the high-wind or storm sail, 40-50 square feet. If a sailor had one of each of these, or even just a full sail and a high-wind sail, he would never be left on the beach if the wind picked up. Generally smaller sails are easier to handle and ideal for high winds, beginners, women and children.

Most sails are made of several panels of dacron (a synthetic woven polyester where the threads intertwine to form a cloth grid with excellent tear resistance weighing from 3.0-3.8 ounces per square yard, sewn together with a horizontal panel alignment using double zig-zag stiches. There is a reinforced sleeve sewn along the luff (front edge) of the sail into which the mast slides and it is called a mast sleeve or sock. There are usually slight curves cut in the panels and along the luff, which is called a luff curve and helps define the shape of the sail. Some sails come with battens and others without. Battens are important on regatta sails for racing since

they provide more power and extra lift when sailing to windward, and help maintain the sail's shape by supporting the leech and preventing curling and flapping. The mast sleeve will have an opening or two in it so that the booms can be attached to the mast. By moving the booms up or down in these openings, you should be able to find a boom height that is comfortable for you.

The sail is attached to the universal with a line coming from the universal and up through a grommet at the tack of the sail. This line is called the downhaul and allows the luff to be tightened or loosened via tension on this line. Another grommet is found at the clew which is where the foot (lower bottom edge) and leech (back edge) of the sail meet. The outhaul line goes through this grommet and around the back of the booms, and when tightened allows the sail to be stretched to the back end of the booms. Outhaul tension plays a large part in determining the shape of the sail. Pulling the outhaul tight will give a flat sail, while leaving it loose will give a full sail. If one drew a straight line from the head of the sail to the clew of the sail this would be called a straight leech. If the edge of your sail extends past this straight line, then the extra area is called the roach measurement and in this case would be a positive roach. If the edge of your sail is inside this straight leech line then you have a negative roach. Windows are clear plastic sections found on nearly all of todays sails and allow you to see objects on the other side of the sail. Most sails supplied with a new board will have the manufacturer's logo near the head, and full sails will usually have a number which no other owner of that particular brand of sailboard should have. Many standard boards will come with a horizontal cut pinhead sail.

Regatta sails or full sails come in two standard sizes, 68 sq. ft. and 57 sq. ft., and are usually made from 3.8 oz. dacron. They may come in one color or in a rainbow of colors. Recently, sailors have been pushing for heavier, stiffer and more durable fabrics in the 4.2 to 4.5 oz. weights, and have a more limited choice of colors - more white than anything else. The larger size is the maximum allowable size for Open Class racing. They are built to perform over a wide range of wind and sea conditions and are usually characterized by battened sections, deep foot curves and stiff, non-stretch material. These sails usually have a luff length of 14'1" to 18'10", and use booms approximately 8'6" to 9' long. Although a high-wind sail is good to learn on, your basic full-size sail is really all you need for quite some time unless you are small, light and not quite as strong in which case you might prefer to own a marginal sail.

A marginal sail is what the factory supplies with most standard boards. Most sailors should master these before moving up to regatta sails. They come in two standard sizes of 54 sq. ft. and 62 sq. ft., and are usually battenless, very flat and have a large luff curve. The 62 sq. ft. sail is probably the most popular size sail in the world. It is designed for 10-15 mph winds and flat or slightly choppy waves. It has a straight leech and a slightly higher clew than a regatta sail and gives good rig control. The 54 sq. ft. sail is intended for 15-25 mph winds, and is very flat with a well balanced leech. It will receive a lot of stress in those conditions and may be built of heavier fabric such as 4.5 oz. dacron

or a stiff 4.5 oz. Yarn Temper.

High-wind and storm sails may also be used for beginners because their size is ideal for learning how to boardsail in light winds if you are a novice, child or light person just learning the sport. Basically they were designed for those windy days in excess of 25 mph when a regular sail seems like a lot of work. But the high-speed thrills that could be derived on windy days if you were accomplished are worth every bit of the effort. Most of these sails are small, between 40 and 50 sq. ft., very flat and made out of heavy materials. They are made for extreme conditions where one wants maximum control in the the rough weather. Their small area puts less strain on the rig which in turn causes less mast bend and they are therefore cut with shallow luff curves.

HiFly 6.5m powerline rig

HiFly 6.0m powerline rig

HiFly 5.5m powerline rig

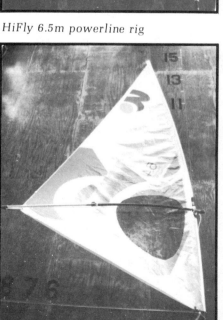
Wayler 5.4m all around sail

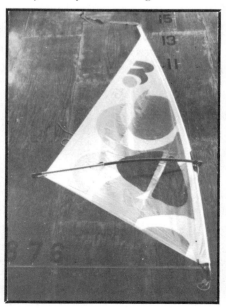
Wayler 4.5m storm sail

Sailrider 5.3m all around sail

Sailrider 3.5m childs rig

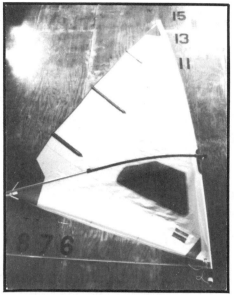
Freedom Sails regatta sail

SAIL CARE AND MAINTENANCE

Caring for your sail properly is not difficult to do and it will extend it's life if done properly. Avoid leaving the sail exposed to direct sunlight. The sun's ultraviolet rays will break down the polymetric bonds in the dacron fibers and in time weaken the cloth and wear down the sail. Another problem is oil, grease and tar stains. They don't hurt the performance of the sail but they are very hard to remove and are unsightly. Always look at the surface first before setting your sail down. Wash your sail in fresh water and make sure it is thoroughly dry before folding and storing it for any long periods. Salt water will break down the sailcloth and stitching over a long period of time and the drying should prevent any mildew from staining the sail. Mildew won't hurt the sail but the stains are next to impossible to remove and looks bad. You may roll the sail around the mast and carry it with the rig. When doing this you should always release the downhaul to eliminate tension, and it is advisable to cover it with a mast/sail bag. This will protect it from deterioration caused by ultraviolet rays and save you from destroying your sail when transporting the rig on top of your car from

the constant sail flapping at 55 mph.

Another method for storing the sail is to take it off the mast, fold it properly and place it in a sailbag. Do not stuff it into the bag and try to avoid folding across the windows. The easiest way to fold a sail is to lay it out flat on the ground with one person kneeling at the tack and a second person kneeling at the clew. Both people should place one hand on the sail about 18-24" above the foot of the sail on their respective luff line and leech lines. The second hand should now grab the sail along this same edge another 18-24" above the first hand. While keeping the sail pressed firmly on the ground with the first hand, the second hand lifts the remaining sail up and over the first hand (a fold is now created between the hands) and places this piece of sail down on the foot of the sail (a fold is now created along the foot). Repeat these two steps until the whole sail is folded up into a strip 18-24" long. Now roll the sail lengthwise from the tack to the clew or vice-versa and place it in your sailbag. You will find a few crease marks on it when you're ready to sail again, but most of these will disappear after a sail or two in strong winds.

The weakest part of the sails are the seams so keep an eye on the stitching. Have them repaired if any come loose. Repairs should be done by a sail loft unless you have a heavy-duty sewing machine. The tip of your mast may start to poke through the head of your sail. Have a sailmaker sew on a piece of leather at the tip. In an emergency duct tape can be used for temporary repairs on small rips. The above suggestions will help you extend your new sail's useful life.

SAIL SELECTOR GUIDE

The question commonly arises of which size sail should be used or purchased. It is safe to say that if you own a high-wind sail and a full-sized sail you should be able to go out on a standard sailboard in most any wind and wave conditions. Considering the millions of participants and variables involved in boardsailing, it is safe to say that each situation encountered would be that much more fun when performed with the optimum equipment. The variables include but are not limited to weight (most sailors weighing anywhere from 65-265 pounds), height (everything from 4' children to 7' tall people), age (sailors from 8 to 80 actively boardsail), strength (from the casual sailor to the die-hard athlete), wind and water conditions and speed (boardsailors will go out in most any type weather) and, of course, the intended use (your first lesson, a recreational outing, a competitive race, speed sailing, wave jumping or wave surfing, or executing freestyle maneuvers). It is easy to see that any combination of these variables could result in two sailors using the same size sail under different circumstances. For instance, and 80 lb. sailor may find an 80 sq. ft. sail manageable in 3 knots of wind while a 210 lb. sailor could use the same 80 sq. ft. sail in 25 knots of wind.

The following sail selection guide should give you a rough idea of what size sail you may want in a given wind speed. Various wind speeds are given on the left side of the chart while body weights of the boardsailor are across the bottom. Find your weight and intended sailing conditions and go up and across to find the recommended sail size. This is only a guide and you should talk with other local sailors and your boardsailing specialist to help find the right sail for you.

SAIL SELECTOR GUIDE

Wind Speed in Knots	Beaufort Scale	66 / 30	77 / 35	88 / 40	99 / 45	110 / 50	121 / 55	132 / 60	143 / 65	154 / 70	165 / 75	176 / 80	187 / 85	198 / 90	209+ / 95+	Unit
41-47	9										40	43	44	49	54	SQ. FT.
											3.8	4	4.1	4.5	5	SQ. M.
34-40	8								40	43	47	49	53	54	58	SQ. FT.
									3.8	4	4.4	4.5	4.9	5	5.4	SQ. M.
28-33	7							43	47	49	53	54	58	60	60	SQ. FT.
								4	4.4	4.5	4.9	5	5.4	5.5	5.5	SQ. M.
22-27	6						43	49	53	54	58	60	64	65	65	SQ. FT.
							4	4.5	4.9	5	5.4	5.5	5.9	6	6	SQ. M.
16-21	5			40	44	47	53	58	60	60	64	69	71	74	80	SQ. FT.
				3.8	4.1	4.5	4.9	5.4	5.5	5.5	5.9	6.4	6.6	6.9	7.4	SQ. M.
11-15	4	40	43	49	54	60	64	64	65	69	74	80	80	80	80	SQ. FT.
		3.8	4	4.5	5	5.5	5.9	5.9	6	6.4	6.9	7.4	7.4	7.4	7.4	SQ. M.
7-10	3	49	60	64	65	69	74	80	80	80	80	80	80	80	80	SQ. FT.
		4.5	5.5	5.9	6	6.4	6.9	7.4	7.4	7.4	7.4	7.4	7.4	7.4	7.4	SQ. M.
4-6	2	54	60	64	69	74	80	80	80	80	80	80	80	80	80	SQ. FT.
		5	5.5	5.9	6.4	6.9	7.4	7.4	7.4	7.4	7.4	7.4	7.4	7.4	7.4	SQ. M.

BODY WEIGHT IN POUNDS: 66, 77, 88, 99, 110, 121, 132, 143, 154, 165, 176, 187, 198, 209+

KILOGRAMS: 30, 35, 40, 45, 50, 55, 60, 65, 70, 75, 80, 85, 90, 95+

MASTS

There are many different brands and types of masts on the market today. Their bend characteristics, stiffness, weight, construction, durability, length, wall thickness, and taper will all vary, providing both merits and drawbacks. Most weigh anywhere from 3 to 5 1/2 pounds, are tapered at the top and come in a standard length of around 15 feet. Many sailors, however, use extensions to increase this height while others use shorter ones for such things as training rig, or if they are a beginner or smaller sailor. The most important elements to look for when purchasing a mast are its stiffness, weight and durability. Beginning boardsailors should be most concerned about finding a durable, lightweight mast. Generally speaking, there are four basic materials used in mast construction; epoxy-fiberglass; epoxy-carbon fiber; epoxy-graphite; and aluminum. Most recreational boards will come with an epoxy-fiberglass mast that was probably built by spinning the fiberglass around a mandril. These masts are available in a wide range of weights and constructions with various bend characteristics. If you intend to do mostly recreational sailing or enter one-design regattas, then the factory supplied mast that came with your board should provide years of good service. Carbon fiber and graphite composite masts tend to be very expensive and are illegal for Open Class racing. But for the Construction Class racer they will provide

very light, very stiff and somewhat brittle masts with the carbon fiber being not quite as brittle as the graphite. Aluminum spars are extremely stiff, and in the past few years they have become lighter and stronger which is helping to increase their popularity.

It is important to note that many custom sails are built with a luff curve set for a mast with a certain amount of stiffness in it. A mast with the wrong characteristics for a custom sail can make an expensive sail look pretty bad. A technique for determining the luff curve of your mast is to peg the base of the mast and the point where the board will be attached and then apply 22 lbs. of pressure to the top of the mast. The resulting flex will be the luff curve. Be sure to consult your local sailboard experts when purchasing a custom sail to see if it will function the way it was designed to with the mast you presently own.

BOOMS

Booms are the wishbone shaped unit that you hold onto when sailing a sailboard. They are your means of steering while at the same time providing support. Steering is achieved by tilting the rig forward to head off the wind and tilting it back to head into the wind. Originally, booms were made out of teak wood, but now almost all are made from aluminum tubing. Two pieces of tubing are bent into a wishbone shape and joined at each end with plastic or metal fittings. The sail is lifted from the water with the uphaul line which is also attached to the forward boom fitting. Some uphauls have shock cord inside them while others may have a piece attached to the end and hooked or tied to the universal so that the uphaul is easy to retrieve. Booms will usually have two or three cleats on them. The first is usually on or near the front boom end fitting and the inhaul lines that attach the booms to the mast are usually cleated off here. The other one or two cleats are usually placed on the tubing on opposite sides toward the back of the booms, and are used for fastening and tying off the outhaul line. It passes through the rear boom fitting and allows the sailor to trim the sail while still sailing and, in the case of two cleats, while on either tack.

Booms also come in different cross-sectional shapes. Round ones tend to be stronger on both axes, and are used in all conditions, including high-wind fun, surf and waves. Oval booms are popular amongst racers, and although they are strong on the lateral axes they can tend to break along the weaker axis

Variety of masts (numbers represent feet)

when taken in the surf. Most aluminum booms have a coating on them for good grip and comfort on the hands. The most popular is a rubber coating which comes in a solid color, or sometimes the right side will be colored green for starboard and the left side red for port. Another popular covering called vulcanized rubber is very strong, hard to tear and almost impossible to remove. These coatings also provide some additional flotation to the booms. Wooden or teak booms have no covering and they should periodically be coated with teak oil to prevent the wood from drying out.

Standard booms for standard boards are generally between 8'6" and 9' in length and are non-adjustable. As shorter Funboards become more popular the trend is for high-aspect sails with short booms. Today, one-piece booms can be purchased in most any length from 6', 6'6", 7', 7'6", 8', 8'6" and 9'. Another popular item is the adjustable or Vario Booms which allows the sailor to own one set of booms that can adjust to most any length, from 6' to 9' in 6" increments. This is either achieved by having one end of the booms push into the other end or by adding or subtracting various extensions to adjust the length of the booms to accept any size sail.

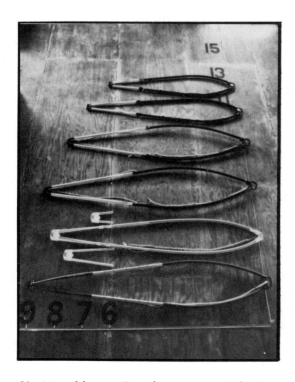

Variety of booms (numbers represent feet)

UNIVERSALS

The universal is the most important part of the board because it connects the hull to the rig while at the same time permitting it to be angled in all directions above the surface of the hull. This feature is what makes up a free-sail system and gives a sailboard its unique characteristics. The universal should stay firmly attached to the board during normal sailing, but be able to release under extreme conditions which could cause injury or damage to the rig.

A safety leash ensures that the rig stays with the board in the event that a universal breaks and they do separate. This is advantageous since the sail is like a sea anchor and will prevent you from drifting too far away. There are a variety of universals on the market today. Two major differences being the design of the unusual joint itself and the way in which it is attached to the hull. The two common designs in universal joints today are the hourglass universal joints and the mechanical universal joints.

The hourglass-shaped universals are the most common ones around and use an hourglass-shaped piece of malleable rubber or polyurethane with threaded bolts on each end to connect the hourglass to the mast base and the mast foot. They are simple to use, light and inexpensive, but should be watched and replaced at the first sign of splitting.

Mechanical universal joints are usually made of stainless steel metal parts or, in some cases, all nylon. These may come with a rubber boot around them to protect toes from getting cut or caught in them. Universals are usually connected to the hull by one of four types of connections; these are friction, suction/expansion, mechanical and pin-locking. The friction connection uses a mast foot slightly smaller than the mast step into which it is being pushed. The degree of friction can be partially controlled by winding duct tape around the insert if it becomes too loose. The suction/expansion connection relies on an air lock which is created after the mast foot goes into the mast step. Basically, a piston screws up into a rubber doughnut causing the doughnut to expand while simultaneously creating suction in the mast step until the sailor unlocks it. Sand and water can affect its performance. Mechanical connections, unlike the first two, can usually be set to release at a desired tension, either to prevent mishaps (like your leg getting caught between the mast and the board and allowing the universal to pop out) or to suit your particular needs. They rely on adjusting tension on a spring loaded knob that tightens and fits securely against the mast step. Pin locking connections use a pin at the top of the mast step that is put into place after inserting the mast foot. They are easy to use and good at resisting sand, but require you to make sure you don't lose the pin.

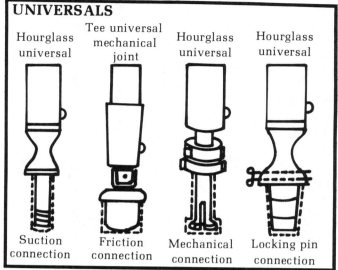

Some universals will have a cleat with an eye, attached to the mast base which can give you the mechanical advantage of a double or triple purchase on the downhaul. On high performance sails this can be helpful in achieving a proper sail shape. Other universals may add extensions of varying lengths to the mast base so that the height of the mast will in effect increase and be able to accomodate sails with longer luff sleeves. There are also universals on the market called vario universals which may have a mast base up to a few feet long coupled with some type of retaining ring which can be adjusted up or down along its length to give you a desired mast height.

From time to time you may find your mast base jammed into the mast. This is usually caused because sand was left inside the mast and, if not removed in time, it could cause the base of your mast or possibly your universal to break. The base may be removed by lashing the universal to a fixed object and then pulling steadily on the mast while at the same time striking the mast foot with a hammer. All standard boards will come with a universal designed for that board. As you advance into high performance boards you may find that many universals have mast bases that are either too big or small for certain masts. Inserts or sleeves are available for many universals and masts to remedy this situation, or you can change mast bases, but it is important to note that not all the accessories and parts from one manufacturer/importer are interchangeable with those of another.

Variety of universals

THE DAGGERBOARD

The daggerboard's main function is to provide lateral resistance which results in the boards forward motion and keeps it from being blown to leeward or sideways in the water. The daggerboard is also called a foil and helps to stabilize the board. Racing daggerboards and performance blades are usually made of high density foam, mahogany, spruce, pine or marine plywood reinforced with uni-dirctional fibers that produce stiffer boards with exact shapes. Most foils have a symmetrical streamlined profile which tapers off at the rear. Standard daggerboards are generally 20 to 28 inches long, 8 to 10 inches wide, and anywhere from 3/4 to 1 1/4 inches thick. With the thickest point generally about 10% of the daggerboard width. Foils come in three different styles: standard daggerboards, kick-back daggerboards and centerboards. Standard daggerboards go straight up and down through the hull. They have less drag underwater since their case is as large as the daggerboard is wide. However it is difficult to sail in heavy air with the board down since the wetted surface area of the daggerboard causes it to hydroplane, thus causing the sailboard to flip up onto its rail. Most sailors will therefore pull the daggerboard all the way out in heavy air when heading off the wind. Kick-back daggerboards pivot back along the hull and help eliminate the possibility of hull damage if the board is run aground. It allows you to put the board straight down for light-wind sailing and going to windward, while at the same time allowing you to sweep it back to form a high-wind daggerboard as the wind increases. This will reduce the weather helm, or turning into the wind on windy days.

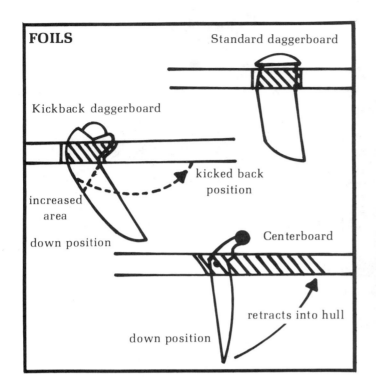

FOILS

Standard daggerboard

Kickback daggerboard

kicked back position

increased area

down position

Centerboard

retracts into hull

down position

Variety of daggerboards and centerboards

Many recreational boards have kick-back foils and some hulls have replaceable daggerboard cases called cassettes. In the unlikely event of damage you can simply replace the cassette and not have to repair the hull. In strong winds, kicking back the daggerboard moves the center of resistance further aft producing smoother performance of the board and making it easier to sail. However, this does not solve the hydroplaning problem as there is even more wetted surface than when the board is in the full-down position. Centerboards, on the other hand, either partially or completely retract into a centerboard box in the hull. This allows it to be easily kicked back in heavy air, and as it retracts into the trunk the wetted surface area can be reduced as much as desired. Smaller swept back daggerboards are also available for most standard boards which will make sailing easier in high winds by moving the center of resistance further aft and reducing the weather helm. As a rule of thumb, a large sail requires a large blade and in stronger winds it is more controllable and efficient to use a smaller blade.

Daggerboards and centerboard; down position

Daggerboards and centerboard; halfway up

Daggerboards and centerboard; kicked back and retracted

THE SKEG OR FIN

The skeg is attached to the underside of the hull near the stern and provides directional stability. Skegs come in a variety of shapes and sizes and these variables, combined with their position, influence the maneuverability of the board. Tracking is improved as flow attaches to the skeg which in turn creates lift. A larger or more swept-back skeg will be better for tracking as it allows flow to attach more easily to it. Maneuverability is achieved by causing the skeg to stall and making flow harder to attach and easier to detach. Smaller, narrower, or more straight-up-and-down skegs are better for maneuverability. Longer and larger skegs may give better tracking but are less maneuverable. Recreational skegs are usually swept back like standard surfboard skegs. Racing boards usually use skegs that are nearly straight-up-and-down with a high-aspect ratio.

Fence fins are large single fins with horizontal fins projecting from both sides of the fin. These help to align the flow of water over the fin and gain a lateral force or lifting advantage from the sail which counteracts the lateral forces of the sail allowing you to sail forward instead of sideways. Under extreme speeds the fence fin will reduce ventilation and cavitation of the skeg. Football fins give you the feel and speed of a single fin as well as the holding power of a multi-fin arrangement by increasing the moment of inertia of the fin. This is achieved by moving the center of the fins area farther away from the bottom of the board.

Wave jumping and surfing boards will generally use more than one skeg and a very small daggerboard or no daggerboard at all. Multiple skegs often replace the need for a daggerboard. One such popular arrangement used today is called a thruster arrangement. Here, one skeg is back and two are forward, providing adequate windward ability as well as good maneuverability off the wind.

Most skegs are usually screwed into a skeg box on the underside of the hull, providing a solid skeg-to-board connection, although some skegs do kick up or pivot back when the board is run aground. This feature may also be helpful when steering the hull. Some boards have skegs that are inserted from the top through a hole in the hull while others may slide in from the back of the hull or slide into a permanently attached fin box located on the underside of the hull. Still other skegs may be permanently glassed into the hull by building up fillets around the base. On a high performance board this will allow flow to reattach more easily after a jump or radical maneuver.

Variety of skegs

Accessories: gear bag, sail/mast bag, mast sleeve inserts, footstraps, carrying strap, bungeed uphaul.

23

RIGGING THE SAILBOARD

Now that all the parts of the sailboard have been described, assembling them will produce a seaworthy sailing craft. The assembly process is called "Rigging" and rigging your sailboard means getting it ready to sail. The steps involved may seem long or complicated but by doing it sequentially you will avoid any mistakes that may haunt you later. After rigging the board a few times it will seem very easy. Before assembling your sailboard check to see you have all the parts: (Fig. 1)

1. The sail and battens (not all sails have battens).
2. The mast and mast tip (not all masts have mast tips).
3. The booms.
4. The universal.
5. The hull.
6. The skeg.
7. The daggerboard.

PREPARE THE HULL

1. Attach a safety leash of strong line to the universal or the bow of the board. (Fig. 2, 3)
2. Attach skeg to the hull according to the manufacturers suggestion with the fin pointing aft. (Fig. 4, 5)

SAIL TO UNIVERSAL JOINT ATTACHMENT

1. Unfold the sail and put in the battens if it has any. All the battens will be a different length so find the right pocket to fit each batten. (Fig. 6, 7)
2. If your mast has a separate mast tip, fit it in the top of the mast and seal it with tape.
3. Insert the small end of the mast into the mast sleeve at the bottom of the sail and push until the mast reaches the very top of the sail. (Fig. 8)
4. Clean out any sand, dirt or small rocks from the base of the mast as this could cause the universal to get stuck in the mast. (Fig. 9)

5. Insert the mast base of the universal joint into the bottom of the mast. (Fig. 10)
6. Tie a bowline at one end of the downhaul line.
7. Pull the opposite end of the downhaul line up through the mast base eye until the bowline stops it.
8. Tie a stop knot on the opposite side of this eye from the bowline to prevent the bowline from moving.
9. Pass the free end of the downhaul line throught the grommet in the tack of the sail and then down and through the bowline. If you still have more line, then you may want to go up and through the tack grommet again which will give you a better power ratio when tightening. (Fig. 11)
10. Pull the downhaul line to the desired tension and tie it off at the grommet with two half hitches. (Fig. 12)

BOOMS TO MAST CONNECTION

This connection is one of the most important parts in rigging your sailboard. In order to make your sail respond to your movements and adjustments you want the booms to be tight against the mast and not wobble or move up and down. This will enable you to feel the forces on the sail better.

1. Make sure that your uphaul line is attached to the booms. If it isn't thread it through the opening in the front boom end fitting and tie it off with an overhand knot. Some people tie one or two overhand knots in the uphaul about 8" to 10" apart to assist you in gripping and for ease in hoisting the sail out of the water. Other uphauls may be of the bungied variety with a piece of shock cord running up the inside of the uphaul. Others may wish to attach a piece of shock cord above the knot in the end of the uphaul line. Both varieties using shock cord are usually then attached to the downhaul so that it will always be in easy reach of the sailor. The uphaul should be long enough to allow you to stand upright on the board as you raise the sail. (Fig. 13)

Fig. 1

Fig. 2

Fig. 3

Fig. 4

Fig. 5

Fig. 6

Fig. 7

Fig. 8

Fig. 9

Fig. 10

Fig. 11

Fig. 12

2. Attach the inhaul to the mast at the boom opening in the mast sleeve with either a clove hitch or double prussic hitch so that either one or two free ends of line exist depending on what type of booms you have and what type of knots they require. The end(s) should pass through the boom opening in the mast sleeve at a comfortable height where you would like the booms to rest. Stand up next to it and raise or lower this knot, until depending on your height, it feels right. If it's too high, lower it. Some instructors recommend placing it at shoulder level to help you develop a better sailing posture with more control. (Fig. 14, 15)

3. The booms are now laid on top of the knot so that the booms run parallel to the mast and the aft end is under the tip of the mast. The uphaul line should lie between the boom handle and the mast and be either on the bottom or forward section of the boom fitting running down toward the universal joint.

4. Different brands of sailboards have different types of front boom end fittings and are attached in different manners. However you tie them, the end result should be a tight fit which joins the booms snugly to the mast. The two most common methods of attachment are for front boom ends without a cleat and for those with a cleat:

A. Boom ends without a cleat usually have 2 holes in the boom handle and are tied off using the double Prussic Hitch with two free ends of line so that they may tie to each other forming a knot. The two lines from the Prussic Hitch are then passed up through the two holes in the boom handle while making sure that the uphaul line falls between these 2 inhaul lines. The 2 lines are now tied off in a loose square knot at the top of the boom handle. The booms are now swung down so they are perpendicular to the mast. This moving of the booms will increase the tension on the inhaul line so care must be taken to make sure the square knot is not too tight as increased tension may cause the mast to be crushed or damaged. If it feels too tight and doesn't want to open to the perpendicular position, then close it back up and loosen the square knot.

B. The second method is used on boards that have a cleat on the front boom end fitting. The best inhaul knot to use is either a clove hitch or a prussic hitch, either one with only one free end of line coming off the knot. The booms are laid on the mast in the same manner as the first method. The inhaul line is then passed over and down through one of the eyes on the front boom end fitting and around the back of the mast and up through the other eye on the front boom end fitting and then cleated. Any extra inhaul line is then usually wrapped around the booms with a half hitch to prevent it coming uncleated. Booms are now swung down so they are perpendicular to the mast. As in the first example, tension will increase on the inhaul when the booms are opened up so care must be taken not to crush the mast. Tighten or loosen the inhaul line until the booms feel tight and comfortable while perpendicular to the mast. (Fig. 16)

SAIL TO BOOMS ATTACHMENT AND OUTHAUL ASSEMBLY

1. Lay the partially assembled rig on the ground and open up the booms so that they are perpendicular to the mast. (Fig. 17)

2. Unroll the sail and bring the clew end towards the back boom fitting.

3. There are two ways of attaching the outhaul depending on whether you have booms that have a single cleat built into the back boom fitting or booms that have two forward cleats.

A. If you have booms with a single cleat built into the back boom fitting then first tie a figure eight knot in one end of the outhaul line. Pass the other end of this line down through the hole on the opposite side of the cleat and out through the grommet in the clew of the sail. Continue to pass the line back up through the other hole in the back boom fitting and then secure it tightly in the cleat.

B. If you have booms with two forward cleats then do the following; Cleat the outhaul line on the side of the booms closest to the ground. Take the free end and bring it back to the back boom fitting. Now depending on what type of back boom fitting you have you will either pass the line through the hole or pulley provided on that side of the boom fitting or around the end and in through a hole in the back of the fitting and then toward the mast. Now pass the line through the grommet in the clew of the sail and then bring it back down through the other hole or pulley provided on the other side of the back boom fitting. Grasp the clew handle of the sail and pull tight. The free end of line is now brought forward on the upper boom side and cleated. (Fig. 18-21)

Fig. 13

Fig. 14

Fig. 15

Fig. 16

Fig. 17

Fig. 18

Fig. 19

Fig. 20

Fig. 21

Fig. 22

Fig. 23

Fig. 24

TRIMMING YOUR SAIL

Once you have rigged the sail assembly you can now trim the downhaul and outhaul tension for the days conditions as well as your sails condition. The downhaul generally controls the position of the maximum fullness or draft in the sail by the amount of tension you apply to it. If you loosen the downhaul the draft will move aft and make the sail fuller. This is good for light winds when less downhaul tension is recommended. Too much tension in light air will cause wrinkles to form that will run up the luff of the sail. Too little tension will cause diagonal wrinkles to appear coming off the luff of the sail. In heavier air, tightening the downhaul will move the draft forward and the sail will flatten. Proper downhaul tension is when the diagonal wrinkles just disappear. The position of the draft gives you your pointing ability. While the downhaul tension controls the location or position of the fullness or draft in the sail, the outhaul tension controls the amount of fullness or draft in the sail. Basically if you loosen the outhaul you will reduce the bend in the mast and increase the draft in the sail. Generally speaking, in light air more draft is desired to prevent the sail from becoming too flat. If it is too loose then long wrinkles will appear in the front. If you tighten the outhaul you will flatten the sail and decrease the draft. This is good for heavier winds and sailing to windward, and it makes the board easier to handle. How much power you will encounter while sailing is determined by the amount of draft. The leech tension may be adjusted at this time by tightening or loosening the leech line.(Fig. 22)

Sail condition is another factor to consider. A blown-out sail will have too much draft and will need more flattening and tightening than a new one will. Once a sail is too stretched out of shape or blown out, you may want to consider purchasing a new one. Different wind and water conditions will warrant different settings for the downhaul and outhaul tensions and some time should be spent experimenting with these settings in order to achieve the maximum performance from your rig. The sail, booms and mast assembly or, as it is commonly called, the rig, is now ready for use. If you are not going sailing now you can simply uncleat the outhaul and furl or roll the sail up. If you are going sailing then insert the universal into the hull   (Fig. 23, 24). There are four common ways of de-rigging your sail assembly. All methods are initiated by uncleating or untying the outhaul first to free the clew of the sail. For sails without battens or ones that have the battens removed, the following methods are good:

DERIG SAIL ASSEMBLY

METHOD 1

Grab hold of the clew and roll the sail toward the universal so that the sailcloth rolls up and around the leech of the sail. Once all the sail has been rolled to the mast sleeve then either put it in a sail/mast bag or tie the sail off to the booms with the outhaul and uphaul lines.

METHOD 2

Grab hold of the clew and roll the sail toward the mast so that the sailcloth rolls up and around the foot of the sail. Once all the cloth has been rolled to the mast sleeve then either put it in a sail/mast bag or tie it off to the booms with the outhaul and uphaul lines. Raise the booms so that the aft end of the booms are touching the mast near the mast tip. A turn of line taken from the back boom fitting and around the mast before tying off the sail should keep the sail/mast tight against the booms for easy carrying.

METHOD 3

If you have battens in your sail and you don't want to take them out and risk losing them you may try the following; Take the clew of the sail and fold it over so that the foot of the sail lays along the mast sleeve. Take the sail area that is left and repeat the procedure a second and third time, each time folding the remaining sail area toward the mast sleeve. Now take the remaining sail area and roll it in toward the mast. This method should avoid any battens being bent or broken, but do keep an eye open just to be sure. This method may also be used on sails without battens but its not the most efficient way.

METHOD 4

The first step is to untie the inhaul and completely remove the booms from the rig. Now take hold of the universal and rotate the sail/mast in circles. This will cause the sail to wrap around the mast. Continue until the whole sail is wrapped around the mast and then put it in a sail/mast bag or tie it off to the booms using the outhaul and inhaul lines as described in Methods 1 amd 3. Alternately, you may simply want to keep the sail/mast assembly separate from the booms for carrying, transport or storage. Methods 1 and 4 keep your sail smooth and don't put any new wrinkles in it.

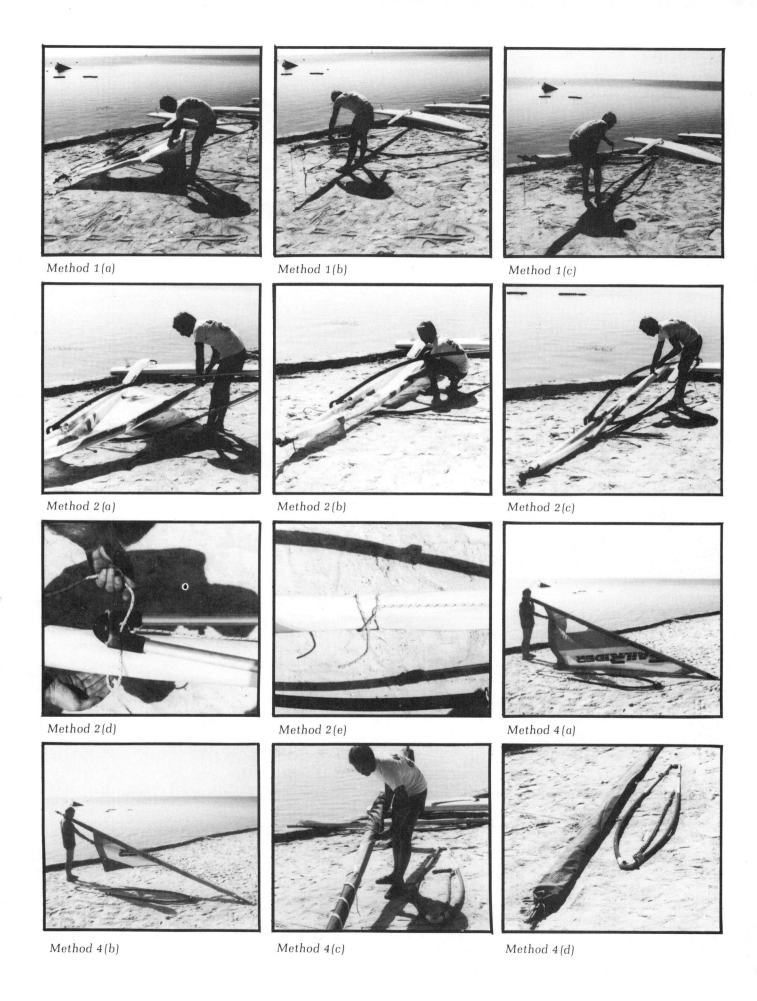

Method 1 (a)   Method 1 (b)   Method 1 (c)

Method 2 (a)   Method 2 (b)   Method 2 (c)

Method 2 (d)   Method 2 (e)   Method 4 (a)

Method 4 (b)   Method 4 (c)   Method 4 (d)

METHOD 5

This method involves completely derigging the sail assembly which is good for storage, long distance cartop transporting, or preparation for shipping. The first step is to untie the inhaul and completely remove the booms from the rig. Next, untie the downhaul and remove the universal from the base of the mast. Step 3 involves pulling the mast out from the mast sleeve. Step 4 is to fold the sail up as described under the sail care and maintenance section and place in your sail bag. Most people leave their skegs attached to the hull between sails. The exceptions are; 1. When shipping it somewhere, 2. During storage, 3. Cartopping when multiple boards on the roof make it impractical to keep the skeg in.

RIG/DERIG/RIG AND DISASSEMBLE SAIL ASSEMBLY

This is an exercise which is very helpful in familiarizing you with your sail assembly and its rigging as well as furling it for carrying or cartopping and folding the sail. This exercise can be practiced by the individual or in groups and lends itself to being perfect for a teaching circuit. It can be practiced in the gym, by the pool or outdoors.

1. Gather together the major parts of the sail assembly (i.e., universal, mast, booms, sail plus battens, if any, and all the necessary lines.) (Fig. 1)

2. Rig the sail assembly. (Fig. 2, 3)

3. Trim the sail properly for open water sailing. (Fig. 4)

4. De-rig and furl the sail assembly and prepare it for carrying or cartopping.(Fig. 5-7)

5. Re-rig the sail assembly and trim it properly for open water sailing as above.

6. De-rig the sail assembly completely and fold the sail properly and place it back in the sailbag. (Fig. 8, 9)

7. Repeat if necessary, let another person try it or move on to the next circuit.

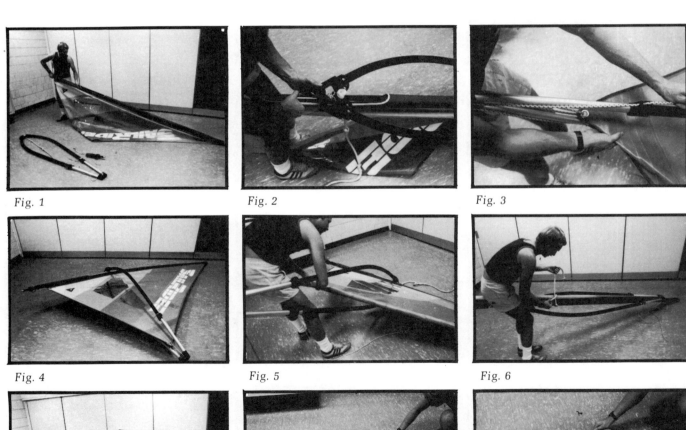

Fig. 1

Fig. 2

Fig. 3

Fig. 4

Fig. 5

Fig. 6

Fig. 7

Fig. 8

Fig. 9

CHAPTER IV

PURPOSE OF TEACHING VOCABULARY

A teaching vocabulary has been established to help make it simple and easy to learn how to boardsail. The instructor and the student can communicate directly and effectively when they both know that what they interpret a word or term to mean, means the same to both of them. Study the words in the teaching vocabulary and learn what they mean. They are simple and basic and are all you need to know when learning how to boardsail.

TEACHING VOCABULARY

BACK: Toward the back (stern) of the hull.
BACK FOOT: The foot closest to the back of the hull.
BACK HAND: The hand closest to the back of the hull, also called the sheet hand. The hand that pulls in on the booms to fill the sail with wind and lets out on the booms to spill the wind from the sail.
FORWARD: Toward the front (bow) of the hull.
FORWARD FOOT: The foot closest to the front of the hull.
FORWARD HAND: The hand closest to the front of the hull, also called the mast hand. The hand that holds the mast on the centerplane.
CENTERLINE: An imaginary line running vertically down the center of the hull from the bow to the stern dividing it into two equal halves. Used as a guide when directing the student's feet into the proper position.
CENTERPLANE: An imaginary plane that extends upward along the center line. Steering the board is achieved by tipping the mast forward and back on this center plane.
BEGINNING POSITION: When the board is perpendicular to the direction of the wind and the sail assembly is in the water pointing downwind.
ACROSS THE WIND: Perpendicular to the direction of the wind.
IN: When the back arm pulls the wishbone booms in toward the center of the board to fill the sail with the wind.

OUT: When the back hand lets out the wishbone booms and the sail moves away from the center of the board to spill wind out of the sail.
LUFFING: When the sailor allows the forward portion of the sail to flutter. The mast is facing the wind and the clew is pointing away from and in the direction the wind is blowing.
PORT: The left side of the board when the sailor is aft and facing or looking forward down the centerline.
PORT TACK: When you are sailing along and the wind is coming from the port or left side of the craft. Your left hand will be the forward hand on the booms and the sail will be out over the right side of the hull.
STARBOARD: The right side of the board when the sailor is aft and facing or looking forward down the centerline.
STARBOARD TACK: When you are sailing along and the wind is coming in from the starboard or right side of the craft. Your right hand will be the forward hand on the booms and the sail will be out over the left side of the hull.
BEARING OFF: Also termed heading off. It is the motion of turning downwind, off the wind or away from the wind.
HEADING UP: Also termed pointing up. It is the motion of turning up into the wind, toward the wind or toward the eye of the wind.
TACK: Also termed coming about. To change the direction of the board by turning the front of the board through the eye of the wind and stepping around the front of the board and the sail assembly to the opposite side, simultaneously changing the side on which the booms are held.
JIBE: To change the direction of the board by turning the front of the board away from the wind while stepping around the back of the board, allowing the sail assembly to swing around the front of the board to the otherside, and simultaneously changing the side on which the booms are held.
SHEETING IN: Pulling in with the back hand so as to harden the sail and fill it completely with wind. Opposite of sheeting out.
SHEETING OUT: Letting out with the back hand so as to ease the sail and let the wind spill from the sail. Opposite of sheeting in.

PREPARE THE SAILBOARD

Rig the sail assembly and prepare the hull for sailing.

1. If you are in the swimming pool, tie off the hull using the tied off tether or anchored technique. Because there is no wind in the swimming pool it is best to use the smallest rig you own to help reduce the possibilities of the rig hitting the side of the pool.

The tied off technique uses two thirty foot pieces of stretch line (or shock cord) which are tied off at four points around the pool. The first piece of line is either fed through the hulls towing eye or else tied or taped off at or around the bow or possibly passed around the hull, up through the daggerboard and down the centerline to the bow before being taped off at the bow. In all cases there should be two equal lengths of line coming off of the hulls bow. The second piece of line is looped over the stern of the hull in front of the skeg and taped off. Leave two equal lengths of line coming off of the stern. Rotate the hull until the bow and stern face the sides of the pool and tie off the hull with the four lines as four points around the pool so that the hull is centered in the pool. (Fig. 1-4)

2. The anchored tether uses a piece of line a few feet longer than the depth of the pool attached to an anchor (could be heavy weights placed a plastic carton or maybe even the drain in the bottom of the pool). Drop the anchor where you want the hull to be situated and bring the free end of line up through the daggerboard well, take up the slack and tie off tightly to the top of the daggerboard. This technique allows the hull to turn 360°, but is less stable than the tied off technique. (Fig. 5, 6)

3. If you are on a simulator, then firmly attach the hull to the simulator using the recommended methods for that model.

4. If you are at the water, then launch the board and push it out into waist deep water.

5. In the swimming pool or at the water, insert the daggerboard and push it all the way down (with the pointed end toward the back of the board).

Fig. 1

Fig. 2

Fig. 3

Fig. 4

Fig. 5

Fig. 6

MOUNTING THE BOARD

Mount the hull in the middle of the board and kneel so that one knee ends up on either side of the mast.

1. In the swimming pool or in the water, try one of the following:

    A. In waist-deep water, spring off the bottom with your feet while lifting with your arms so that either one or both knees land on the board. If necessary, raise the second foot aboard.

    B. In deep water, while treading water with your feet either spring or use your arms to lift yourself out of the water, getting one knee up on the board first before lifting the other.

2. At the simulator, place both hands on the hull for support before climbing up and kneeling on the deck.

BALANCE

1. Assume a kneeling position and get a feel for the boards stability and balance.

2. After kneeling on the board and feeling comfortable, stand on the board, going up from one knee first.

3. Practice standing in the center of the board with the feet on and at right angles to the centerline.

4. Move slowly towards the bow and stern or towards either edge and feel how the hull responds to the various weight placements.

5. Practice the self rescue paddling technique in the 3 balance positions.

    A. Sitting.

    B. Kneeling.

    C. Lying.

6. Once you have completed this exercise, bring the sail assembly to the hull and attach the two with the universal and safety leash.

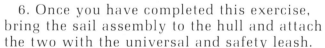

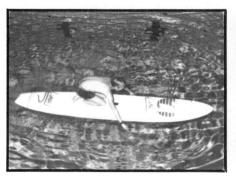  

GETTING THE UPHAUL

Position your body in the center of the board in a kneeling position. Retrieve the uphaul using one of these two methods:

1. Lean on the mast with one hand and take hold of the uphaul line with the other by leaning out over the sail and grabbing it. Resume your original position.

Common Error:
- Leaning on the mast too long and the mast goes under water.

2. Scissor the mast and board together and crawl forward to take hold of the uphaul line. Return to your original position and scissor the board back so that it is again across the wind.

Common Error:
- Crawling too far forward will cause the stern to rise. Leaning too far out on either edge of the board may tip it over and cause you to fall in.

PROPER FOOT STANCE

Maintain your grip on the uphaul line. Stand, with your body over the centerline and your feet on and at right angles to the centerline. Your forward foot is in front of the mast, your rear foot is approximately 15"-18" (shoulder's width) behind the front foot, centered on the daggerboard.

Common Error:
- Faulty balance, your weight too far toward the outer edges of the hull.
- Foot position.

PULLING THE SAIL UP FROM WINDWARD TO LEEWARD

From time to time, after a fall or if you've been sitting on the board drifting for awhile you may find the sail assembly floating to windward of the hull. In order to get in the beginning position you must maneuver the sail so it's pointing downwind at 6 o'clock. The following 3 methods will be helpful.

METHOD 1 (Good light air method)

1. Grab the uphaul line and stand up on the board while maintaining pressure on the uphaul.

2. Maintain pressure on the uphaul and pull the rig to the right or left until the rig is aligned at right angles to the hull.

3. Pull the rig up part way until the water starts to run off the sail. Use your legs and upper torso to help initiate this action. The wind will now fill the underside of the sail with air and help lift it up and reduce the tension on the uphaul.

4. Continue to pull on the uphaul until the back end of the booms have cleared the water. The wind will now push the sail across or over the bow or stern as it swings to a downwind position.

5. The sailor must make sure that he continues to face the rig as it turns and move around the mast from the lee to the windward side. If you don't move your feet the sail will most likely knock you off the board as it swings around. Take note that the stronger the wind; the faster the sail will be blown from the windward to the leeward side and you must respond quicker to these actions or end up in the water.

METHOD 2 (Good Medium Air Method)

1. Grab the uphaul line and stand up on the board while maintaining pressure on the uphaul.

2. Pull the uphaul until the mast tip is a foot out of the water.

3. Maintain pressure on the uphaul and pull the sail assembly towards the right or the left and bring it across and over either the bow or the stern. Keep the mast a few feet off the water so the wind will help you to pull the rig around.

4. Since the rig is moving over the hull you must remember to move your feet as the rig turns and constantly face it. If you don't remember to move the feet, the wind could force the mast and mast base down on your foot and start to crush it. This is an excellent method to try using a board with both ends tied off in the swimming pool.(Fig. 1-6)

METHOD 3 (Good Heavy Air Method)

1. Grab the uphaul line and stand up on the board while maintaining pressure on the uphaul.

2. Pull the uphaul until the mast tip is a foot out of the water.

3. Maintain pressure on the uphaul and swing the sail assembly towards the right or the left so that the wind catches it and forces it and the hull to begin to rotate in a half circle to the vertical position. Maintaining a pull on the sail is important as it is doing the work for you in this technique. The feet can remain in the same position throughout the turn.

Method 2

BEGINNING POSITION

When you get on the board you should establish what is called the 'Beginning Position', and check the following points:

   1. Is the wind at your back (coming from 12 o'clock)?

   2. Is the mast pointed straight downwind (toward 6 o'clock)?

   3. Is the sailboard across the wind and at a right angle to the sail (with the board pointed between 3 and 9 o'clock)?

   4. Are you facing the sail (looking toward 6 o'clock)?

Common Errors:

- Position of the board in relation to the mast.
- Determining the wind direction.

PULLING UP THE SAIL

Pull on the uphaul line with a steady hand-over-hand motion until the mast comes straight up toward you with the sail pointing downwind. Pull until the aft end of the booms are approximately 2" out of the water. Make sure that the board stays pointed across the wind and the feet stay on the centerline. Keep your buttocks in and your shoulders out while maintaining leverage with your legs.

Common Errors:

- Pulling up too fast or not having a sustained pull.
- Not keeping the board across the wind or feet on the centerline.
- Body position is poor with the buttocks too far out over the water.
- Not continuing to pull the uphaul until the aft end of the booms are completely out of the water, otherwise the sailboard may begin to sail.

NEUTRAL POSITION

Hold the uphaul line with both hands, close to the booms. Both hands will be directly in front of the body with the arms bent at a right angle and keeping the mast slightly away from the body. The feet should remain on the centerline, one on each side of the mast with the knees slightly bent. The shoulders and body should lean back to counterbalance the sail which still has the aft end of the booms a couple of inches out of the water. This position should feel comfortable and the board should be stable. This is called the Neutral Position.

Common Error:

- To take hold of the booms, or handle.

BOARD CONTROL AND TURNING

1. Move the sail assembly toward the back (stern) of the board. Face the rig and keep your back to the wind, keeping the sail pointing downwind. The front (bow) of the board will start turning into the wind. Stop moving the sail and the turning will stop. Move the sail toward the bow and return to the starting position.

2. Move the sail assembly toward the front (bow) of the board. Face the rig, keep your back to the wind, and keep the sail pointing downwind. The front (bow) of the board will start turning away from the wind. Stop moving the sail and the turning will stop. Move the sail toward the stern and return to the neutral position.

Common Errors:
- Lifting the boom ends too far up from the water, or holding booms too close to body.
- Not facing the sail.

BASIC TURNING OF THE BOARD
(Using Crossover Technique)

The board may be maneuvered through a 360° turn merely by pushing the sail assembly to either the left or right while still holding the uphaul line. During this maneuver, the sail will be luffing and heading downwind. As the board turns, move the feet around the board while continuing to keep the mast between you and the sail. The basic turn starts with the board pointing from 3 to 9 o'clock or vice versa. The 360° turn is completed when the board returns to the original starting position.

1. Your board should be across the wind, pointing from 3 to 9 o'clock or vice versa.

2. Move the sail assembly toward the back of the board (and the boom end toward the water).

3. As the board turns, step around the front of the mast as the front of the board passes through 12 o'clock. The wind will still be at your back and one foot will now be on either side of the centerline of the board.

4. Continue moving the mast and your feet in the same direction until the board has moved a total of 180°. It now points in the opposite direction as the starting position. (If it originally pointed from 3 to 9 o'clock, it will now point from 9 to 3 o'clock).

5. Continue turning the board and step behind the mast. As the front of the board passes through 6 o'clock, let the sail assembly swing around the front of the board. The wind will still be at your back and one foot will now be on either side of the centerline of the board.

6. Continue moving the mast and your feet in the same direction until the board has moved a total of 360° and points back to the original starting position. (If it originally pointed from 3 to 9 o'clock, it will again point from 3 to 9 o'clock).

7. Your feet should now return to the centerline position.

Common Errors:
- Moving feet faster than the corresponding sail turn.
- Lifting the boom ends too far up from the water or holding booms too close to the body.
- Not facing the sail and not keeping back to the wind.

BASIC TURNING OF THE BOARD (Using Mast Hand Technique)

Another common method for executing the above mentioned maneuvers is using the mast hand technique. In this technique, the moment of the aft end of the booms are lifted from the water the boardsailor releases the uphaul line and grabs the mast itself about 6-10" below the booms. The maneuvers of the basic turning of the board are all executed while holding onto the mast.

BEGINNER'S CHECK LIST

1. You are now ready to start boardsailing. Let's check and make sure we are back in the neutral position.

2. Make sure the board is across the wind with the sail assembly pointing downwind and at right angles to the board.

3. The sail should be luffing.

4. The feet should be at right angles to the centerline of the board with the front foot in front of the mast and the back foot on or in back of the daggerboard well about shoulders width apart.

5. The sail assembly should be a couple of inches out of the water with the body leaning slightly to windward to counterbalance the sails pull. The knees are slightly bent, the buttocks in, and more than half of the body weight is placed on the back leg.

6. Both hands should be holding the uphaul or the mast, near the booms with back hand on top.

Common Errors:
- Sail not at right angles to the board.
- Feet not positioned properly.
- Not keeping the aft end of the booms out of the water.
- Keeping the legs straight.
- Bending at the waist while keeping the arms straight.

READY POSITION
(Using the Crossover Technique)

1. Grab hold of the uphaul, with the back hand on top and closest to the booms.

2. Take the front hand and cross over your back hand and grab the booms about 6-10" back from the front boom end.

3. Pull and snap the mast forward so that it is straight up and in front of you blocking your view of the bow of the board. Release the uphaul with your back hand and let that hand fall to your side. There should now be a straight line running from the back of the board through your back shoulder, front shoulder, front elbow, mast and bow of the board. The mast will be touching the shin of the forward leg at this time.

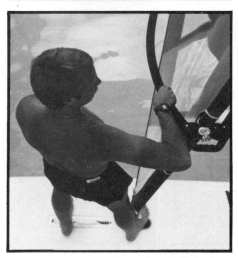

4. Take the back hand and grab hold of the booms about 2' back from the front hand. You are now in the ready position. Tip the mast straight forward towards the bow of the board with your front arm and pull (sheet) in the booms with your back hand just enough to fill the sail with wind. The mast is still on the centerplane and you are sailing. This is the sailing position. To sail in a straight line, keep the booms parallel to the water.

Common Errors:
- Not going through the entire sequence and having improper hand placement on the booms.
- Sail not at right angles to the board.
- Feet not positioned properly.
- Not keeping the mast on the centerplane.

READY POSITION
(Using the Mast Hand Technique)

1. Pick a heading. Grab hold of the mast with both hands with the back hand on top and closest to the booms.

2. Drop the back hand. Draw the mast across the centerline and directly towards the wind until you can site your heading through the window. As you draw the sail across, rotate your upper body towards the bow to face your heading. The front foot should now be angled forward in a comfortable position next to the mast.

3. The back hand is then placed on the booms directly in front of the shoulders.

4. You are now ready to begin sailing by placing the front hand on the booms about 6-10″ behind the mast (making the arms about shoulders width apart). Until you sheet in there should be no wind in the sail. This is the ready position. Rotate your upper body until the sail just fills with air. You are now sailing. This is the basic sailing position. To sail in a straight line., keep the booms parallel to the water.

Sailing techniques using the mast hand or crossover techniques are the exact same except during the acts of tacking or jibing when, depending on the technique, the boardsailor will either grab the mast or the uphaul while executing these maneuvers.

TACKING

In order to reach a destination that is dead upwind or head to wind of you, you will have to learn how to tack. Tacking in conjunction with close hauled sailing allows you to zig zag your way upwind changing from port to starboard tack and vice versa until you reach your destination. When tacking, the bow of your board will pass through the wind while you step around the front of the mast and resume sailing on the new tack. The board will turn through a minimum of 90° as you go from a close hauled port tack to a close hauled starboard tack or vise versa. It is not a difficult process and with a little practice, changing direction can be a quick and easy maneuver.

TACKING
(Using the Crossover Technique)

1. Head up into the wind by raking the mast back and, without changing the trim of the sail, tilt the aft boom end down towards the water. Constant pressure should be maintained on the sail with the back hand until the bow of the board has headed into the wind.

2. Step in front of the mast with both feet so that one foot will now be on either side of the centerline of the board and continue to maintain pressure on the sail. As the bow passes through the eye of the wind, let go of the booms with your back hand and grasp the uphaul with this hand and help the board to continue turning while the booms sweep across the stern onto the new tack. As the board turns, continue to walk around the front of the mast, taking small steps and keeping your feet close to the mast. Remember to keep your body between the mast and the eye of the wind as you turn.

3. Continue to turn until you have once again reached the basic starting position only this time pointing in the other direction.

Remember to change your hand positions and return your feet to the centerline position.

4. Take the front hand and cross over your back hand and grab the booms about 6-10" back from the front boom end.

5. Pull and snap the mast forward (as in the ready position).

6. Grab hold of the booms with your back hand, tilt the rig forward, sheet in with the back hand and begin sailing on the new tack.

TACKING
(Using the Mast Hand Technique)

1. Head up into the wind by raking the mast back and, without changing the trim of the sail, tilt the aft boom end down towards the water. Constant pressure should be maintained on the sail with the back hand until the bow of the board has headed into the wind.

2. Step in front of the mast with both feet so that 1 foot will now be on either side of the centerline of the board and continue to maintain pressure on the sail. As the bow passes through the eye of the wind, let go of the boom with the front hand and grasp the mast with this hand. Continue turning the board by placing both hands on the mast and moving the aft end of the booms across the stern onto the new tack.

46

3. Continue to turn until you have once again reached the basic starting position, only this time pointing in the other direction.

Remember to change your hand positions and return your feet to the centerline position.

4. The front hand grabs the mast and brings it across the centerplane and directly into the wind (as in the ready position).

5. The back hand is then placed on the booms about 3' back from the mast.

6. Place the front hand on the booms about 6-10" behind the mast. Tilt the rig forward, sheet in with the back hand and begin sailing on the new tack.

7. By repeating this maneuver and executing another tack you will return back to the other side. The techniques for tacking are the same whether you change from port to starboard or starboard to port.

JIBING

Another technique for altering your course is called a 'Jibe'. When jibing, the sail passes across the bow of the board while the sailor steps behind the mast around to the other side of the board. Jibing is different from a tack since the change of course is executed while sailing downwind and is begun by heading off or bearing away from the wind.

JIBING
(Using the Crossover Technique)

1. Head away from the wind by sheeting in with the back hand and, without changing the trim of the sail, tilt the mast forward and to windward towards the bow of the board. This will raise the aft end of the booms. Constant pressure should be maintained on the sail with the back hand. By stepping towards the back of the board you will be able to counterbalance the pull of the sail. As the stern passes through the eye of the wind and the sail assembly becomes perpendicular to the board, move your front foot aft and bring your rear foot forward until your feet are on either side of the centerline, about shoulder's width apart, with the body facing forward.

2. Let go of the booms with your front hand and take hold of the uphaul.

3. As the board passes through dead downwind, push the booms, away from you and towards the bow of the board with your back hand. As the rig passes around the front of the board, continue to lean the rig towards the original windward side with the hand holding the uphaul.

4. The old back hand simply crosses over the hand holding the uphaul and re-grasps the other side of the booms about 6-10″ back from the mast and now becomes the new front hand. Continue to turn and take small steps around the mast until you have once again reached the across the wind neutral position only this time pointing in the other direction.

5. Release the uphaul with the old front hand, drop it to your side, and return your feet to the centerline position. Begin sailing on the new tack by reaching up with your back hand and re-grasping the booms, tilting the rig forward and sheeting in.

JIBING
(Using the Mast Hand Technique)

1. Head away from the wind by sheeting in with the back hand and, without changing the trim of the sail, tilt the mast forward and to windward towards the bow of the board. This will raise the aft end of the booms. Constant pressure should be maintained on the sail with the back hand. By stepping towards the back of the board you will be able to counterbalance the pull of the sail. As the stern passes through the eye of the wind and the sail assembly becomes perpendicular to the board, move your front foot aft and bring your rear foot forward until your feet are on either side of the centerline, about shoulder's width apart, with the body facing forward.

2. Place your front hand on the mast below the booms.

3. Release the booms with your back hand, take hold of the mast with both hands, and let the sail swing around the bow of the board. Use both hands to help make sure the board continues to turn by pushing the sail to the right to go left and vise versa. The old back hand will become the new front hand.

4. Continue to turn and take small steps around the mast until you have once again reached the aross the wind neutral position, only this time pointing in the other direction. The new front hand will be on the mast while the new back hand holds the booms about 3' back from the mast.

5. Return your feet to the centerline position and begin sailing on the new tack by tilting the rig forward and sheeting in with the back hand.

JIBING (Alternate Method 3)

An alternate method to try if you are using the cross over technique and are heading downwind is to let go of the booms with your back hand and reach under the front hand and take hold of the uphaul. As the board passes through dead downwind let go of the booms with the front hand as well and also grasp the uphaul. With both hands on the uphaul continue to push and move the rig to the original windward side until the hull has turned in the opposite direction and is across the wind. Remember to keep your body between the mast and the wind at all times and take small steps around the mast as the hull turns. Return your feet to the centerline position and as you stand holding the uphaul line you are now ready to begin sailing by executing the basic cross over technique starting sequence.

If you own a sinker short board you may find that jibing is the only way to turn the board, even when trying to head upwind, since there is usually not enough room or floatation in front of the mast to enable the sailor to execute a tack. Jibing is not a difficult process in light air. However, as the wind increases, it can become a little trickier and will require more practice. Sometimes a sailor, due to a variety of variables such as waves and currents may find it faster to sail on a broad reach rather than dead downwind. In order to reach a downwind destination the sailor may have to zig zag downwind on these broad reaches using a series of jibes. Although the sailor is physically performing jibes, this is sometimes called tacking downwind.

STARBOARD TACK/PORT TACK

STARBOARD TACK

When you are sailing along and the wind comes over the starboard (right) side of your board and causes your rig to extend out over the port (left) side of your board then you are on a starboard tack.

PORT TACK

When you are sailing along and the wind comes over the port (left) side of your board and causes your rig to extend out over the starboard (right) side of your board then you are on a port tack.

STEERING - HEADING UP

Heading up or pointing up is the act of bringing your board towards or into the wind. To head up, pick a new heading slightly upwind. Then, without changing the trim of the sail, lower the aft boom end towards the water, until the board heads towards the new target. Make sure the aft end of the booms does not go into the water. To stop the board from turning past your target, slowly raise the aft boom end away from the water until the turning is neutralized. This will cause the board to continue moving in a straight line.

Common Error:
- Not keeping constant pressure on the sail assembly.
- Tilting the body instead of the booms.
- Trying to sail directly into the wind.

STEERING - HEADING OFF

Heading off or bearing off is the act of turning the board downwind or away from the wind. To head off, pick a new target slightly downwind. Then, without changing the trim of the sail, lift the aft end of the booms up and away from the water. To stop the board from heading off, lower the aft boom end back towards the water until the booms are approximately parallel to the water. This will cause the board to stop turning and continue in a straight line.
Common Error:
- Not keeping constant pressure on the sail assembly.
- Tilting the body instead of the booms.

STEERING - HEADING DOWNWIND

If you head off until the hull is pointing dead downwind then you will be sailing downwind or on a run. The feet are moved so that both are behind the mast foot, near the daggerboard about shoulder's width apart with one foot on either side of the centerline of the board with the body facing forward. The sail assembly will be at a right angle to the hull. If you use the centerline as a guideline, when there is an equal amount of sail area over the left side of the rig as there is on the right side, then the sailboard will point straight downwind. Raising or lowering the aft boom end will still cause the board to turn. If you tilt the rig to the right so that more sail area is on the right side of the centerline then the hull will turn left. You can also speed up this turning to the left motion by putting additional weight on the right side of the board. While executing these maneuvers, constant pressure should be maintained on the sail with the back hand. Consequently, tilting the rig to the left and putting weight on the left side of the hull will cause the board to turn to the right.

Steering straight

Steering left

Steering right

ANGLE OF ATTACK, SAIL ADJUSTMENT

The ideal angle of attack that will generate efficient sail lift for any point of sail exists somewhere between luffing and stalling. It is the angle at which the apparent wind meets the sail. If measured it would be the angle between the apparent wind and the longitudinal axis of the booms. The ideal angle of attack will vary slightly depending on the wind and its strength, wave conditions, board speed, the cut and trim of your sail and other variables. The apparent wind interacts with the true wind. Therefore, the velocity and direction of the wind you feel will probably change as your board's speed changes, so try to be aware of and react to these changes in wind direction.

Sheeting in until the sail is just full and stops luffing is generally the best angle of attack although in heavier winds you may want to sheet in a little more. Try to avoid luffing on nearly all points of sail, except a run when the angle of the sail to the wind is the same but it is the hull and its relation to

the wind which will change so much. That is why you find a tight sail (one that is sheeted in a lot) when sailing close to or toward the wind and a loose sail (one that is not sheeted in a lot) when sailing down and away from the wind. In light winds your arms should be bent slightly with the body straightened and the chest parallel to the sail. As the winds increase, the arms should extend while the hands move along the booms until a comfortable position is found where the rig is balanced and the forces equally distributed. As the winds increase you may have to tilt the mast to windward and at the same time lean your body out more to windward. You will not fall backwards since the force of the wind on the sail will hold you up compared to lighter winds when you may find yourself holding the sail up. With practice, you will find yourself in heavy air in a totally effortless comfortable position where your arms are extended with the body leaning back being counterbalanced by the force of the wind holding the sail up.

HANDGRIPS

Amongst boardsailors, a common complaint is that the forearms tire quickly and they want to lengthen their sailing time. Since the forearms are worked harder than any other part of the body when boardsailing, one of the best cures is to sail longer and more often which will naturally strengthen your forearms. Using straight arms when cruising might also help to relax you as some of the pressure will be taken off your upper arms. Some sailors, especially when going upwind, have been known to take their back arm and loop it over the booms so the booms are under the inside of their upper arms just below the armpit and they sheet in by using body weight. Another upwind technique, which is actually a freestyle trick, is to place your whole body inside the booms, facing the sail, with your back resting on the booms and draping your arms over the booms. Another method to help relax your forearms is to periodically invert the position of your hands on the booms. Start sailing with the traditional overhand grip (both hands on top of the booms, fingertips down). When you get tired, switch to an underhand grip (both hands on the bottom of the booms, fingertips up). Alternately, you may try the mixed grip where either the front hand remains in an

overhand grip and the back hand goes to an underhand grip or vice versa. This gives you four different handgrips to try.

Finger position can also vary depending on the grip. Normal finger position is with the 4 fingers on top of the boom and the thumb underneath it. Others, especially on the back hand (sheet hand) may keep all 4 fingers and the thumb on top of the booms. Some people even place the thumb along the side of the booms. The whole key is to find a comfortable grip and hand position that allows you to spend the most time possible on the water. Some may not feel at all comfortable, but try them if you're tired. Sailing for a long period of time increases your forearm strength, but may develop some painful blisters on the palms of your hands. If the blisters are too bad, you may have to rest for a few days to let them dry up so you don't tear your hands apart. If they are just forming, you might purchase a pair of sailing or waterski gloves to get over the crisis. These gloves should be padded around the palm area and will probably help relieve the pain. Just as increased sailing will increase your forearm strength, it will also help your hands get calloused and in better condition for boardsailing.

Overhand grip

Underhand grip

Mixed grip

Mixed grip

Overhand grip, Thumbs forward

Overhand grip, Thumbs in

SHEETING IN

Sheeting in on a normal sailboat would be the act of pulling in the main sheet (a line) which in turn pulls the boom in toward the center of the boat. In boardsailing, the same expression is used to explain the act of the aft hand pulling the booms in toward the centerline of the hull, which will cause the sail to fill with wind. This action trims the sail to the proper angle of attack. The tighter you sheet in, the more pull you will feel on your arms. This may also be accompanied by an increase in speed. If the wind drops suddenly and you feel you are falling back to windward, sheeting in may give you the power to pull you back up on the board. Tightening or pulling the sail in is sheeting in and the hand that you sheet in with (the back hand and the one furthest from the mast) is the sheet hand. It acts in the same manner as the main sheet would on a regular sailboat.

SHEETING OUT

Sheeting out or easing the sail lets the booms back out by letting out your back hand. It is helpful for slowing down or lessening the pull on the arms. In gusty winds be prepared to sheet out and lean to windward if the sail pull gets too strong.
Common Error:
- Sheeting in or out too fast and not keeping constant pressure on the sail.

LUFFING

Luffing is the end result of sheeting out to a point where the sail starts to luff by fluttering first near the mast and continuing out towards the clew. There is no wind in the sail at this time and the board will slow to a stop.

STALLING

Stalling is the end result of oversheeting to a point where the aft end of the booms are pulled in past the centerline. The board will first stall out and come to a complete stop before starting to move in reverse if the rig is kept oversheeted.

OVERPOWERED

If you start to feel overpowered by the sail, then sheet out.

1. Remember to sheet out by easing off and loosening the back hand. If you must release one hand from the booms, the back one is always the one to release first.

2. Bending at the waist and letting the mast lean out to leeward may tempt you to release the front (mast) hand instead of the back (sheet) hand. This error will cause the mast to swing further out to leeward, make the sail feel heavier and most likely result in a fall or at least a drop of the sail.

Sheeting in

Sheeting out

Luffing

Stalling

When overpowered never let go of the front hand

When overpowered release the back hand

FAST TACK

Before executing a fast tack it helps to have good boat speed to carry you through the turn. To achieve this, keep the hull flat on the water, the mast vertical along the centerplane and possibly bear off just a little if you have been sailing very close to the wind.

1. To initiate the tack, lean the mast back to help the board head up and move your back foot about 6-12" toward the stern. Sheet in the sail so the board turns into the wind while keeping the arms fully extended to insure the sail stays leaned back. At this time take your front hand off the booms and place it on the mast just below the booms. When the board is head to wind, over sheet the sail and pull the clew of the sail across the centerplane and push the stern away from you with your back foot. Continue to hold

this position until the bow of the board has passed through the eye of the wind.

2. Move toward the bow of the board and place your old back foot just in front of the mast. At the same time release the booms with your old back hand. Your body should be close to and facing the mast at this time with equal weight on each foot.

3. Place the new back foot onto the centerline of the board, on or just behind the daggerboard and pivot on your new front foot until you are facing the booms. Simultaneously, throw the mast forward along the centerplane with the hand that had been holding the mast before re-grasping the booms with both hands to stop its forward motion. While keeping the front hand forward, sheet in with the back hand and sail off on the new tack.

HEAVY AIR JIBE

A heavy air jibe is a controlled jibe where you jibe around the daggerboard. It is a smooth turn with very little loss of board speed. It requires much practice to perfect so that you don't get overpowered by the rig or have the hull rail up on you.

1. Head off the wind by tilting the mast to windward and sheeting in slightly.

2. As you start to jibe, sheet out with the back hand to de-power yourself so the hull doesn't rail up. Lean the mast to windward while maintaining a firm hold on the booms and step back slightly to help elevate the bow. At the same time put pressure on the windward foot and bring the sail downwind towards you. This action will start to turn the board to leeward.

3. As the board turns past dead downwind pressure will start to build on the back hand.

4. Release your back hand from the booms and start to bring the mast forward to a vertical position with the front hand. The sail will start to swing around to the opposite side of the board.

5. Grab the mast just below the point where the booms are connected with the back hand. At the same time release the booms with the front hand.

6. Grab the new side of the booms fairly far back with the old front hand (now the new back hand) and start to sheet in. Simultaneously step forward as fast as possible so the board doesn't round up into the wind. Without a daggerboard you will not jibe as fast and you must step further back and put more pressure on the windward rail.

LAUNCHING

Launching your sailboard is the act of getting your seaworthy craft together and off the land and into the water. Once you have arrived at your sailing locale, unload the sailboard and bring it to the water's edge or wherever you plan to sail. Unless you have completely derigged the rig assembly, you should have three parts. These are the hull, daggerboard and rig (sail, mast and boom assembly).(Fig. 1)

First, rig the sail assembly and trim the downhaul and outhaul to accommodate whatever the current or projected wind and water conditions are. Before every sail, it is a good precaution to check all the lines on the rig. If any are chafed or worn, then they should be replaced. Frayed ends can be melted smooth for ease in passing through eyes and into cleats. There are five possible methods of launching.

LAUNCHING METHOD 1

The rig assembly will be put in the water first as it won't drift away or get washed back on the beach as fast as the hull would. The rig is carried above the head so that the front of the booms are pointing into the wind while the mast is perpendicular to the wind. One hand will usually be grasping the mast above the booms, while the other hand is on the booms itself. When balanced correctly the wind will literally carry the rig for you. If you do not hold it properly, the wind may keep forcing the tack, clew or head of the sail into the ground, making it difficult to carry. One should experiment in carrying the rig at different angles in an effort to find an easy method where the wind works for you. Carry the rig to the water's edge and throw it out into the water. It will float. The board is usually carried at waist level under one arm with the top toward your body. The hand on the side of the body at which the board is carried is placed into the daggerboard well on the bottom side. The other hand is now placed in the mast step. A proper balance can be achieved by moving the hand in the daggerboard well up and down its length. The daggerboard is looped over the wrist of either hand before picking the board up. Alternately, the daggerboard can be put in the hull and the back hand holds onto it while the front one still grabs the mast step. Carry the board down to the water's edge and wade into waist deep water. Insert the daggerboard and push it down all the way in the daggerboard well. Now paddle out or reach out and grab the sail assembly and insert the universal into the appropriate mast step. Finally, you should

attach the safety leash. This will prevent the rig from floating away should it come loose from the hull.(Fig. 2-5)

LAUNCHING METHOD 2

Fully rig the board on land and then stand between the board and the mast, and lift the board up on it's side before taking hold of the nose of the board under one arm and then grabbing the uphaul with the other hand. Since you will be dragging the sailboard to the water's edge you should do this maneuver only on soft surfaces like sand, mud or grass that won't scratch the equipment. Whichever way you launch, make sure you go in deep enough water to put the daggerboard in before starting.(Fig. 6)

LAUNCHING IN THE SURF

Surf can take the form of the playground for high performance craft and Funboards and stretch for a few hundred yards, or it can merely be a short series of waves, called a shore break or surfline, that may be either rough or calm and one that must be broken through before reaching the vast expanses of open water just beyond it. Launching in the surf or waves can present many problems for beginners and experts alike. If there is another area from which to launch, use it. If not, then you might try one of the following: First, check the wind for its strength and direction. Weak winds coming straight onshore accompanied by moderate waves will present problems. You will have to leave the shore at an angle to the waves and you may not have enough wind to power you through them before a wave or whitewater pushes your bow back towards land and knocks you over sideways with the next wave. If you must launch in these conditions, do the following; Wait, watch and study the waves before trying to go out. Waves come in sets, sometimes in groups of seven, getting progressively bigger and when the last of the set breaks there is sometimes a lull before the next set starts in. You want to launch in this lull.

LAUNCHING METHOD 3

Similar to Method 2. Stand on one side of the hull while facing both the nose of the board and the sail assembly, while both point towards the water. Lift the nose of the board up on its side and put it under one arm before crossing over with the other hand and grabbing the uphaul up high or the handle on the front boom end fitting. Hold both close together at waist level and carry it into the water while dragging the stern along the ground. Once in waist deep water, drop the nose of the board and make sure you keep the sail out of the water. Quickly climb on the board while making sure you don't drop the rig and start sailing. This method is great for launching in a rough shorebreak where speed in getting on the board and not dropping the sail may determine whether you make it out or not. (Fig. 7)

LAUNCHING METHOD 4

This was developed in Hawaii and is good for calm shorebreaks. Standing at the water's edge, point the nose of the board toward the water. Hold the sail up to see which way the wind is blowing. If the aft end of your booms points to the left of the board then grab the mast or booms with the right hand. If it points to the right, then grab the mast or booms with the left hand holding whichever hand at eye level to keep the sail and booms above the water. The free hand now reaches down and grabs the stern of the board, lifts it to waist level, and proceeds to push the rig, nose first, into the water. Since the sail is already out of the water and ready to go you simply step onto the board once you are in water deep enough to accomodate the skeg(s) and/or daggerboard and off you go.(Fig. 8)

LAUNCHING METHOD 5

Entering the shorebreak in the self rescue position with the rig assembly rolled up and placed on top of the board and you lying on top of the rig in a paddling position. Again, try to start paddling out during a lull in the waves. If a wave comes toward you then paddle into it as fast as possible in an effort to punch through it. Keep paddling to keep up your speed, especially when going through a wave to avoid being washed back to shore. Once you are out past the shorebreak and well clear of any surf and waves, then rig your board and sail away. Most standard boards are not designed for sailing in breaking surf and it is not recommended to play in the surf on one, especially if you are a beginner.

LANDING

Landing is easier than launching since you are going in the same direction as the waves. If you have the time, wait and try to sail in during a lull. If you end up surging in on a wave then beware. Shooting down a wave will increase your speed maybe to the point of having the sail backwind in your face. If this happens, board control will be achieved only with precise balance. Many times the board will want to head up, putting you sideways to

the wave before it probably knocks the board out from under you. Keep the nose pointed toward the beach. Another problem is the bow plowing forward into the next wave before it pearls or nose dives to the bottom like a submarine. Standing further back on the board should help if you see this problem starting. If you successfully ride the wave to shore, then sail until you can touch bottom. Step off beside the board and while still holding the mast or boom with one hand, lift the stern with the other hand and push it nose first up the beach in much the same manner as you launched in Method 4. If you aren't successful on your first attempt and fall, then be aware of the power of a wave. Even a small wave can break a mast or twist a set of booms before you know what happened. Floundering in the waves can be a frightening experience but need not always be an expensive one. If you fall and your rig is still totally together and you don't have enough time to get back on the board and pull up the sail before the next wave hits you, then quickly swim and grab the mast tip of your sail and try to swim with it as fast as you can out to sea and into the face of the oncoming wave. As the wave breaks, dive down into it while still holding the mast tip. Because of the high buoyancy content of the board, the wave will try to lift it and carry it to shore faster than it would a rig assembly. If you are close to shore hold on as a few more waves may even take you into the beach. If you don't keep the mast tip toward the breaking wave and let the rig assembly get between the hull and the shore, then the oncoming wave will probably lift up the board and try to carry it toward shore while simultaneously flipping the rig over or pushing the rig toward the bottom. Either situation will most likely break your mast. If you are still a distance from the beach you should wait for a break in the waves before quickly trying to get up and get started. In some falls, the universal may pop out and maybe even break your safety leash. If so the hull might quickly float away on the next wave. Ideally you want to stick with your hull. In any potentially dangerous situation this is the first priority.(Fig. 9)

Sometimes a series of waves may sweep your board away faster than you can swim after it or catch it. If this happens, the hull will end up at a point on the beach. If so, and you know you can't catch it, let it go. If you are a strong swimmer and have a PFD or wetsuit on, try to save your rig. Swimming with a fully rigged sail assembly is slow and tiring. Untie the outhaul and do your best to roll the sail up and tie the rig assembly into as small a package as possible. This should also help prevent a mast breaking which would happen a lot easier when fully rigged. Now swim toward shore with the rig and try to conserve as much of your strength as possible. Let the waves work for you and try to ride them in. Whatever you do, don't panic.

Stay calm and remember your emergency procedures. Anyone who has ever gone out in the surf has fallen at least once. Some experts have spent hours at the beach, broken 2 or 3 masts and never got to sail. If trying to save the rig puts you in danger, dump it. Remember that equipment is replaceable; you are not!

Fig. 1

Fig. 2

Fig. 3

Fig. 4

Fig. 5

Fig. 6

Fig. 7

Fig. 8

Fig. 9

FALLS AND FALLING

Falling while learning how to boardsail is as common as apple pie is American. At some time you may get overpowered by a gust of wind, watch it die completely or even have it come at you from the opposite direction before you have a chance to react to it. Any of these situations and a whole variety more may cause you to fall while learning how to boardsail. Recognizing that this will happen and becoming aware of the various types of falls and learning how to fall may avoid a potential agony down the line. The most common falls you will encounter are the;

1. Catapult Fall.
2. Into the Sail Fall.
3. Body to Windward/Sail to Leeward Fall.
4. Body and Sail to Windward Fall.

CATAPULT FALL

This is by far the most dramatic fall. It usually occurs in high winds when sailing on a reach. First a strong gust of wind hits the sail and the sailor sheets in and leans back in an effort to harness this power and go faster. Sometimes the sailor doesn't brace the forward foot fast enough or sheet out quick enough. Before you know it the sail is being propelled to leeward at high speeds. By the time the sailor releases his grip on the booms he has built up forward momentum and usually is catpulted over the bow of the board in a diving manner or has little choice but to run off the bow of the board into the water.

BODY TO WINDWARD/SAIL TO LEEWARD FALL

This is a very common fall and usually occurs when the sailor, feeling that he is being overpowered and pulled towards the sail, decides to totally let go of the sail and push it away from himself rather than to just sheet out. This slight push to windward coupled with the fact that he now has nothing to hold onto to maintain his balance causes him to walk or fall back off the board to windward and into the water, while the sail assembly falls to leeward.

BODY AND SAIL TO WINDWARD FALL

This is also a fairly common type of fall and is the one that could cause potential panic to a timid beginner. Sometimes you may be leaning out to windward and the wind dies suddenly or you start to fall backwards so you sheet in and there is not enough wind to hold you up. The end result is that you usually fall to windward and sometimes you may even pull the sail assembly right on top of your head as you go under. Your body and head are usually under the water when the sail hits the water so the chances of hitting yourself with the rig are very slim. However, the one real danger is in coming up under the sail and needing air only to find the sail and lots of water over your head. If this happens remain calm and don't panic. When this type of a fall occurs, come up with your hands over your head. If you feel the sail overhead then spread your arms and turn 360° until you feel one of the 3 edges of the sail or the booms and then pull yourself out to that edge before popping your head up for air. Remember that there is usually not a pocket of air under the sail so hold your breath until you know you are surfacing in the air.

Any of the above mentioned falls may also be practiced in the swimming pool. This safety procedure will enhance the boardsailors sense of comfort and well being.

INTO THE SAIL FALL

Usually comes in two varieties. The first works on the same principle as the catapult fall but instead of being launched or thrown over the bow, the sailor doesn't release his grip on the booms fast enough and gets pulled into and on top of the sail either face first or after executing some sort of somersault over the booms.

The second variety is a log gentler and occurs when the sailor again doesn't sheet out fast enough in a gust of wind and gets pulled into and on top of the sail as it falls to leeward. This usually happens a lot slower and the sailor may find himself sitting, kneeling or maybe even standing on the sail. If he is quick, he may jump back on the board before he even gets wet. A practice should not be made of falling on the sail as it may damage or rip the sail if its done continously.

EMERGENCY STOPS

If you want to slow down then simply sheet out (loosen the pull on the sail) with your back (sheet) hand. However, there are certain times when you may find yourself on a collision course with another moving boat or even a docked yacht.

DROP THE SAIL STOP

In any emergency situation when you have to stop fast a simple method is to drop your sail. It will act as a sea anchor and slow you down and stop your forward progress. If this doesn't stop you quick enough then drop the rig and immediately jump in yourself. Grab hold of the board and try to swim it and you away from the obstacle. (See Fall #3)

STOP JIBE

Another method that advanced boardsailors use to stop themselves and also to prevent getting wet is called a stop jibe. Here the sailor basically executes a jibe in a small area without doing a lot of the heading off and downwind maneuvering associated with a normal jibe. The sailor sheets out with the back hand, tilts the mast to windward and continues to push the booms away from him with the back hand. This causes the sail to backwind and fill with wind from the other side. Keep pushing on the booms with the back hand and force the clew to pass around the bow of the board. Remember that you are on the leeward side of the sail and as the board turns you should take small steps around the mast to maintain your balance. Once the sail passes over the bow, regrab the booms on the other side with the old front (mast) hand and continue to pull the sail to complete the turn. Release the booms with the old back hand and bring it around to the other side of the booms where it will become the new front (mast) hand. You are now on a new tack going away from the obstacle and should execute the appropriate maneuvers to head up or off depending on your new destination.

POWER JIBE

Another techinque which is similar to and has the same end results as the Stop Jibe is called a Power Jibe. Step forward of the mast with the front foot and release your front hand from the booms and regrasp them on the opposite side well back from the mast. As the board slows down, back wind the sail around to the other side with the old front hand. The hull will now pass through the dead downwind position and start to head up on the new tack. Continue to pull the booms in while simultaneously raking the mast back with the old front hand (now the new back hand) and transfer the old back hand around to the other side of the booms so it becomes the new front hand and head off on the new tack.

INTERNATIONAL DISTRESS/EMERGENCY HAND SIGNALS

If you find yourself in difficulty and stuck out on the water then you should signal passing boats or people on shore by means of the international distress/emergency hand signals. The visible signal is communicated by the sailors arms.

I'M OK.

1. Sit or kneel on the board as upright as possible.
2. Raise your arms over your head and form them into a loop and hold this position.

HELP - SOS (I am in trouble)

1. Sit or kneel on the board as upright as possible.
2. Straighten your arms and keep raising and lowering them up above your head and down by your side repeating several times.

I'm O.K.   *HELP-SOS*   *HELP-SOS*

SELF RESCUE

There are many practical reasons for self rescue. It is important to recognize these conditions and start a self rescue before you are too exhausted or blown miles offshore.

1. If you can still sail, but are unable to make upwind progress, then you may find it safer or easier to sail to a shore that may be across or downwind from the launch site.

2. If for some reason you are unable to sail back to shore you can still safely make it back by executing a self rescue.

3. Paddling a sailboard with a fully rigged sail assembly attached to it is very difficult, even in light winds. Self rescue may take a few extra minutes to roll up the sail onto the rig and place it on the board, but the paddling to shore will be much quicker.

4. Sometimes you may leave the beach with a sail that is too large for your abilities and you may have to return to shore to change to a smaller sail.

5. Sometimes you leave the beach with the right sized sail, but the wind gets stronger until there is too much wind for you to handle. Return to shore for a smaller sail.

6. Sometimes a line or part of the craft may break or fail to function properly and it may be necessary to return to shore and make the necessary repair.

THE MOST COMMON FORMS OF SELF RESCUE ARE:

1. Rig on stern, paddle with hands.
2. Sit down and paddle with one hand.
3. De-rig and paddle with mast.
4. De-rig and paddle with hands.
5. De-rig and paddle with daggerboard.

RIG ON STERN, PADDLE WITH HANDS

(Only for no wind situations - Flat Water)
A method of self rescue which doesn't require you to de-rig the sail assembly in no wind situations is to lay and balance the rig on the stern of the board facing aft while still attached to the hull.

1. Make sure the rig is balanced correctly or else the mast or clew will dip into the water and upset your steering and slow you down.

2. The sailor then kneels down facing forward, in front of the universal and paddles with both arms to his destination.

SIT DOWN AND PADDLE WITH ONE HAND

(Only for no wind situations - Flat Water)
A method of self rescue which doesn't require you to de-rig the sail assembly in no wind situations is to sit forward of the mast on your fully rigged sailboard, facing aft with your legs straddling the mast.

1. Grab hold of the mast about 3' up from the universal with one hand making sure the clew end of the booms are raised out of the water.

2. With the free hand, reach down into the water and paddle the sailboard in the direction you want to head. It is difficult to hold the mast up and is advisable not to let the clew of the sail drop into the water as you sit down.

DE-RIG AND PADDLE WITH MAST

(Only for No Wind Situations - Flat Water)
1. Totally disassemble the rig and place the booms, sail and universal on the deck while keeping the mast to use as a paddle.

2. Stand over the rest of the rig and use your mast like a kyak paddle and paddle to shore (most masts will sink, so don't let go of the mast and don't kick the universal overboard as it will probably sink as well).

3. An alternate method is to kneel or straddle the rest of the rig and paddle to shore in the same manner.

DE-RIG AND PADDLE WITH HANDS

This is probably the most common method of self rescue.

1. Disconnect the sail assembly from the hull (including untieing the safety leash).

2. Release the outhaul and roll and furl the sail tightly up onto the rig as you would when preparing it for carrying or transporting on the roof of your car. The outhaul and uphaul lines can be tied around the mast and booms to hold the rig together.

3. Center the disassembled rig assembly on top of the hull.

4. Lie face down on top of the sail assembly and use your hands as paddles much as a surfer would.

5. An alternate method here is to straddle, sit or kneel on top of the sail assembly and use your hands as paddles.

6. Another method is to straddle and sit on top of the sail assembly facing forward and use your daggerboard as a paddle much like a canoeist would.

ERRORS AND CORRECTIONS

Errors are quite common when learning how to board sail and being able to see and recognize these errors as they develop should help you to correct them immediately and hopefully prevent a fall in the water. Sure a fall here or there may seem fun or even a cooling experience on a hot day but for a beginner, repetitive falls are frustrating and tiring. Example: You are just about ready to sheet in and begin sailing. You are in a rush, sheet in before you're ready and get pulled into the water. You have really done a lot more than fall. First you have to recover from the fall, climb back on the board, retrieve the uphaul, pull up the sail, get back in the starting position and go through the same steps to the original position where you made

the error. Before, instead of waiting and thinking for 5 seconds about the right next move, you rushed the sequence and fell. True, you're now back where you started but instead you are now wet, possibly a little colder, potentially a little more frustrated and for sure a little more tired. You have repeated all those steps and lost 3-5 minutes of class time and have less time to enjoy the finer points of boardsailing. The most common areas where mistakes are made are:

1. Beginning Position
2. Foot Position
3. Neutral Position
4. Sailing Position
5. Sheeting In
6. Sailing
7. Posture
8. Board Control

BEGINNING POSITION

When you get on the board you must check and see that:

1. The wind is at your back.
2. You are facing the sail.
3. The board is across the wind.
4. The mast is pointing downwind.

FOOT POSITION

Proper foot placement is very important. Check to see that:

1. The feet are in the proper position, on the centerline, not too much to windward or leeward.
2. The legs are relaxed. Stiff and tense legs may make the board shakey.
3. Check your feet occasionally to insure they are in the proper position.

NEUTRAL POSITION

Before you get ready to sheet in and fill the sail with wind you want to make sure that the board is across the wind. If you start with the board pointing too high to the wind, it will head up and get backwinded from the leeward side knocking you for a fall. If you start with the board heading too far off the wind, the initial pull on the arms as the sail fills with wind might pull you over.

SAILING POSITION

The hull of a sailboard sometimes acts in the same manner as a bicycle. At rest, both a sailboard and a bicycle can appear very tippy and unstable. However, forward motion causes both to feel very stable. You can now concentrate on more important matters such as steering. When you begin to pull the sail in make sure that:

1. The board, sail and feet are in their proper positions.
2. When you begin to pull the sail in concentrate on the following 3 areas:
   A. The mast is on the centerplane.
   B. The mast is tipped slightly forward and to windward.
   C. The back arm is pulled in.

SHEETING IN

Sheeting in too fast or too much may cause the mast to lean out to leeward instead of staying on the centerplane.

1. The sail gets heavier and the body is forced to bend at the waist out of its proper position to help fight this pull. When this happens, sheet out or release the back (sheet) hand. This will spill the air out of the sail, cause it to luff, make it lighter and easier for you to pull the sail back up to its centerplane position.

2. Bending at the waist and letting the mast lean out to leeward will cause another error which is the tendency to release the front (mast) hand instead of the back hand, which helps lessen the load on the sail assembly. Remember, if the sail assembly starts to get away from you to leeward always sheet out or release the back (sheet) hand and never the front (mast) hand.

SAILING

1. Practice steering and staying on a proper course.
2. Avoid pointing too high and sailing into the no sail area or you may get backwinded and loose your balance.
3. Avoid heading off too far away from the wind or you may have trouble getting back up wind.
4. Avoid sheeting in too fast when heading off since this sudden force might pull you into the sail and cause you to fall.
5. Practice sailing in a straight line by picking a point on shore and heading for it. If you head above that point, then, without changing the trim of the sail, raise the aft boom end a few inches to head off. If you start to head below it, rake the sail back and without changing the trim of the sail, lower the aft boom end a few inches to head up.
6. Try to avoid oversteering. Without changing the trim of the sail, raise and lower the aft boom end just a few inches at a time, rather than a few feet. Remember, steer and move the rig with the arms and not the upper part of the body.
7. Concentrate on the sails position, trim and your proper course. Beginners also tend to stare at their feet and risk heading off course.

POSTURE

Check to see that your body is aligned correctly on the board.

1. The knees are slightly bent.
2. Your buttocks is in.
3. Your shoulders are back.

A common mistake is to bend at your waist and let the mast lean out to leeward. This will put excessive strain on the lower back and this awkward position doesn't give you much chance to pull yourself up and recover if a strong gust of wind hits the sail.

BOARD CONTROL

Practice board control which includes:

1. Keep your feet in the proper position.
2. Keep the hull under control.
3. Keep the mast on the centerplane.
4. Keep wind in the sail.
5. Stay on course.

CHAPTER V

TRANSPORTING YOUR BOARD

Unless you are one of those fortunate few that live on the shore of a lake or an ocean, or are a member of a waterfront club or organization that has facilities for storing a board, you will have to face the problem of transporting your sailboard. Weighing in at under 70 lbs., the sailboard is not heavy, but due to the length of the hull and mast, putting it in most cars can be next to impossible. If you own a van with a long wheel base or have a trailer you may be all set. If not, you will find that the easiest way to transport your board is by means of a roof rack attached to the roof of your car. Most racks consist of two equal and identical parts which can be adjusted to match the width of the car's roof. Racks are most effective as the distance between them increases so one rack is usually placed on the roof as close to the front windshield as possible, and the other as far back as the curvature of the car's roof will allow so that the sailboard itself never touches the roof. Roof racks could consist of your homemade rope-and-towel rack to a manufactured soft roof rack to some of the more elaborate solid aluminum or steel racks which are capable of holding four or more boards and rigs. Many hard racks also come with a variety of attachments and accessories.

Generally racks are attached to the car via the rain gutters. While driving, the board will generate lift and store energy. This will put a lot of strain on both the car rack to gutter connection as well as the sailboard to car rack connection. The failure of either of these is unsafe and could cause an accident, or loss or damage to your equipment. It is therefore advisable to purchase the strongest and sturdiest rack you can afford. Even when the car is parked, boards can generate considerable lift if it is blowing really hard and once untied, could blow right off the top of the car onto the ground, someone elses car or even a person. Use caution!

Also note that not all gutters can support the weight of a hard roof rack plus multiple sailboards, and some might not be able to support even one sailboard, especially while driving. Check this before purchasing a hard rack. Soft racks are great for short hauls at slow speeds, whereas long trips with multiple boards on highways are better with hard racks. Soft racks use the rain gutter to hold them in place, but the actual weight of the sailboard is placed directly on the car's roof. Make sure there is not so much weight that it dents your roof. Soft foam pads help prevent the roof from getting scratched. They are quick and easy to attach and just as easy to steal when you are out sailing so it is advisable to remove them whenever the board is not on the car's roof.

A sailboard should be carried upside down with the bow forward unless the board is wider at the front than in the back. This will allow the skeg to catch against a tie-down and stop any forward motion in the event of a quick stop. A good tie-down knot to use is the trucker's hitch. Strong nylon ropes 1/4" diameter or larger, or straps are best for tying the board to the rack. Clothesline, stretchy rope, and rubber bungee tie-downs or shock cord are probably too weak and are not recommended for this connection. If you are going on a long trip or you have a short roof and your racks are less than 4-5' apart, or if the bow of your board extends 3-4' forward beyond the rack, then it is advisable to also tie the mast and/or bow of the board to the car's front bumper, so it doesn't ride up while you are driving. You may also run an extra line around the board, down through the daggerboard well and through an open car door or window before tying off in the event that the roof rack or rain gutter fails.

When purchasing your first set of roof racks, follow these simple guidelines. Determine; 1. The number of boards you will be carrying. 2. The type of car on which you will be carrying them. 3. Consider the distances you will normally be transporting the boards and if any overnight trips are planned where you may want the capabilities of a lock-on system. 4. Check your budget. See your local sailboard specialist and ask advice from other experienced boardsailors and you can probably find an affordable rack with the features you desire.

A hard rack, soft rack and towel rack

Hard rack

Soft rack

Towel rack; both ends tied off to the cars bumpers

BUYING A NEW SAILBOARD

A sailboard is basically a free-sail system in which the sail and board operate independently of each other. You control the rig and position the sail to make the board move forward and in the direction you want to go. Large or small, light or heavy, strong or weak, beginner or expert - whichever you are and regardless of your level of expertise or income, there is a sailboard for you and purchasing the right sailboard will increase your enjoyment of the sport tremendously. Your goal is to find a sailboard which compromises the least while fulfilling your personal needs be they skill, family, finance or plain personal preference. To maximize your chances of getting what you need, the preceding descriptions on the various parts of the craft should help alleviate some of the confusion when walking into a sailboard shop seeing all the products available. But there is

much to consider when purchasing a sailboard. It is recommended choosing the most professional sailboard shop you can find. Assess your pesonal needs and educate yourself on the available equipment for the activity you desire. Search out a boardsailing specialist shop by talking with experienced boardsailors in your area. Check the various trade magazines and publications. Go to the shops and determine which ones are professionally staffed by people who know what they are talking about and who know the boardsailing products.

A top sailboard shop should carry everything you need for boardsailing which include such things as: accessories, replacement parts, wetsuits, clothing, roof racks and a full range of sail sizes. They should provide excellent service, offer lessons through a sailing school with certified or competent instructors. There is a board out there that is perfectly suited for your intended use. You must choose a board that suits your present needs yet offers room for growth as time on the water increases your level of expertise. Beginners learn how to boardsail fast and some beginner models may be outgrown quickly. On the other hand, a good sailor may become confused with all the choices on the market. If your likes and desires still leave too many choices, then start to analyze your dislikes to help you avoid getting a board that has those qualities. Finally, you must decide what the intended use is and where you will use it. Certain designs are better than others under certain conditions.

Maybe you live on an ocean and you don't care about racing, but you have plenty of wind and waves. If so, you may choose a Funboard and try your hand at water starts, wave jumping and wave surfing. Maybe you just want to cruise or use it as a mode of transportation to get from Point A to Point B. Maybe you want to become a freestylist or go out with a friend and try your hand at tandem or tandem freestyle. Once you know what your intended use is you should analyze the wind and waves in your area and whether the prevailing winds are strong or light as this may also affect your choice of equipment. It may seem like a lot of questions or things to think about, but with all the variables involved in choosing a sailboard a definitive statement of what the perfect board is for you is difficult. Only you can determine who you are, what your current and projected levels of expertise are, and what the intended use of your new sailboard will be, and the prevailing conditions of your intended sailing locale. Once you have answered these questions, you can go back to your sailboard specialist and pick the right equipment for you. Remember your personal needs and pick a board that will grow with you. When you find the equipment you like, make sure it has a good warranty and a dealer system to back it up. If you follow these guidelines, you will have a sailboard that is good for you!

BUYING A USED SAILBOARD

Purchasing a used sailboard is a good choice for someone on a tight budget or for one who finds a deal that can't be ignored. Used sailboards are sometimes difficult to find but if you do find one, try to evaluate its condition and acertain why its being sold. It could be because there is something seriously wrong with it or maybe just the fact the owner is buying a second generation board, upgrading the equipment, or has to move and won't be able to bring it along. Before purchasing, check the following:

1. Condition of the hull. Look to see if it is delaminated or if there are any soft or mushy areas. Check any seams for splits or if any major repairs have been performed on the board.

2. Shape of sail. Check to see if it is blown out or if it has lost its shape. Check the stitching, mast tip, grommets and examine the window for splits or cracks.

3. Condition of the skeg box. This is a hard area to repair so remove the skeg and look for cracks.

4. Condition of the mast. Vertical white colored cracks in the epoxy usually indicate areas of potential breakage. Check the area where the booms attach as this is a common area for cracks. The base of the mast should also be examined for any splitting.

5. Condition of the booms. Check to see if they are bent or twisted. Examine the boom-end fittings for fatigue cracks and see if they are on tight. Listen for water sloshing around inside the tubing. Check the covering on the booms for splits and tears and feel whether it twists or rotates around the tubing - it should be glued down tight and look to see if there is a front boom bumper.

Examine all the areas mentioned and use your best judgement to determine if this is a fair market value. If you feel the price is too high, point out any damage as a negotiating point and make another offer. Because of all the variables there are no laws or rules regarding resale value except "caveat emptor" or "let the buyer beware".

BOARDSAILOR'S TOOL KIT

It is a good idea to put together a handy tool/repair kit so that you can deal with any minor problems. After a long drive to your favorite boardsailing spot, nothing is more frustrating than to discover that you need to perform a minor repair on part of your sailboard before you can go out and enjoy yourself. Being unable to make this minor repair could prevent you from sailing that day, making the long trip a wasted effort. Kits are not designed for major repairs and we assume that when you get home you will take the time to make a thorough and proper repair of the problem. A good tool/repair kit for sailboards should include the following items:

Duct Tape: If a tool/repair kit contained only one item, this would be it. For beginners and experts alike, a good roll of duct tape is essential. It can be wound around loose fitting universals to create a tight rig to board connection. Similarly, the fit of your daggerboard can be adjusted with duct tape. It will patch a minor tear in a sail or patch a crack in the hull to prevent water absorption. You can wrap the base of the mast with it if its cracked or wrap up equipment for transport or even use it for general tie-downs. You can even patch your wetsuit or build up the mast base of a universal if it fits too loosely in the base of the mast. The possibilities are endless and it's certainly a good investment.

Rip Stop Tape and a Piece of Sailcloth: Good for patching minor rips or tears in a sail. If you have a major rip or tear, try to avoid using the sail and get it repaired by a professional sailmaker before the rip gets too big and the damage is irreversible.

Flatheat & Phillips Head Screwdrivers and Allen Wrenches: Be it a skeg, universal, daggerboard cap, mast track or other part of a sailboard, something ususally needs tightening or adjusting, fixing, removing or replacing. These three items can usually take care of this minor problem. Also, a line that won't go through a cleat due to a frayed end can usually be pushed through with one of the above tools.

Extra Line: Always a good idea to keep on hand, in a variety of diameters. No matter how often you check your lines for chafing, or wear and tear, there is always the possibility of something going wrong. Spare lines can replace broken outhauls, inhauls, downhauls or uphauls, or serve as a towing line. Always carry a few feet of line somewhere on the sailboard when sailing. It may be wrapped around the booms, placed on the mast or put in a harness backpack. They can be used to construct a rope universal or lash together a broken mast to help get you home and can serve as a tie-down on your car's roof rack.

Knife: Good for cutting lines, sailcloth or rip stop tape, and can help in retrieving nuts, bolts, screws or inserts caught in sliding mast tracks or skeg boxes.

Pliers or Vice Grips: Besides the recommended uses of tightening or loosening nuts and bolts. They can also be helpful in untying tight knots that don't want to come loose.

Standard File or Rasp: Useful for smoothing down sharp rails or cosmetic imperfections that can be irritating and possibly scratch or cut you during general sailing or freestyle maneuvers. Filing these down will not affect the board's quality. A rasp on the other hand can be used to add scratches to the hull's surface, creating a new non-skid surface. Files can also be used in preparing a board for the sanding and smoothing out of any dings.

Sandpaper and/or Sanding Blocks of Fine Grain: Wet/dry quality is best for working on sailboards. If you are a racer, this can be helpful for smoothing out the leading and trailing edges of your daggerboard or skeg. Some people use it for removing minor scratches on a stock board while others may sand the bottom prior to a race although this is not recommended.

Wax: Good for increasing the non-skid quality of the deck's surface. In some areas, oily waters may make what was a good non-skid surface a poor one and wax may help restore the traction.

Spare Battens: Good to carry if you are at a regatta and lose or break one of them since a racing sail relies on its battens. Many fathead sails would be useless without the long compression battens and spares are recommended.

Skegs, Inserts & Screws: Also handy to have as you never know when you'll break one or pull it out. A freestylist may keep four different lengths on hand to choose from just before a competition starts while a racer may want to choose between a high-aspect and standard skeg prior to a race. On Funboards, inserts and screws are easily lost and good to keep on hand.

Biodegradable Soap: For washing suntan oil off your body and the board since suntan oil can make parts of the sailboard very slippery.

Although these are the basic ingredients for a good boardsailing tool/repair kit, it never hurts to keep some sunblock or suntan lotion, a T-shirt, sneakers or bootees, and a wetsuit and towel in the car whenever you plan to go sailing. These should insure that you get in all the fun you set out to find.

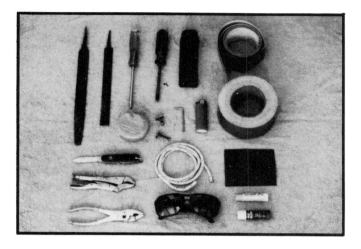

A well equipped tool/repair kit

LINES AND KNOTS
Lines on sailboards should be stretch resistant and hold in the cleats provided. Most lines supplied on sailboards contain polyester or nylon and come in 3/16", 1/4" or 5/16" thicknesses. Nylon lines stretch too

much for sailboards whereas a dacron/polyester or a prestretch which is basically a polyester multi-filament line with very little elasticity are highly recommended for replacement lines. Most of these lines are braided or woven and the ends should be singed after cutting to prevent fraying which will make it easier to slide through cleats or grommet eyes. When replacing lines use 3/16" to 1/4" for outhauls, 3/16", 1/4" or 5/16" for inhauls, 3/16" for downhauls and 1/4" or 5/16" for harness lines. It would be impossible to tell you exactly what thicknesses or lengths to buy since the size of the cleats you have on your booms and their placement in relation to the boom end fittings as well as the length of your booms will all affect this decision. Uphaul lines very rarely need replacing due to wear although some beginners may prefer to substitute a bungied uphaul over what may have been supplied by the factory.

The knots pictured are the most important ones for boardsailing students and should be practiced in class sessions with lengths of rope and simulated craft parts. A rope board of mounted knots and enlarged transparencies of these instructions could be utilized in class and dry land sessions.

Every knot should be checked for tightness and security against coming untied. Proper knots will make the sailboard rig feel smoother, tighter and more balanced on the water.

BOWLINE: Called the "King Of Knots" makes a loop in the end of a line which won't shrink, jam or become too tight to untie. The Bowline can be used to attach the downhaul to the tack grommet or the outhaul to the clew grommet.

Step 1: Place the loose end from right to left across the standing part leaving a small loop.

Step 2: Grip and hold together the small loop with one hand. Take the free end with the other hand and bring it up and through the small loop from underneath leaving a lower loop of the desired size.

Step 3: Pass the free end behind the starting part.

Step 4: Pass the free end down through the loop and pull up tight.

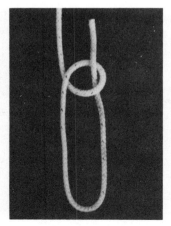
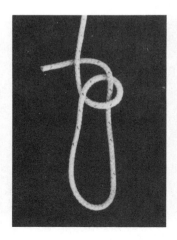
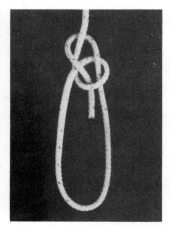

OVERHAND KNOT: This is the simplest of all knots. It can be tied around the boom to secure a line after it has passed through a cleat. It can be tied at one end of a rope as a stopper, but can become impossible to untie.

(A figure 8 knot is better as a stopper if it is to be untied later.)

Step 1: Take one end of the line and pass it over a piece of the remaining line.
Step 2: Pass it through itself and pull tight.

OVERHAND KNOT #2: Some front boom end fittings require a large knot at the end of the inhaul line to set in around the male fitting. An Overhand Knot works well here.

Step 1: Take a one-foot length of line and fold in half.
Step 2: Hold the two ends together and tie both off with an overhand knot.

Step 3: Place the line around the mast so the knot is on one side and the loop on the other.
Step 4: Place the knotted end through the loop and place knot in front boom end fitting.

FIGURE-OF-EIGHT KNOT: This is like an overhand knot with a twist. It is easier to untie than the overhand knot and is larger, stronger and does not injure rope fibers. It can be used at the end of a line, can prevent rope from unraveling or from running through a cleat. By using the Figure-Of-Eight as a stopper, it can be used at the end of the inhaul, outhaul, uphaul and at intervals along the uphaul to provide a handgrip.

Step 1: Make an underhand loop.
Step 2: Bring the end around and over the standing part.
Step 3: Pass the end under, and then up through the loop.
Step 4: Draw up tight.

THE SQUARE KNOT (or Reef Knot or Binding Knot): A common knot used in reefing or furling sails or in packaging parcels and bundles. It is often used for tying two ropes together although this is not recommended since it unties easily when either free end is pulled.

Step 1: Pass the left end over and under the right end.
Step 2: Curve what is now the left end towards the right.
Step 3: Cross what is now the right end over and under the left.
Step 4: Draw up tight.

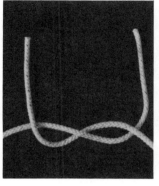 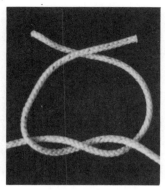 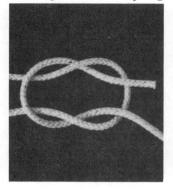 

CLOVE HITCH: This is a quick simple method of fastening a line around a mast, spar, or post. A clove hitch with a stopper knot is useful for tying the inhaul to the mast and for tying harness lines to teak booms. (some classes of boards have a sleeve on the mast to which the boom is attached with a click-in mechanism and therefore doesn't use an inhaul line.) It can be tied in the middle or end of a line, but has a tendency to slip to the end of a line and a stopper knot is helpful.

Step 1: Take one round turn on one side of the standing part and cross over the original line.
Step 2: Make a second round turn on the other side.
Step 3: Tuck the free end through the second turn so it lies between the rope and the part.
Step 4: Tighten the knot by pulling on both ends. Alternately you may tie a stopper knot on one of the free ends and pull until the stopper catches at the knot.

 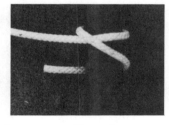 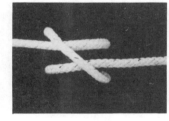 

PRUSSIC HITCH: This is an excellent knot for securing an inhaul line to the mast when a single free end of line or two free ends coming off the mast are desired. When tight, the knot will not slip down the mast.
  Step 1: Fold the inhaul line in half. Bring the looped end around the mast and pass the two ends through the loop.
  Step 2: Bring the loop around the mast a second time.
  Step 3: Pass the two ends through the loop once again.

Step 4: If only one free end of line is desired, tie a stopper knot at the end of one of the free ends of line. Pull on the line without the knot until the loop locks down on the knot and line respectively and tightens around the mast. If two free ends are desired. Don't tie a stop knot on either end. Instead pull on each end until you have two ends of equal length and the loop has locked down tightly on the mast.

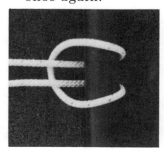 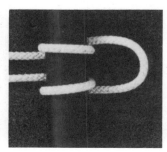  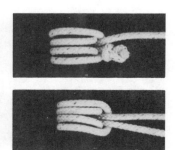

ROLLING HITCH KNOT: This is an excellent knot for securing an inhaul line to the mast when a single free end of line coming off the mast is desired. It is also useful in suspending something from a vertical pole.

Step 1: Make two round turns on the mast.
Step 2: Cross the end over these two turns.

Step 3: Make another turn around the mast and under the line in Step 2.
Step 4: Pass the free end through the second turn so it lies between the line and the mast. Secure the end of the line with a stopper knot.

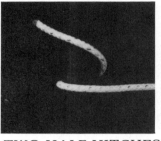

TWO HALF HITCHES: Basically this knot is a half hitch tied twice, it's quickly tied and reliable. It is used when a line needs to be secured at a right angle to an object. It can be used for tying off an outhaul (instead of cleating), for tying boards onto a roof rack or when tying up or mooring.

Step 1: Take a turn around the fixed object and pass the free end around and back through itself.
Step 2: Bring the free end around behind the main line a second time.
Step 3: Pass the free end back through the new loop.
Step 4: Pull tight.

THE TRUCKER'S HITCH: The Trucker's Hitch is a slip knot which pulls right out when you wish to move its posision. It is a great knot to use for tying equipment securely to the roof rack of your car or when you are trying to get proper downhaul tension on mast bases of universals without cleats. It is easily tied and untied.

Step 1: Make a loop as shown in the first photo.
Step 2: Next bring the loop around the line, creating a smaller loop and pass it through the other loop.
Step 3: Pull tight.
Step 4: Use the new loop to secure tension or the knot will pull out. The remaining line can be tied off with one or two half hitches.

CHAPTER VI

SAILING THEORY

A sailboard handles differently than a sailboat in both its maneuvers and steering and even experienced sailors require some time and practice to master the fundamentals of boardsailing. The theory behind it and the forces that prevail can be somewhat confusing. Understanding these principles and familiarizing oneself with the basic terms will help you understand the way in which the wind affects the sail and what boardsailing is all about. Practice on the water combined with this theory will shorten the time needed to learn to boardsail.

THE WIND

The sail is the sailboard's engine and the fuel that powers it is the wind. You should familiarize yourself with the wind and how it affects the sail which in turn affects the steering. A boardsailor is really dealing with three different types of wind. These are; 1. True wind. 2. Induced wind. 3. Apparent wind. The true wind is the atmospheric wind we feel on dry land. We can determine its direction by looking at a flag, watching the motion of a tree, throwing a handful of grass or sand in the air or looking at the smoke coming from a cigarette. Wind is referred to by the direction it comes from. For example, a north wind is one that moves from north to south. Being able to determine where the wind is coming from is probably the most important question a beginner can ask himself. Knowing this will help the inexperienced sailor figure out where he will end up if he is unable to make proper use of the wind to sail where he wants. For instance, you may be taken out to sea, into a swimming area, onto some rocks, into a busy channel and another boat, or close to some other area considered dangerous for the inxperienced boardsailor. If you are out on the water, the true wind can be found by letting the sail luff or flutter in the wind and the direction it points is the direction of the true wind. Induced wind is created by the forward motion of the board. It moves at the same

speed as the board but in the opposite direction. However, when boardsailing, the wind you perceive and feel is not either of these. It is called the apparent wind and it is a result or factor combination of the true wind and the induced wind. This is the wind that affects the sail and is the force that actually propels the sailboard.

To understand the effect of the wind on the sail, think of your sail as an efficient foil that functions like the wing of an airplane. As air flows over the surface, it generates an upward force known as lift just as air flowing past your sail generates lift, only in a horizontal dirction. Once the wind strikes the leading edge of your sail, as in a wing, it is split into two air currents. Because of the wing's shape, the top airflow has to travel further behind the mast and around the entire forward side of the sail than the bottom airflow that passes to windward of the sail. The airflow that passes to leeward has farther to go to get past the sail's curvature and in the process creates a partial vacuum or low pressure area on the leeward side of the sail. Meanwhile, the air that passes to windward compresses as it hits the sail, while simultaneously pushing the sail into a curve and causing a high-pressure area on the windward side of the sail. The resulting pressure differential in turn pushes the sail toward the lower pressure area on the leeward side and produces the lifting phenomenon. This lift is generated perpendicular to the angle of the booms and consequently pulls the sail, board and sailor with it. However, when you are on a run or running, the sail is pushed and not pulled by the wind. This occurs because the induced wind blows in the opposite direction of the true wind. The true wind hits the sail at a 90° angle and cannot effectively flow past the leeward side of the sail. As you travel with the wind on a run and approach the speed of the wind, the push of the wind on the sail decreases creating less apparent wind and less speed. If one traveled as fast as the wind, the apparent wind on the sail would be zero and the wind pushes the board along without lift. One might think that running is a fast point of sail but since the induced wind is equal in strength to the board's speed, but from the opposite direction, it is theoretically possible that your actual speed could drop to zero. This principle of aerodynamics explains how sailboards develop their lift. When a sailboard is heading downwind on a run it is powered by push in the sail. On all other points of sail, sailboards are powered by pull or lift caused by air flowing over the sail's surface. Generally speaking, sailboards are 2/3 pulled and 1/3 pushed. The energy of the wind caught in the sail is then transmitted through the sailor's body to the sailboard itself.

Your sail is most efficient when held at the correct angle to the apparent wind or as otherwise stated the angle between the boom

and the longitudinal angle of the board should be correct. This angle will change as your point of sail does. If the angle between the sail and the apparent wind is too small, then the sail will luff, and become inefficient because part of its area is not being used to generate force. On the other hand, if the angle between the sail and the apparent wind is too large the sail will stall. Air can't flow smoothly past the leeward side of the sail and breaks up, preventing low pressure from forming on this side which would have been used to create lift or pull. Consequently the sail is pushed along as if you were heading downwind on a run. Between the angles of luffing and stalling exists a multitude of sail angles that will generate efficient sail lift. As a general rule of thumb, allow the sail to just begin to luff and then pull the booms in about one foot.

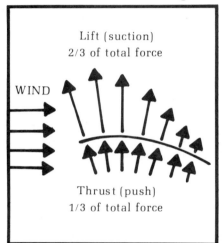

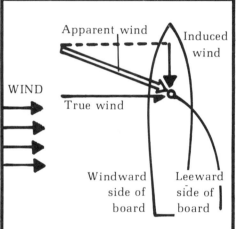

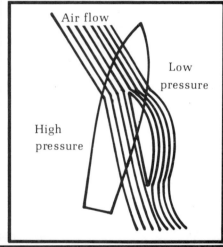

CENTER OF EFFORT

All of these forces we have just discussed act on the sail to produce a single point called the center of effort (CE). This is the point where all of the aerodynamic forces, or lift, can be assumed to act. It is a moveable point and when your sail luffs, the center of effort (CE) will move further aft which will put more pressure on your back hand. The opposite effect occurs when the sail stalls causing the center of effort (CE) to move forward. Efficient and accurate sail trimming will produce a balanced center of effort.

CENTER OF LATERAL RESISTANCE

The forces pushing on the sail act in a sideways direction, especially when close hauled. To prevent moving in this direction we use a daggerboard or centerboard. The daggerboard's foil shape provides very little

forward resistance and allows it to move readily through the water in a forward direction. At the same time, it produces much lateral (sideways) resistance which prevents the board from moving sideways. These combined forces allow the sailboard to move forward in the direction the bow is pointing. There exists a moveable point usually around the daggerboard's midpoint where the resistance to sidewards motion is balanced. Technically, this point is called the center of lateral resistance, or also called the center of resistance (CR). All of the forces which act on the lateral plane act through this point. This position will vary slightly as the board moves through the water. If your board has a kick-back daggerboard or fully retractable centerboard then the center of lateral resistance (CR) will change as the daggerboard's relative position to the board changes. Basically, as the daggerboard is pivoted further aft, the center of lateral resistance (CR) also moves further aft.

STEERING

A sailboard is steered by properly positioning of the sail's rig. Steering is a function of the sail (CE) and its relationship to the daggerboard (CR). By changing their relative position to each other, the direction in which the board moves is changed. However, if one wants to sail in a straight line or on a straight course, you want to maintain directional balance and align the CE with the CR. This is achieved when the CE is just ahead of the CR as viewed from the side. You will notice that the sail area forward of the CR is almost equal to the area aft of the CR.

HEADING UP

Similarly, if we lower the aft boom end without changing the trim of the sail, the CE is moved aft of the CR. This causes the sail area behind the CR to become larger than the sail area ahead of the CR. The stern is now pulled to leeward which causes the board to head up toward the wind.

HEADING OFF or BEARING OFF

By raising the aft boom end without changing the trim of the sail, the CE is moved ahead of the CR. This causes the sail area in front of the CR to become larger than the sail area behind the CR. Leeward side force is now provided against the bow which causes the board to turn to leeward away from the wind and head or bear off.

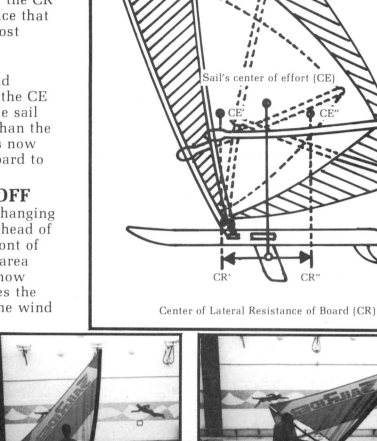

CENTER OF EFFORT AND CENTER OF LATERAL RESISTANCE

Sail position for sailing straight ahead

Sail position for heading off

Sail position for heading up

Sail's center of effort (CE)

CE′   CE″

CR′   CR″

Center of Lateral Resistance of Board (CR)

Heading up

Sailing straight ahead

Heading off

RUNNING

When you are sailing downwind on a run, the sail's forces act in a forward direction while encountering the equal and opposite resistance of the induced wind. Because of this, steering is achieved by tilting the sail from side to side instead of forward and back.

ALTERNATE STEERING

We have just explained how the sailor changes directions by moving the CE relative to the CR by tilting the sail forward or aft.

Similarly, although not quite as effective, the sail assembly (rig) can be leaned to windward or leeward to achieve the same results. A third method involves changing sail trim and consequently moving the CE in the sail. There are two methods of doing this. In the first, the outhaul is either tightened or loosened to change the camber or degree of fullness in the sail, which will in turn change the CE. In Method 2, sail trim is achieved by luffing (undersheeting) or stalling (oversheeting) the sail. As explained earlier, luffing reduced the effectiveness of the forward portion of the sail and moves the CE aft which will cause you to head up. Stalling or oversheeting, reduced the effectiveness of the aft part of the sail and moves the CE forward which causes you to head or bear off. These principles may come in useful when sailing and handling your board in heavy air although its not recommended to use this method when racing.

Now that we have introduced you to the basic of wind and water on the board and sail, and presented some new sailing terms and discussed their applications, we have probably clarified a few questions and possibly raised many more. This section is only an elementary guide to basic sailing theory. Other books on general sailing theory will discuss this subject in more detail. Becoming aware of the forces that prevail

may help you handle various situations that you may encounter with more ease and help you react faster in certain situations. But don't panic if you didn't understand everything in this chapter. I could introduce you to World Champion boardsailors who have been on the circuit for 8 years who still don't know what or where the CE or CR are, and you can be sure it hasn't detracted at all from their enjoyment and proficiency in the sport. Most of you will have no interest in the prevailing forces and will enjoy the simplicity of the sailboard by just getting out there and going for it. It isn't important to know where the CE or CR are at any given point in time. But for those of you who do want to know, this summary should help to strengthen your knowledge of this subject while adding to your learning experience.

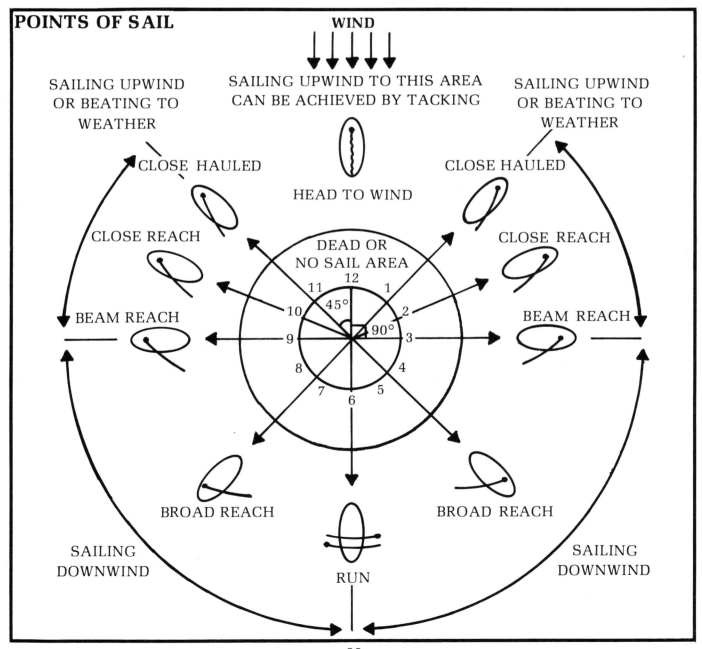

POINTS OF SAIL

WIND

SAILING UPWIND OR BEATING TO WEATHER

SAILING UPWIND TO THIS AREA CAN BE ACHIEVED BY TACKING

SAILING UPWIND OR BEATING TO WEATHER

CLOSE HAULED

HEAD TO WIND

CLOSE HAULED

CLOSE REACH

DEAD OR NO SAIL AREA

CLOSE REACH

BEAM REACH

11 12 1
10 45° 2
9 90° 3
8 4
7 6 5

BEAM REACH

BROAD REACH

BROAD REACH

SAILING DOWNWIND

RUN

SAILING DOWNWIND

COURSES - POINTS OF SAIL

Now that you have familiarized yourself with how to determine the direction of the wind, we will discuss the sailor's ability to sail on different courses or points of sail. It is possible for you to sail to any point although you may not always be able to get there by going in a straight line.

The apparent wind allows you to sail on many different points of sail but the sail must always be filled from an angle more than 45° off the wind. Heading higher than this angle will cause the sail to luff and forward progress will be halted. This 90° area (45° to the left and 45° to the right of where the wind is coming from) is often referred to as the "Dead Area" or "No Sail Area". When luffing, turning into the wind or tacking, you may find yourself in this area, but you will not be making forward progress.

If where you want to go is in this area you will have to tack to get there. This is something we will discuss later. Just remember you cannot sail directly into the wind. That leaves approximately a 270° direction in which you can sail. Just as a compass gives its 360° names like north and south, so we give various points of sail or courses names. The points of sail are called close hauled, close reach, beam reach, broad reach and running. They can be best explained when laid out in a circle. If we think of this circle as a clock face we can more easily associate the points of sail with the hours and better introduce you to the nautical terms of points of sail. Where the wind comes from is also referred to as the eye of the wind and is at 12 o'clock. Sailing upwind or close hauled occurs at 1:30 and 10:30, or roughly 45° from the direction of the wind. Sailing on a close reach occurs at 10 and 2 o'clock. Close hauled and close reaching are also called beating as they allow you to sail upwind or to weather on a windward course. Sailing across the wind or perpendicular to the wind happens at 3 and 9 o'clock and is also called a beam reach. Sailing on a broad reach happens between 4 and 5 and 7 and 8 o'clock, and finally, sailing downwind or on a run occurs at 6 o'clock. The wind will come from a number of directions and these ratios and hours are always the same whether its a north wind or south wind or anything in between. These courses and points of sail differ from each other due to their orientation to the wind causing the board to approach or go away from the wind at a different angle or direction than the other points of sail. It is interesting to note however, that the angle of the sail and its

setting in relation to the wind changes very little as compared to the boat's heading. Basically, you will find a tight sail (one that is sheeted in a lot) when sailing close to or toward the wind and a loose sail (one that is not sheeted in a lot) when sailing down and away from the wind.

ACROSS THE WIND

This means perpendicular to the wind. It is the easiest starting position with the wind at your back. Here the hull points between 3 and 9 o'clock while the sail points downwind to 6 o'clock.

HEAD TO WIND

"Into The Wind" or "In Irons" occurs when the board and the sail points toward 12 o'clock. The board will make no forward progress in this area as it is in the "Dead Area" or "No Sailing Area".

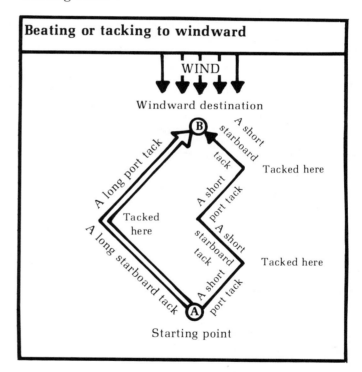

BEATING OR TACKING TO WINDWARD

Sailing directly into the wind at 12 o'clock is impossible to do. But what happens if you want to go to that point? Then you must beat your way upwind by tacking to windward. When beating, you sail close hauled on the alternate tacks of port and starboard sailing first on one and then tacking over to the other. You will eventually cross the point dead upwind that you set out for. Reaching this destination can be achieved by making two or more long tacks (assuming no obstacles are in the way) or a series of short tacks that would create a zig-zag pattern. Each time you tack you will probably start drifting downwind so tack as quickly as possible. Although sailing close hauled is relatively slow, maintaining this point of sail and tacking will probably be the quickest route upwind in the long run.

JIBING

It is possible to sail dead downwind to 6 o'clock by going on a run but sometimes obstacles or waves make it too difficult to follow this straight line route. If this is the case, you should try jibing or as it's sometimes called, 'Tacking Downwind'. One or more downwind turns or jibes can be made in the same manner as our upwind tacks to reach our desired destination.
Helpful Hints:

1. When sailing close hauled, don't "Pinch" or sail so close to the wind (inside the 45° area) that the sailboard almost stops moving (or stalling).

2. Keep the board "Footing" or moving along. You may have to head off on more of a close reach and lose the higher pointing angle, but the speed you gain by "Footing" may actually allow you to cover more ground in a shorter time on a close reach than you may have covered heading higher, yet slower,

while sailing close hauled. Racers constantly ask themselves that question of whether to sail close to the wind and go slower or to keep the board "Footing".

3. Keep an eye out for windshifts. Clues to windshifts are to watch other boats, flags or trees while others are only noticed when they reach you. When heading upwind, a wind shift will either help or hinder your progress. If you were sailing close hauled and heading for a certain point and a wind shift occured so that you could now head upwind or higher than your previous point then you received a "Lift" or "Lifter" which will help you to get to your destination quicker. However, if you were sailing close hauled toward that same point and the wind shifted and all of a sudden you started luffing and had to head off in order to keep sailing so that you now headed below that point, then you were "Headed" or received a "Header". This will hurt your forward progress. If this happens then you should immediately tack. Why? If you tack when you get headed, you will be lifted on the new tack. However, if you tack just after you've been lifted you will be headed on the new tack. Successful racers take advantage of every lift and header to help them get to the upwind mark before their competition.

TOO MUCH WEIGHT TO LEEWARD

Taking your feet off of the centerline and placing them too much to leeward is incorrect and will probably result in a fall. As the leeward rail digs into the water, the hull becomes unstable. To avoid a fall, you will

usually bend at the waist into a position which will not give you the needed leverage to hold the sail up properly. As the sail leans further to leeward, steering by tilting the mast fore and aft becomes ineffective. Additionally the sail becomes heavier and even a slight gust of wind will probably pull you over into the sail or water.

TOO MUCH WEIGHT TO WINDWARD

Another error is to take your feet off the centerline and place them too much towards the windward rail. As it digs into the water, the hull becomes unstable. To avoid a fall you will usually bend at the waist which will again let the sail out to leeward while forcing the rail deeper into the water. The foreward hand may grab the mast and in pulling down on the booms to lift you back up, the board will head up until you have no wind in the sail or is becomes backwinded. No wind and poor balance on an unstable board will probably result in a fall.

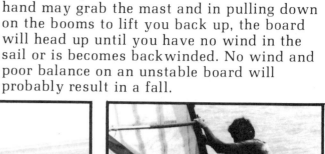

CLOSE HAULED

This is one of the slower points of sail and occurs when sailing at 10:30 or 1:30 or roughly at a 45° angle to the wind. This is as high as the sailboard will effectively and efficiently sail to the wind. The sail is sheeted in or held "Close Hauled" so that the ends of the booms approach the centerline and rest off the downwind corner of the hull allowing you to catch the wind coming diagonally from the front. In light wind, the booms are held close to the body with your arms bent, feet forward and close together. This will allow the sail to pivot around your hands and adjust quickly to true wind direction changes as well as apparent wind changes caused by an increase in your boat speed. Your back hand should assume more than 60% of the total load. The mast is straight up and should not lean to leeward (the side of the board away from the wind). Both feet should be close together and behind the mast while on and at right angles to the centerline. The body is fairly erect and should lean slightly in the opposite direction of the face of the sail (to windward). The hull will be flat although some racers induce a leeward heel by putting weight on their toes. As the wind speed increases, the arms will move farther aft and apart and will also become more extended. When the wind becomes really strong, the feet should move out to the windward rail while still remaining close together and the hands should move farther aft and spread to shoulder's width apart while simultaneously straightening the forward arm. If you start to sail too close to the wind (toward 12 o'clock) the sail will start to luff and the front part will start to flap. If this starts to happen then head off some by raising the aft boom end without changing the trim of the sail. A proper close hauled course is when you are sailing just on the edge between having a full sail and a luffing one.

CLOSE REACH

A close reach is still a form of upwind sailing or beating although not the highest possible, and occurs when sailing at 10 and 2 o'clock. You will not be heading as high as when close hauled, but your speed will be greater allowing you to cover a greater distance in a shorter time. The sailing stance and hand and foot positioning are almost the same as when close hauled with the exception that the sail is not sheeted in quite as much. Beginners will find balance easy and it is an easy point of sail to maintain. By heading upwind, you are counteracting the effects of falling down and the subsequent drifting downwind so that you should still gain ground upwind enabling you to return to your starting position.

BEAM REACH

Sailing on a beam reach occurs when sailing across the wind at 3 and 9 o'clock. The wind will be blowing at right angles to the board and is abeam of you. In most cases the wind waves or chop will be parallel to the board. The sail is sheeted in about halfway (not as much as on a beat) with the boom at about a 45° angle to the board. The arms should be slightly bent and at shoulder's width or wider and carry the load evenly. The sail will feel heavier and want to pull forward so the body should be braced slightly more toward the stern to counteract this force. While the back foot remains on and at a right angle to the centerline, the front foot should now be pointed forward and placed either beside or just behind the mast. This action will cause the rest of your body to face more toward the bow to help balance the sail. As the wind increases, the body is leaned further out to windward and aft to counterbalance the increased forces.

BROAD REACH

A broad reach and the beam reach are the two fastest points of sail. If you bear further away from the wind until it is coming diagonally from the rear and side at 4 and 5 or 7 and 8 o'clock, you will be on a broad reach. The sail is sheeted in almost at right angles to the hull. The arms will still remain slightly bent but spread a little farther apart than shoulder's width, 60% or more of the load on the forward arm. The sail will again want to pull forward so the mast is tilted slightly windward to reduce the forces. The body is now angled so that the rear foot moves slightly across the centerline to leeward while still remaining at right angles and the front foot still points forward, placed beside and/or behind the mast. The body is rotated more toward the bow than on a beam reach. As the wind increases, the arms are moved further aft due to the rearward shift of the center of effort. To help counterbalance this pull on the sail, the weight is also moved further aft and increased weight is placed on the forward foot to help brace it and prevent the rest of the body being pulled forward at this point. You will find planing on a broad reach one of the greatest thrills.

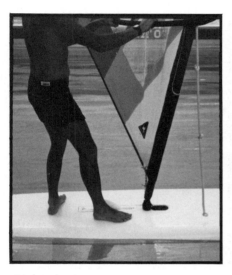

Light air stance

Heavy air stance

RUNNING

Sailing on a run occurs when you are sailing at 6 o'clock. Tilting the mast forward and slightly to windward while sheeting in the back hand causes the board to head or bear off the wind until you are heading dead downwind. At this point, the sail is shifted until it is at right angles to the hull. Move your body so that you now stand facing the sail and bow with your body perpendicular to the center line and over the daggerboard. Your feet are shoulder's width apart with one on either side of the daggerboard. In heavier air the feet should be moved further aft.

Remember to look through the window when sailing downwind to avoid collisions. Steering the board on a run is achieved by tilting the sail to the left or right sides of the board rather than fore and aft as you did on the other points of sail. Tilting the sail to the right will make the board turn left while tilting the sail to the left will make the board turn right. This is a very tricky point of sail for balancing, especially if the daggerboard is pulled out, so keep your weight low and nees flexible to counterbalance any passing boats wake or waves and chop.

Light air stance

Heavy air stance

86

PRACTICE

One of the most important exercises you can do is to sail on all points of sail, including tacking and jibing before you venture out too far from shore. The best way to do this is to practice sailing in a circle. Start off sailing on a close reach or close hauled to get upwind of the starting point and allow for some downward drift if you have problems or are slow at tacking. After sailing a short distance upwind, tack onto the other tack. Tilt the sail forward and experience sailing on a close reach, beam reach, broad reach and finally on a run. Now execute a jibe and start raking the sail aft passing through the broad, beam and close reach before returning to a close hauled positon. Practice this routine while varying it slightly each time to keep it interesting. You might try going in the opposite direction or making larger or smaller circles or tacking and jibing around buoys or obstacles.

One problem for beginners is called the beginner/obstacle syndrome. Put a beginner in an open body of water, give him a few pointers and he'll be sailing. However, put a boat, buoy or even a floating soda can in that body of water and it's like the board is made of metal and the obstacle is a magnet. Without fail, the two will be drawn toward each other and have a collision. To prevent the beginner/obstacle syndrome and to avoid the work (or potential embarrassment) involved in self rescue, practice what you've learned near the shore. Once you feel comfortable on these different points of sail and avoiding obstacles you can venture farther away from shore or search for heavier winds.

WIND DIRECTIONS

When first learning how to boardsail, one of the most important questions you need to be able to answer is, "Where is the wind coming from?", so you can determine where you might drift if you are unable to return to your starting position. Wind can come from any one of 360°. When asked what the wind is, we might say it is a north wind. Wind direction is explained in the direction it comes from, therefore a north wind is one that moves from north to south. Although wind can come from 360 directions, it is generally broken down into four larger categories of north, east, south and west. Each of these categories can be further split in half to include northeast, southeast, northwest and southwest.

When speaking of the wind, its direction can also be referred to by its relationship to the shoreline. The 5 general categories include dead onshore, crosshore or sideshore, dead offshore and splitting these in half we come up with the other two categories: cross offshore and cross onshore. Let's for a minute assume that the shoreline runs east to west and is north of the water. Examine the diagram.

Obviously the north, south directions will be different if the shoreline runs in any other direction than east to west, but it will always move proportionately to this. Wind does not always come from the same directions. It is constantly changing be it minute shifts or major direction changes. Determining the wind's direction can be achieved by looking at indicators on shore such as flags or trees or by luffing your sail and seeing which direction it points. There are generally two types of winds. Steady winds will come from

WIND DIRECTIONS

WIND DIRECTIONS

1. dead offshore (north)

2. cross offshore (northeast and northwest)

3. cross shore or sideshore (east and west)

4. cross onshore (southeast and southwest)

5. dead onshore (south)

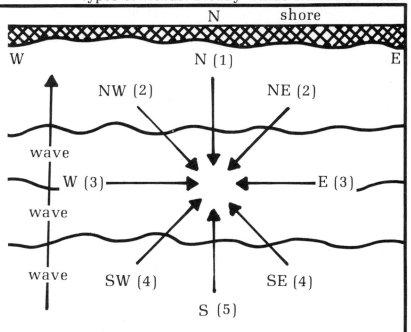

the same direction for at least 20 minutes whereas shifting or oscillating winds move a small amount every few minutes. For example, a north wind might shift to northwest for a few minutes and then oscillate back to north and after shift to northeast before oscillating back to north.

When determining where you will end up if you are unable to return to your starting position, you may want to keep the following pointers in mind:

Dead offshore and cross offshore winds will give most beginners the biggest headaches. The wind is blowing out to sea and away from the shore. The water will generally be flatter as the waves haven't had a chance to build. However, the farther out you go, the bigger they will get and usually its accompanied by a stronger wind the further offshore you get since wind right on the shore may be light due to tall buildings or trees. As the beginner struggles to master the fundamentals he may fail to notice himself getting farther from shore. Couple this with a few falls, fatigue and frustration, and the increased winds offshore, and you have a situation that is beyond the novice's capabilities and may prove too much to handle. This situation may require a self rescue paddle back to shore or help from another party. It is very important to recognize and be able to deal with this wind direction.

Cross shore or sideshore winds are generally ideal for beginners. They are usually accompanied by a steady wind which is not blocked by tall buildings or trees and offer reasonably flat, calm waters since waves don't build too easily in this direction. This will enable the beginner to sail in and out with relative ease. If you get into trouble you will be blown along the shoreline and unless you have sailed out a long way will not have too far to go to reach land again.

Dead onshore and cross onshore winds are winds that blow onto the shore. They tend to be steady and are accompanied by waves or chop that have had a chance to build depending on how large or wide the body of water is. This forces the novice to learn how to sail upwind quicker than he might want to since heading off will put him right back on shore. A beginner can feel safe in these kinds of winds since he will always be blown back to shore if all else fails.

Wind strength can also be observed by watching the angle of the sails of other sailing boats or sailboards. Remember that as the wind increases, a normal sailboat will tend to lean more toward leeward (both the mast and hull) whereas a sailboard's hull will tend to remain flat while its sail is leaned to windward, exposing less sail area to the forces of the wind and making it easier to hold on.

This only gives you a feel for wind directions. Other varaibles such as wind strength, wave size, type or height, currents, rocks, potential shorebreaks and the use of a tether may make any one wind direction more favorable than another for the beginning boardsailor.

PLANING

When a sailboat moves through the water it pushes the water in front of it aside. Sailboards moving at slow speeds in light winds perform the same function. However, in heavier air, many light displacement boats such as sailboards are capable of skimming over the surface of the water. This action is called planing and happens when the craft goes fast enough to rise to the water's surface. Planing can happen once the wind speed rises above 12 knots. Your board speed increases greatly when planing and the thrill of going that fast makes mastering sailing in heavier air worth the effort of learning.

BEAUFORT WIND SCALE

Throughout sailing history, many different scales have been used for measuring the speed of wind. In 1805, Admiral Beaufort devised a simplified wind speed scale that has become standard among the world's seamen. It was appropriately named after him and called the "Beaufort Wind Scale". It divided into twelve increments various wind velocities and accompanied each with a brief description of the appearance of the water's surface at that wind speed. Without an anamometer, the sailor can still estimate the prevailing wind speed by observing the water's surface. This chart relates the numerical Beaufort values to wind speed in knots, miles per hour and meters per second as well as the appearance of the water's surface at a given wind speed.

To translate knots into miles per hour, figure that 1 knot will equal 1.15 mph, or 7 knots equals 8 mph. To translate knots into meters per second, figure that 1 knot equals .514 meters per second, or 10 knots equals 5 meters per second. Remember, there is no right or wrong weather for boardsailing; with the appropriate attire, sail size, board shape and equipment, someone - somewhere - can handle most anything Mother Nature provides. But don't be foolish - think safety. When in doubt, don't go out!

BEAUFORT WIND SCALE

FORCE	DESCRIPTION	SEA SPECIFICATIONS	EQUIVALENT SPEEDS			RECOMMENDED OR SUGGESTED BOARDSAILING CONDITIONS
			KNOTS	MILES PER HOUR	METERS PER SECOND	
0	Calm	Sea like a mirror	-	-	-	In calm, boardsailing impossible
1	Light air	Ripples with the appearance of scales are formed	1-3	1-3	.5-2	Good for beginners
2	Light breeze	Small wavelets, still short but more pronounced	4-6	4-7	2-3.5	Good for beginners
3	Gentle breeze	Large wavelets, crests begin to break	7-10	8-12	3.5-5	Too strong for beginners
4	Moderate	Small waves becoming longer, fairly frequent white horses	11-15	13-18	5-8	Fun for the experienced
5	Fresh	Moderate waves taking a more pronounced long form, many white horses, chance of spray	16-21	19-24	8-11	Fun for the experienced
6	Strong	Large waves beginning to form, extensive white foam crests everywhere, probably some spray	22-27	25-31	11-14	High-wind sails needed, only for the experienced
7	Moderate gale	Sea heaps up, white foam from breaking waves blown in streaks along the direction of the wind	28-33	32-38	14-17	
8	Fresh gale	Moderately high waves of greater length, edges of crests begin to break into the spindrift	34-40	39-46	17-20	
9	Strong gale	High waves, dense streaks of foam along the direction of the wind, crests of waves begin to topple, tumble and roll over, spray may affect visibility	41-47	47-54	20-24	
10	Whole gale	Very high waves with long overhanging crests, the resulting foam is blown in dense white streaks along the direction of the wind	48-55	55-63	24-28	
11	Violent storm	Exceptionally high waves, sometimes concealing small and medium ships, sea completely covered with long white patches of foam, edges of wave crests blown into froth, poor visibility	55-63	64-73	28-37	
12	Hurricane	Air filled with foam and spray, sea white with driving spray, visibility bad	64	74	37	

CAUTION: This is no weather for boardsailing

RIGHT-OF-WAY RULES

Whenever you approach an intersection or rotary in your car, you will probably encounter a stop or yield sign or even a traffic light. These motor vehicle laws have been designed to help reduce accidents and to establish some order on the roads. In the middle of a large body of water, with no defined highways, streets or roads, it is easy to imagine the variety and the number of situations that could arise between boats if no rules were established. There are general right-of-way rules and there are yacht racing right-of-way rules which will be discussed in the section on racing. Safety is the prime concern in learning the rules. You will encounter many situations where you may have the right-of-way, but to try and claim that right may cause a confrontation which you will probably lose. Remember to use your common sense at all times and stay alert, watching out for the other person.

A sailboard is small and hard to see by larger craft, and when you are sitting down on your board between an approaching craft and the sun, the glare on the water may make it impossible for someone to see you. At all times think safety and be careful. The following basic right-of-way rules will most directly affect you as a boardsailor (as well as most other sailing vessels and sailboats). The boat with the right-of-way is called the favored vessel and the boat which must yield is called the burdened vessel.

1. In a crossing situation, when sailing on opposite tacks boats on starboard tack (with the booms to the left or port side) have the right-of-way over boats on port tack (with the booms to the right or starboard side).

2. When sailing on the same tack (both booms on the same side) the leeward (downwind) boat has right-of-way over the windward boat. Similarly, when on the same tack, the boat on the higher point of sail has the right-of-way (close hauled has right-of-way over beam reach.)

3. An overtaking (passing) boat must keep clear of the boat ahead being overtaken.

4. When tacking, the boat changing direction (tacking) must keep clear of a boat underway.

5. A capsized or anchored boat has right-of-way over a moving boat.

6. A boat giving right-of-way to another boat can in turn ask for right-of-way to maneuver and navigate around an obstruction or shoaling water which may lie in his path.

7. Generally speaking, sailboats have right-of-way over powerboats. This includes a right-of-way over rowboats and paddleboats.

8. Towing boats have right-of-way over other boats. A boat with another in tow (even if its a powerboat) has right-of-way over a smaller craft (even a sailboard).

9. Large commercial ships or fishing boats or boats with limited maneuverability have right-of-way over smaller crafts (including sailboards).

10. Service craft (including power boats) such as police or ambulance have right-of-way over other craft.

11. When two boats are approaching each other head on (most often two powerboats) then both should stay to the right of the oncoming traffic (like two passing cars on a road).

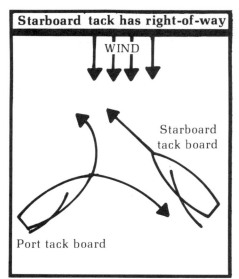

Starboard tack has right-of-way

WIND

Starboard tack board

Port tack board

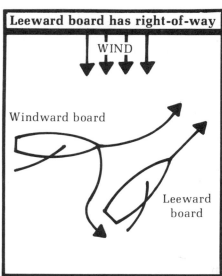

Leeward board has right-of-way

WIND

Windward board

Leeward board

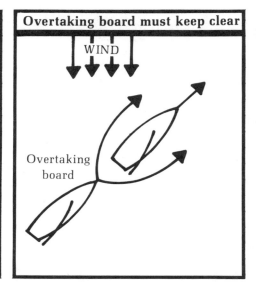

Overtaking board must keep clear

WIND

Overtaking board

Like all rules, these will be broken and interpreted by other people sharing the same body of water in different ways. Safety is the prime concern, so follow these guidelines;

1. Try to avoid a collision, even if you have the right-of-way.

2. Keep a safe distance from other vessels and watch out for the other person.

3. Learn to recognize potentially dangerous situations before they happen and react accordingly in plenty of time to get you out of the area. Just because you are in control of your craft doesn't always mean the other person is in control.

4. Use common sense.

5. Be flexible and avoid confrontation. You may think you are right and the courts may rule that you were dead right, but the medical examiner might say you lost if you were dead and right.

SAFETY

Boardsailing is a safe sport for people of all ages. Over the years, sailboards have acquired the best safety record of all boats. It was thought so safe that in 1973 the Coast Guard granted sailboards an exemption from the PFD (lifejacket) rule that governed other boats. (However, this has recently been changed due to the Coast Guard's relinquishment of its control on the issue and it is now in the hands of the individual states. More on this subject later in this section). Other watersports such as motorboating, waterskiing, scuba diving, surfing and even yachting have had many more injuries and fatalities over the years. If you fall off your sailboard, the unique free-sail system permits the rig to fall into the water, and act as a sea anchor, causing the board to come to a complete stop. Sailboard hulls are unsinkable, and even when cut up into small pieces, each piece will float. They can act as a PFD yet at the same time be paddled for a self rescue. Many beaches around the country use sailboard hulls to aid in rescuing swimmers, sailors and motorboaters from less reliable craft. Yes, boardsailing is a fun sport as well as a safe sport. There are very few rules and regulations that must be observed. In order to increase your enjoyment of the sport, take note of the following safety suggestions and precautions. It will reduce your chances of experiencing a less than enjoyable day at the shore.

1. Stay with your board. Sometimes after a bad fall or under extreme conditions, the mast foot may come out of the mast step or the universal may break. This breakdown could cause the board's mast-to-board safety leash to break and the board and sail assembly to separate from each other. In heavy winds and waves, the board, without the sail assembly, will drift away very quickly. If so, swim to the board at once. You can always paddle back to your rig once you get the board. If you wait too long in heavy winds and waves to make this decision, the board could take off and you'll never have a chance to catch it again. Do not stay with the sail rig. The hull will keep you afloat indefinitely and besides being visible from the land, air and sea, it will keep you out of the water, be it warm or cold.

2. Make sure the sail assembly (rig) is connected to the board with a mast-to-board safety leash. At least if the universal pops out, the rig and board will stay together.

3. Check the local rules on PFD's (life jackets). Some states require PFD's to be worn at all times. If you are not a good swimmer or can't swim, wear a PFD. It may save your life. Novice boardsailors should always wear a PFD.

4. Wetsuits - Always dress warmly enough for the prevailing weather conditions. Inadequate protection from the cold can cause such things as weakness, fatigue and poor balance which could lead to hypothermia (read the detailed description on hypothermia in this section). The longer you intend to sail, even on a warm day, the more important it is to wear some sort of a wetsuit (wetsuits and the varieties available are discussed later in this section).

5. Inspect your equipment before going for a sail. Make any minor repairs needed with your tool/repair kit before you leave the shore. Replace any chafed or worn lines at ths time. Try to be as sure as possible that nothing will break when you go out.

6. Take a spare line with you. Some people lash it to the forward or aft end of the booms. It may be carried inside the mast or in their harnesses backpack. It may be used to replace an inhaul, outhaul or downhaul line. It may also be used to lash a broken mast together.

7. Try not to sail alone. Whenever possible, sail with a friend or at least tell someone you are going out, where you are going and when you expect to return. Since most parking lots close or empty out at night, you might, if you have no one to contact or tell of your plan, put a note under your car's windshield wiper with any important information. A passerby, or security guard or parking lot attendant may find it and get help if the situation warrants it. It never hurts to be cautious since there are so many variables you

encounter every time you leave the shore. You may even want to bring along a sailor-to-board safety leash for security in case of an unforseen circumstance many miles from shore.

8. Do not sail at night or in fog. Sailboards don't carry navigation lights and other boats will have a hard time seeing you.

9. Study the conditions. Observe storm warnings and don't go out in conditions that you think are beyond your capabilities. The National Weather Service broadcasts at 162.3 and 162.55 megahertz the weather conditions in your area.

10. Local knowledge. When sailing in new areas, check first with the local officials or boardsailors for any important things you should know. This could include local PFD regulations, potential launching fees, local winds and strengths, currents, tides, shorebreaks, underwater obstructions, water depth, or warning systems to call you back to shore in an emergency. In offshore winds, be sure you can get back to your starting point. Offshore winds seem calm on the sheltered beach when you can only see the backs of the waves but remember, the further out you go, the stronger the wind and the higher the waves.

11. Keep your distance from swimmers, swimming areas, other boats, fishing areas, docks or obstructions. Many times, only a swimmer's head is visible above the water. Use caution near swimming areas.

12. Learn the right-of-way rules and comply with them (described later in this section).

13. Avoid shipping channels, harbor areas or anchoring grounds. Be ready to alter your course in plenty of time and try to avoid potentially dangerous situations. Think safety.

14. If you see a thunderstorm approaching, always try to head for shore in good time to avoid getting caught in the strong gusty winds that come from all directions and bring lots of rain. If you do get caught in a storm and self rescue seems too hard, then keep the sail assembly in the water to serve as a sea anchor to prevent you drifting too quickly. When the calm comes, then try to resume sailing or self rescue back to shore.

15. Know your limitations. Don't be afraid to ask for help. If you are cold, tired, exhausted and can't make it back to the starting point, and are too tired to self rescue and paddle back, ask a passing boater for help. Above all, never leave the hull. It is similar to a PFD and can be paddled faster than you can swim.

16. When sailing a long distance along the coast or even if you plan on a long days voyage offshore, it is a good idea to carry some change in your pocket or tape it to the board somewhere so that in the event that you have equipment failure, the wind gets too strong or even dies on you, and you land at any point other than where you launched from, you can always call somebody on the phone to come get you.

HYPOTHERMIA

Hypothermia refers to lowered body temperature. The loss of heat from the body core, which includes the head, neck, chest and groin area is one of the potentially dangerous aspects of boardsailing. Protection of these areas is most important.

For the beginning boardsailor, the frequency of falling off and remounting the board may be very high. The high frequency of falls, coupled with a cool wind and cold water, can lower the body temperature rapily and cause hypothermia. Advanced sailors are not immune to hypothermia. They are susceptible anytime they encounter prolonged exposure to a combination of wind and water temperatures which may cause a decrease in their body core temperatures.

If the boardsailor is exposed to the following conditions: cloudy skies, cool winds, and water temerature lower than 70° and frequent contact with the water, uncontrollable shivering and loss of manual dexterity may occur. When body temperature drops to 94°, extensive shivering occurs. If the body temperature continues to drop to 90° or below, many changes take place. A numbing of the extremities, lack of coordination, disorientation, general sluggishness and slowing of the mental process indicates hypothermia has set in. The ability to reason will be somewhat lowered and the novice boardsailor may be in for a tough time. If the novice should find himself out on the board and the above mentioned situation comes about, he should attempt to get to the shore immediately and seek attention or help.

A point that should be emphasized in the treatment of hypothermia is not to increase muscular activity. When an increase in muscular activity is begun, a quick return of chilled blood to a warmer heart takes place. This causes an irritation of the heart and may cause the heart to stop pumping. Do not make the sailor move about causing circulation which puts further strain on the heart. It is important to follow these simple procedures when treating hypothermia.

1. Get victim into a warm area.
2. Remove all wet clothing.
3. Dry the skin.
4. Get on dry clothing.
5. Insulate the body from cold surfaces.
6. Use warm sugary drinks until the body temperature has been restored.

Once you start the rewarming process, the central core of the body is taken care of first: head, neck, upper and sides of the chest, and the groin area. There are don'ts that we should follow with hypothermia victims:

1. Don't give the victim anything to drink that is very hot, keep liquids at body temperature.
2. Do not let the victim exercise or rub the extremities. This action stimulates circulation and sends chilled blood to a warm heart.
3. Do not give victim alcohol or caffeine.
4. Do not wrap the victim in a blanket without providing another source of heat.

If you find yourself in a situation completely immersed in water, a technique for survival is the H.E.L.P. (Heat Escape Loss Position). This position may also be used on the sailboard, if the boardsailor realized he/she may be going into a bout with hypothermia. It is a simple procedure to follow. You must cover all the major areas of heat loss. In a sitting position, pull knees up to chest, wrap arms tight around knees, keep elbows close to sides as possible. You will definitely increase the survival time by maintaining this position. Folding the arms across the chest, crossing the legs and bringing them up to the chest is also a position that may be used. Long sails in waters where the weather conditions may change rapidly could force the sailor to stay out longer than anticipated or force him to seek safety on an unprotected or barren beach.

If you feel cold, a little lethargic and you have 'stopped' shivering, you are a good candidate for the exhaustion exposure syndrome, hypothermia. Once on the beach the sailor may derig his sail system and wrap the sail blanket-style around his body to help regain a normal body core temperature. This method may also be effective if you find yourself becalmed out on the water without any wind to return to shore. When wrapping the body with the sail, the most beneficial body position for conserving body core temperature would be in the H.E.L.P. position.

HEAT ESCAPE LOSS POSITION

H.E.L.P.

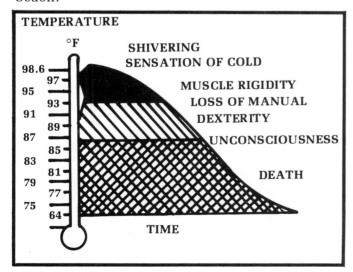

TEMPERATURE

°F

SHIVERING
SENSATION OF COLD

MUSCLE RIGIDITY
LOSS OF MANUAL
DEXTERITY

UNCONSCIOUSNESS

DEATH

98.6 · 97
95 · 93
91 · 89
87 · 85
83 · 81
79 · 77
75 · 64

TIME

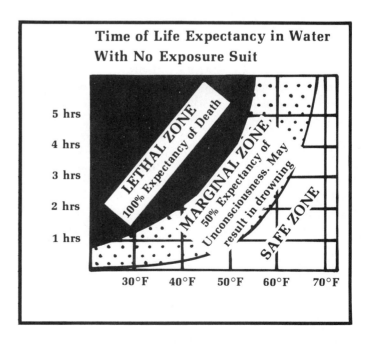

Time of Life Expectancy in Water With No Exposure Suit

5 hrs
4 hrs
3 hrs
2 hrs
1 hrs

LETHAL ZONE 100% Expectancy of Death

MARGINAL ZONE 50% Expectancy of Unconsciousness. May result in drowning

SAFE ZONE

30°F 40°F 50°F 60°F 70°F

WIND CHILL FACTOR

Wind chill factor refers to the cooling power of the wind and wind chill is the rate of heat loss in kilocalories per square centimeter per minute from skin as 91.4°. For simplicity, in still air there is no wind chill factor and whatever the outside temperature is, is in effect the temperature the body will feel. However, as the wind increases, the temperature the body feels actually reduces. For example, if the air temperature is actually 35°. and the wind speed is 5 mph, the equivalent temperature the body feels is 33°. But if the windspeed increases to 30 mph, then the equivalent temperature the body feels is 5°. Wind chill is an important concern in cold climates, expecially for snow skiers where human flesh may freeze and cause frostbite.

For boardsailors, frostbite is not a concern but it is important to understand that the principles still remain in force on the water. For example; staying dry and sailing in light winds in 70° air and 70° water on a sunny day will feel very comfortable in a bathing suit. However, if the wind picks up in the afternoon and possibly brings with it a cool wind and then you fall in once or twice, then the cooling power of the wind will cause a heat loss from the body and could cause you to enter a hypothermic stage. Just remember that increasd winds accompanied by the cooling effects of the drying of water and spray off the body are forms of wind chill which may result in heat loss and under the right conditions could cause hypothermia.

FIRST AID FOR MARINE INJURIES

As boardsailors search for new horizons above the water, there are few things in and under the water that could affect or prevent this enjoyment. Some have stings, spines or poison like cone shells, coral, jellyfish, sea anemones, sea snakes and sea urchins. If you come into direct contact with any of these, the following symptoms may occur and the suggested remedies may help ease the pain. It is recommended to seek medical attention as soon as possible.

CONE SHELL:
Symptons: varies from a slight sting to severe pain, tingling, numbness, tightness in chest, difficulty swallowing, impaired vision, partial paralysis and collapse.
Cure: apply a tournequit or constricting band 2-4" above the wound. It should not be too tight and you should be able to slide your finger under it. Immediately soak in hot water for 30 minutes or apply hot compresses to help inactivate the venom. After 30 minutes remove the band.

CORAL:
(Found only in tropical and sub-tropical waters over 50° and not more than 32° north and not more than 27 degrees south of the equator and lives in shallow waters). It injects venom through stinging cells and produces multiple sharp cuts which can become infected by particles of broken off calcium containing materials. Very common in Hawaiian surf.
Symptoms: Burning or stinging pain.
Cure: wash thoroughly with soap and water and then wash with hydrogen peroxide. If white bubbles start coming from the cut then it's working and needed washing. Once clean, apply an antiseptic oinment such as Neosporin cream. Afterwards bandage and keep clean and dry. If you must sail the next day, just remember to repeat this procedure after each sail to prevent any infection.

JELLYFISH:
Can have long tentacles that trail below the surface and are armed with stinging cells.
Symptoms: mild sting to burning pain, shock, cramps, swelling, nausea, difficulty breathing, vomiting or collapse.
Cure: tentacles sometimes cling to skin and should first be removed. Apply sand, flour, or a paste of baking soda and water and then wipe off with a towel or cloth. Then apply diluted ammonia or alcohol to deactivate the toxin containing nematocysis. Analgesic creams may also help relieve the discomfort as well as Adolph's meat tendorizer.

SEA ANEMONES AND HYDROIDS:
Symptoms: Burning or stinging pain, stomach cramps, diarrhea and chills. Cure: Soak in hot water or apply hot compresses for 30 minutes.

SEA SNAKES:
No one has ever died from a sea snake bite and there are no sea snakes in the Atlantic Ocean.

SEA URCHINS:
(Are covered with sharp brittle spines containing a potent nerve poison, which break off when they penetrate a hand or foot!)
Symptoms: pain, dizziness, muscle tremors, partial paralysis. Cure: use the same cure as you would for a cone shell sting. Other sources say that human urine will dissolve the spines. Another ingenuous approach was tried in the movie "Thunderball" where James Bond was seen sucking a spine out of a young lady's foot after she stepped on a sea urchin. You decide which is best for you.

INTERNATIONAL DISTRESS/EMERGENCY HAND SIGNALS

If you find yourself in difficulty and stuck out on the water, then you should signal passing boats or people on shore by means of the international distress signal. This visible signal is communicated by the sailor's arms. First, sit on the board as upright as possible. If you are okay, then raise your arms over your head and form them into a loop and hold this position stationary. This means, "I'm Okay". If you are in trouble, then keep raising and lowering your straightened arms up above your head and down by your side, repeating several times. This means, "Help - S.O.S!!".

PERSONAL FLOATATION DEVICES (PFD'S)

The excellent safety record of boardsailors granted them a PFD (personal floatation device, or life jacket) exemption from the Coast Guard in 1973. Until recently, the choice of whether to wear a PFD or not was left up to the individual. Recently, all this changed when the Coast Guard left the enforcement of PFD laws up to the individual states that want them. Now many state and local authorities require a PFD when boardsailing. A recent survey found that 28 states now require PFD's to be worn or carried at all times when boardsailing.

Safety on a sailboard and boardsailing's excellent safety record overall can be credited to a combination of things. These include proper instruction, good equipment, wetsuits, knowledge of hypothermia and the advantages of dressing properly, safety leashes and PFD's. Advantages in wearing/carrying a PFD:

1. If you are a weak swimmer it could save your life if you become separated from the sailboard.

2. If you are a good swimmer, it could save your life if you become separated from the sailboard.

3. If you fell into the water or a piece of equipment knocked you unconscious and into the water, then a Coast Guard approved PFD would keep your head above water and prevent drowning.

4. It will provide warmth to the upper body in the hope of preventing hypothermia.

5. When sailing long distances, any number of situations could arise which may warrant needing a PFD. Disadvantages in wearing/carrying a PFD:

1. When falling backwards, sometimes you pull the sail down with and on top of yourself. Without a PFD, you hit the water first and sink for a second while the mast hits the water right behind you. Because you are under water for a split second, you avoid getting hit in the head with the mast. With a bulky PFD on, you may find yourself pulling the mast and hitting yourself on top of your head since you won't break the surface of the water this time.

2. When sailing in big surf and waves, wearing a PFD may restrict the freedom needed to naneuver to safety, prohibiting you from diving under breaking waves and white water or in your effort to swim to your board and recover your equipment.

The preceding were a few advantages and disadvantages of personal floatation devices (PFD's). If you have the choice, try to make as intelligent a decision as possible on whether you choose to wear a PFD or not. When you buy one, look for one that is both comfortable and Coast Guard approved. Shop wisely and remember, the life you save may be your own.

SELF RESCUE

If you are unable to sail back to land for any reason, never leave your board. These reasons may include frustration, increased winds, no winds, exhaustion, broken equipment or a number of other situations, but no matter how close to shore you are, don't abandon the board. Instead, try a self rescue. Remember that the hull can't sink. Stay with it. If you have broken an arm or can't sail or paddle, then sit on the hull and keep the fully assembled rig in the water. It should minimize your drift caused by wind and waves by acting as a sea anchor. Don't panic and wait for help. If possible, try to use the emergency hand signals when another boat or person on shore notices you. If you can paddle, then you should attempt a self rescue, using one of the methods detailed in the 'How To' section on self rescue. Two alternate methods of self rescue are:

1. If you are not too far from shore, but can't make it sailing is to pull the sail assembly about 3/4 of the way out of the water and leave the aft end of the booms in the water. Tilt the mast slightly toward the bow which should cause the sail to fill with enough air to pull you across the water and back to land.

2. If you are in the self rescue position and another boardsailor comes along to help you, then simply pull your hull parallel to his, either to windward or to leeward, and hold onto his daggerboard strap and catch a free ride home. Just have confidence that your rescuer doesn't fall back and sit on you, or worse, drop his rig on you.

WARNING AND DISTRESS SIGNALS

Signals are used on the water for general safety in the same manner that signals are used on roads and highways. Many watercraft are required by law to be equipped with certain safety features such as lights, horns, whistles, flags or sirens. These signals may vary from locale to locale so check with the local officials when sailing in a new location. For example, if you were at the ocean in New England you might find a gale warning nothing more than the unceremonious raising of a large red square flag with a smaller black square in its center hoisted at the local marina. However, if you were at an inland lake in California you might find that same gale warning announced by a series of different colored flashing lights displayed at various high points around the lake accompanied by acoustic signals such as horns or sirens which are supposed to tell you

to make your way to the nearest shore as quickly as possible. Different areas have different systems and you might find some of the following at your locale.

Warning Signals:
Visual - Flags, Flashing Lights, Balls or Baskets.
Acoustic - horns, sirens, whistles, bells, p.a. systems and announcements.
Audible signals are also used by watercraft to say certain things and these are expressed by using a code-like series of dots and dashes as in the Morse Code. This may seem unnecessary in local areas where one can pick up a radio and talk in English with an approaching ship, but in international waters or shipping lanes or even in port where an American ship approaches a German ship and neither speaks anything but his native tongue, it could become difficult to verbally communicate one's next move. In this code, a dot (.) lasts for approximately 1 second while a dash (—) lasts about 4 seconds.
The most common audible signals formed by this code are the following:

.	Short tone. Approx. 1 second.
—	Long tone. Approx. 4 seconds
.	Changing course to starboard.
..	Changing course to port.
...	I'm reversing.
—	Attention.

COMPASSES

Whenever you take a long trip offshore, even if you only plan on going a few miles out, it is advisable to carry a compass with you and try to make note of the shore direction. The purpose being that sometimes a fog bank can roll in which sometimes brings a drop in wind and as the wind increases again it may be coming from another direction. You may have determined that a beam reach would aim you back to shore but during the lull the wind may have shifted 180° and your beam reach would have you heading further offshore. In dense fog you have no visible reference points and a compass could be very helpful.

However, it must be noted that compasses are illegal to use when racing sailboards. The theory being that it would give a competitor an unfair advantage in determining headers and lifters offshore when there are no land references to confirm this. Some companies have come up with a tactical wind tracking device which works like a compass and divides a 360° circle into 8-45° incremental segments. By comparing the relationship of the centerline to these segments one can determine when the wind has shifted and whether to tack to avoid a header or hold the tack and gain with a lifter.

Tactical wind tracking device

WETSUITS

If you live in the tropics and always get to sail in bright sunshine on warm sparkling waters then there is a good chance you may never need to purchase a wetsuit. However, if you don't live in a tropical paradise then you should consider purchasing a wetsuit for your warmth and protection. It will result in an increased enjoyment of the sport. The type and thickness of your wetsuit should depend on the climate where you live, the seasons of the year in which you are likely to be sailing and the average wind strengths you will enjoy. While boardsailing, exposure to the elements of wind and water can cause a lowering of your body core temperature due to the cooling effects of the evaporation of water spray and body perspiration. The stronger the winds, the faster the cooling process will take place. This is called the wind chill factor. The end result of this is one of the few real dangers in boardsailing, called Hypothermia. It is discussed elsewhere and should be reviewed. Choosing the right wetsuit and using it at the proper time is very important since hypothermia can occur even when the air and the water temperatures seem comfortable and safe.

You will find wetsuits that do little more than reduce the windchill on a warm, windy day to dry suits that will allow you to sail in arctic conditions. As a guide, if the water temperature is under 70° a wetsuit that covers everything from your thighs to your shoulders should be worn. If the water gets as low as 50° then a full wetsuit that covers you from your toes to neck is advisable. This is assuming that the air temperature is over 70°. Once the air temperature drops below 70°, then even if you are in warmer waters, wetsuits are advisable. What is the difference between a good wetsuit and a poor one? A good wetsuit is designed to fit tight, yet comfortable. Once wet, a layer of water is retained between your body and the wall of the wetsuit. This layer of water is then warmed to a body temperature of 98.6° and forms a thermal barrier between your body and the surrounding air. It is this trapped wet layer that keeps you warm. If your wetsuit fits too loosely and water can flow freely between your body and the inside of the suit then this water will never have a chance to warm and the wetsuit is not performing properly. Another consideration is that almost 1/3 of your body heat can be lost through your head, feet and hands, so you should consider the extra protection of a hood, booties or gloves in extremely cold conditions. There are many different styles and brands of wetsuits to choose from on the market and the following factors should be considered:

1. Most wetsuits are made from neoprene and come in thicknesses ranging from one sixteenth to one quarter of an inch (or 2mm to 6mm). Generally, the thicker the wetsuit, the warmer it is but the increased thickness can also affect its maneuverability. Thick arms can start to ache fast when kept bent for a long time.

2. Neoprene is usually covered with nylon on one or both sides. Nylon inside makes the suit easier to slip on and off while nylon on the outside reduces the risk of tears or rips and extends the life of the material. The disadvantage of nylon on both sides is that it retains water and may make it cooler as the water evaporates. Solid rubber on the outside may tear a lot easier and break down faster but it usually keeps you a little warmer and allows less wind to pass through the suit.

3. Good zippers are usually made of rust proof plastic and not metal.

4. Areas of high wear and abrasion, like the knees, should have extra material and be reinforced at these points.

5. Areas of high stress like the crotch and armpits should be well designed and also reinforced.

6. All seams should be well stitched and either be glued or taped as well.

Choosing what brand of wetsuit to buy and the thickness you desire are all personal preferences, but the following guidelines should help inform you what is on the market and its intended use.

VESTS: are sleeveless with large neck openings and come down to your waist. They help to retain heat in the covered torso and protect it from wind and water spray. Vests also prevent a harness from chafing your skin and are mostly commonly used on warm, windy days.

NEOPRENE SLEEVE JACKETS: are similar to the original scuba diver wetsuit jackets. They come to your waist, have a neoprene body and neoprene sleeves. Although they keep the arms very warm, they tend to constrict the flow of blood and the muscles lose some of their freedom of movement because of arm tightness. They are great on very cold days but the restricted movement in the arms causes you to tire quicker.

FABRIC SLEEVE JACKETS: breezebreakers, or wind breakers, are the names given to jackets that have neoprene in the torso area for warmth and some sort of waterproof material on the sleeves like Speedflex, Goretex, oxford nylon or a variety of other materials. The purpose is to provide an effective wind break on the arms that also allows the arms to be free and flexible without the loss of circulation that can occur in tight neoprene sleeves.

LONG JOHNS: or Farmer Johns cover the legs and torso, protecting them from the wind and water spray, yet they leave the arms and shoulders completely free to move. They are perfect for sailing in warm winds on cold waters. The combination of a long john and a jacket can extend your sailing season considerably. If you plan on purchasing two wetsuits, these are the two to buy, to be used alone or layered.

SHORT JOHNS: cover the thighs and torso and will have either no sleeves or short sleeves. They are generally for warm conditions and provide minimal protection. They are a good compromise between the vest and the long john.

FULL SUITS: or body suits are great for providing protection in extra cold weather. They are one piece and cover your whole body including the legs and arms (However, not the head, hands and feet). They come with either neoprene or fabric sleeves and have the same advantages and disadvantages that both offer in the jacket version. Some of the fabric sleeve ones come with a slip on neoprene sleeve liner that can be worn over the arms (and inside the suit) on really cold days. If you only own a full suit, then on a hot day it can be unzipped with the top half rolled down to your waist and the sleeves tied off in front of you. As it cools off or the wind increases, put the top back on and leave it unzipped or zipped depending on the temperature. If it really gets cold, then add the extra slip on sleeves for full protection. If you wanted to own one wetsuit only, then this is probably the one to buy.

WIND SUITS: are very popular in Europe and quite fashionable. They are similar in design and function to all the suits mentioned above except they are usually not made out of neoprene but instead of thinner and slicker (wet look) type fabrics. They block the wind and spray very well but are lacking some in the warmth department. However, they are high fashion and do tend to make the wearer look attractive.

DRY SUITS: are for those extra cold locales or those winter sails when ice floating past your board would not be a visual shock to the system. They offer waterproof protection and many allow you to wear your clothes under them, letting you go out in the coldest conditions without getting wet. Many have permanently attached booties (although some also require an overshoe to provide protection of the material) and airtight seals at the neck and wrists to prevent water from entering the suit (the zippers used at the point of entry are also waterproof). However, even if the rest of your body will be warm, you must protect the head and hands with adequate coverings.

HATS: considering the amount of body heat that can be lost through your head, a hat should be considered when completing your boardsailing wardrobe if you live in cold climates or sail in cold waters. If you don't expect to fall in, then a woolen ski hat will keep your head very warm and since it retains over 80% of its heat when wet, the occasional fall won't leave you cold. If you plan on falling in a lot or have a short board that requires you to waterstart all the time, then the purchase of a neoprene wetsuit hat may be a wise investment.

SHOES OR BOOTIES: there are a variety of specialty shoes and booties on the market today. Some are used to improve your traction and grip on boards where the surface is too slippery to stand on comfortably. As the wind strengthens, these boards will feel even more slippery and shoes or booties should give you that added control you need. Some of these shoes have tiny suction cups on the bottom much like the arms of an octopus and they provide excellent traction. Shoes or booties can be advantageous when sailing in new waters where you don't know what is on the bottom and the beach may be less than ideal, be it shells, rocks, sand or broken bottles. These will provide protection for your feet. In warm waters, one can use one of the slipper type shoes on the market or even an old pair of tennis, deck or running shoes. However, as the water gets colder, you can invest in some neoprene type products to help keep the feet warm. These could include neoprene socks (not to be worn on the ground as they will wear out easily), which can be worn inside a pair of tennis shoes or specialty shoes that may be made completely of neoprene with some sort of solid bottom on them such as the tiny suction cups.

Vest

Vest

Neoprene sleeve jacket

Fabric sleeve jacket

Long john

Short john with sleeves

Short john without sleeves

Full suit

Dry suit

GLOVES: another accessory that may or may not be needed. Gloves can be used to prevent blisters and callouses, potentially increase your grip on the booms or provide warmth against cold water or the wind. Gloves used to prevent blisters or callouses can be in the form of sailing, or golfing gloves which have flexibility and reinforced palms yet offer little warmth. This type of glove will also give you the best grip on the booms. For relief from the wind and cold waters, one can use ordinary rubber household gloves but they may stay very cold when wet. Some companies make a rubber glove with an excellent wrist seal which keeps the inside of the glove dry and with the addition of a liner will provide warmth. These thin gloves give your hands more sensitivity to feel the booms. For warmth, a pair of neoprene gloves will probably be the best. There are generally three types on the market. There are the scuba diver gloves that come in a variety of thicknesses and are usually cut flat. Gripping the booms actually stretches the material passing over the backside of your hand which offers a resistance by wanting to pull back to the open postion. It actually takes effort just to grip the booms. Another type of scuba glove is the type that are cut in the half-closed position so there is extra material on the backside of your hands making it no effort to grip the booms. These are better than the first type. The third and best type of gloves are the specially designed boardsailing gloves made of neoprene that incorporate both the half closed grip with the reinforced leather palms and provide both warmth and a positive grip. Like the wetsuits, the thicker the neoprene, the warmer the gloves, but remember that thicker gloves may lessen your sensitivity or feel for the booms although this is secondary to the protection, comfort and safety they provide.

When searching for a wetsuit or wetsuits, consider the climate where you will be sailing and the degree of protection you need. Thicker suits may be warmer but they can also restrict your freedom of movement.

Increasing your sailing comfort is secondary. A suit must protect you from one of the few dangers of boardsailing, Hypothermia.

BATHING SUITS

An expensive or flashy bathing suit may look excellent on you and attract lots of attention but it may not be what you want to wear when learning how to boardsail. Repetitive climbing onto a sailboard with a rough textured surface may cause certain types of suits to wear fast and may cause the fabric to run or tear. Nylon suits wear well but can be slippery when sitting on a board which has minimal non skid on the deck. The tops of ladies two piece suits have also been known to disappear after a catapult fall. Stomachs and elbows have also been seen with rashes or redness after repetitive mounts on the hull which in the case of a lady in a one piece suit could result in excessive wear to that part of the suit. This is not to say that all beginners fall in alot. It's just a word of advice that until you have reached the stage where you spend more time standing on the board than you do climbing on and falling off, it is recommended that you wear one of your less prized suits and even wear a T-shirt over it.

SUNGLASSES

Sometimes when sailing for prolonged periods of time, the sailor may find his eyes starting to hurt. This is usually caused from the severe sun rays reflecting off the water or just from the constant spraying of water in your face. The glare from sailing in intense sunlight for just a few hours can actually lead to sunburning of the eyes. Sunglasses are your best solution to remedying both problems. Price isn't the only assurance of good quality. You are looking for a pair that offers adequate protection from damaging rays. This should encourage you to try several types and styles in an effort to get a good fitting pair. Many sailboard shops carry eyeglass straps that are made of neoprene which may keep the glasses afloat if they still do fall off.

Hats and inner sleeves

Boots

Gloves

SUNBURN

Whenever one is outdoors for a long time, the risk of getting sunburned is very high. You can get sunburned even if you already have a tan and on days that may seem overcast or hazy as it is exposure to the sun's ultraviolet rays, not just direct beams of sunlight that burn you. A burn will come fast but it also will go away fast as the burn layer of skin dries out and peels off. When sunburned, the skin will usually appear white for a second or two after being touched and the finger is removed. Your skin will also feel hot and very tight. It can also cause pain, swelling, fever and a headache.

Ideally, one wants to prevent getting sunburned. The best solution is to cover the exposed areas of one's body with a waterproof suntan lotion. Many lotions contain PABA and come in varying strengths. Strengths will be labeled on the container usually on a scale of 1-15 with 1 being the weakest, and allowing most of the sun's rays to reach the skin, while a 15 is the strongest and will block out almost all of the sun's harmful rays. Suntan oils are used for getting a tan, and do not mix very well with sailboards as they create very slippery and unsafe surfaces. Another preventive measure to avoid getting sunburned is to wear a wetsuit, shirt, long pants, gloves, a hat or visor in an effort to cover up the exposed parts of the body.

If you do get sunburned, the following suggestions should help to relieve the general discomfort;

1. Stay out of the sun.
2. Take a long bath in cold water.
3. Cover the burned areas with cold wet compresses.
4. Later blot dry with a sterile cloth.
5. If no blisters have developed, you may apply an antiseptic ointment or spray. Do not use butter or margarine.
6. If blisters have developed, do not break them or remove the shreds of tissue and do not apply any ointment. Instead apply a dry sterile cloth for protection.
7. If severe burning has occured, treat for shock and obtain medical attention.
8. Take an aspirin or two to help relieve the pain.
9. Drink lots of liquids and keep from getting dehydrated.
10. A sunburn on the first day of your vacation, regatta or boardsailing season will put a damper on some of the potential fun. Next time be more careful!

WEATHER

Most boardsailors only go out sailing for a few hours at a time and generally don't go too far offshore. They can usually pick and choose the good days to go sailing. Becoming familiar with terms used in weather reports may add to your enjoyment of the sport and potentially increase your chance of having a safe sail by avoiding getting caught in some unexpected situations.

Weather is referred to as the general atmospheric condition with regard to temperature, moisture, winds, cold, heat, atmospheric pressure and storms and the interaction of these forces and how they affect us here on land.

Let's take a look at those things that will affect us, our day at the beach, and our sailing. The movement of air over the earth's surface is affected by differing forces of high and low pressure areas which create what we feel as wind. High pressure areas (also called anticyclones) tend to stay in one place. At the center of the high, the air is dry which usually means good weather. A rising barometer, say above 30 millibars, usually means good weather. Winds spread out from the center of a high and in the Northern Hemisphere (above the equator) move in a clockwise direction. If you lived in the Southern Hemisphere, they would move counterclockwise. Low pressure areas (cyclones or depressions) tend to move rapidly. At the center of the low, there are usually strong winds and rain. A falling barometer, say below 29 millibars, usually indicates rain and poor weather. Winds spiral into the center of a low and in the Northern Hemisphere they move in a counterclockwise direction. If you lived in the Southern Hemisphere, they would move clockwise. Wind will generally blow from areas of high pressure to areas of low pressure while the speed of the wind is affected by the pressure differential between the two. The grater the difference in pressure, the faster the wind will move toward the low pressure area.

If you were to look on a weather chart, you may see a series of lines running through places having the same air pressure. These are called Isobars and are usually drawn at intervals of 4 millibars. When you see isobars close together, it indicates high winds and if they are far apart it indicates light winds. Fronts are boundaries between masses of air of different origin. The symbols you may see on a weather chart to indicate a warm front are solid half circles on one side of a solid line and a cold front are solid triangles on one side of a solid line. These symbols are placed on the side of the line toward which the front is about to move. Local temperature differences between land and water, caused by the sun's heat will also effect the local weather. It is here that the sun causes another form of wind movement called thermals or thermal winds.

It is a fact that water takes longer to heat than land, but once heated, it will retain that heat much longer than land. You can prove this by going to the ocean in the summer and although the water temperature may change only a degree or two between morning, noon and night, the air temperature may change from 60° in the morning up to 90° at noon and down to 50° at night. This heating and cooling of the land produces two types of thermal winds, sea breezes and land breezes. In a sea breeze, or onshore breeze, the land is heated up during the day by the sun until it is warmer than the neighboring water, and as the warm air rises, a local low prssure area is formed over the land. This low pressure draws in the cooler and heavier air from the sea, causing the onshore breeze (sea breeze). These breezes are usually steady. Since the land also cools off quicker than the water, then at night, the reverse process happens. Hence, when the land cools to a temperature lower than the neighboring water, the warm air over the water begins to rise creating a

local low pressure area over the water. This low pressure area draws in the cooler air from the land causing a land breeze or offshore wind. These breezes tend to be more flukey or puffy. This phenomenon usually occurs at the ocean and on larger inland lakes. Generally speaking, sea breezes usually occur between noon and sunset with late afternoon producing the strongest winds. Land breezes generally occur between midnight and mid-morning with the strongest winds around sunrise.

You should also become familiar with the weather patterns and characteristics in your area for whatever time of year it is, since these patterns do change. Locally you may notice how at one time of the year the air always seems to blow on shore while at other times of the year it always blows offshore. Similarly, certain months may be called the rainy season while others may be the dry season. Perhaps some months are always foggy in the morning and others aren't. Knowing more about the weather can help you predict what could happen on the day you decide to go sailing. Remember to watch the cloud formations. Some racers watch clouds to help predict a wind shift. For example, if the clouds are coming from a different direction than the wind, then it could mean a shift to the direction the clouds are coming from.

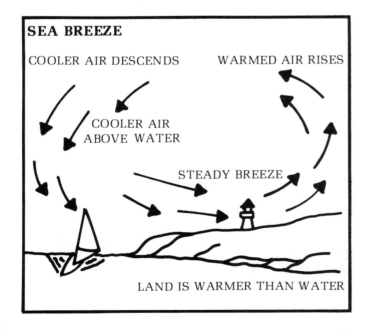

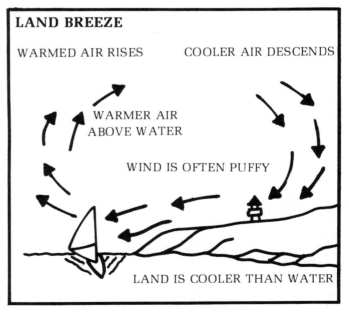

If the winds are calm and its muggy out this could be a sign of an approaching thunderstorm. The gathering of dark cumulus clouds with their typical anvil shaped top are a sign of worsening weather and usually the wind will increase fast until it is strong and gusty. Rain usually follows which causes the wind to drop, sometimes to zero, before it usually repeats the pattern of strong gusty winds followed by rain. This combination of wind and rain is sometimes called a "squall" or "line squall" since you can see it approaching like a moving wall. After it passes, the wind may have shifted to a new direction. Your proficiency on a sailboard may not proliferate by learning about the weather but your chances of avoiding a potential confrontation with a storm, getting becalmed or blown offshore, doing well in a race, maintaining your suntan or picking an overall good day to go sailing can be increased by any knowledge that you have about the weather.

THUNDERSTORMS

Thunderstorms can and do occur anytime of the year and in any part of the country and they normally occur when a cold front collides with a warm front. The cold air pushes the warm air upwards which will form cumulus or thunderhead cloud formations. These may start as little fluffy cumulus clouds on a clear day that quickly grow bigger, taller and darker until they turn into a storm. While the ice falls from the top of these clouds, rain falls from the bottom to the ground. The ice keeps getting carried back to the top of the cloud by strong air currents until this action of rising and falling eventually builds up a strong positive charge at the top of the cloud and a strong negative charge at the bottom. This buildup of electricity gets so strong that the current flashes and we on land see lightning. Lightning can occur inside the cloud or between the cloud and a positive charge on land. When lightning strikes, it heats the air to white heat which expands very fast to produce the sound we know as thunder.

As a boardsailor, it is not important to know how thunderstorms occur, but to be able to identify them as they approach in time to take evasive action. Thunderstorms move fast and can hit in as little as 30 minutes after sighting. If you see one, it is advisable to head for shore immediately. If you get caught in one there are two potentially dangerous situations to consider. The first is being struck by lightning. However, this has never caused injury to a boardsailor. One of your biggest problems will be overcoming the mental worry of getting struck. Thunderstorms are usually characterized by heavy winds and waves accompanied by torrential rains, followed by periods of flat calm and no wind before resuming the sometimes violent winds and rain. Sailing can be extremely difficult under these conditions as the wind may come from all directions at great speeds before dropping to zero and then resuming without warning. If you do get caught in a thunderstorm you may want to keep the sail assembly in the water to act as a sea anchor and prevent your drifting too quickly and then try sailing back when the wind drops or try a self rescue if it's not too far to paddle. Make sure that the sail assembly is attached to the board in case you get knocked over in the waves.

WAVES

There are generally three types of waves that one may encounter while boardsailing. These are wind waves, or chop; ground swells or swells; and boat wakes. Wind waves or chop are the direct result of the local wind conditions. The wind's strength and direction, as well as the size and depth of the lake or sea, will have an effect on the wave's height. The farther offshore you go, the larger the waves will be but they are also less powerful and don't break as often whereas near the beach they may be breaking constantly and rolling in one after the other.

Ground swells or swells are generated by storms hundreds of miles away from the shore on which they break. They travel for miles as rolling swells until they reach land and shallow water. When they hit the shallow waters they usually increase in height and steepness before breaking and forming the waves that surfers love to ride. There can be zero wind but these waves may keep coming and some may be quite large depending on the configuration of the ocean floor prior to its reaching the beach. At the ocean, unprotected shorelines may have these ground swells break on them causing a shorebreak, which depending on its height, can make getting off the beach a real problem for the beginning boardsailor.

Another kind of wave is a boat wake. It is generated by powerboats and comes off their sterns in two directions, each at an equal and opposite angle to the straight line course of the boat. If you are a novice boardsailor or you are in the middle of a race then boat wakes can be an unwanted visitor. However, if you want a little excitement from the flat waters, it is very possible to both surf and jump these boat wakes depending on the strength and direction of the wind. Just make sure that they aren't trailing any fishing lines or towing a water skier or another boat.

By definition, the top of the wave is called the peak, the distance between two peaks is called the wave length, the bottom of a wave is called the trough, while the distance between the trough and the peak is called the wave height. The back of a wave is called the backside, and the inside part of the wave is called the wave face, while the part that breaks is called the lip and the distance between this lip and the trough is called the height of the face. Waves are either measured by the height of the face (this will give the higher measurement) or by the distance from the flat water level (not in the trough) to the lip.

HOW THE WAVES BREAK:

The waves we discussed break in a variety of different ways. When the sea bed gradually gets shallow, waves that roll over it slowly build getting higher and steeper, until a peak is formed that breaks at the top and tumbles toward shore, pushing a wall of white water in front of it. The whitewater disappears when the wave reaches deeper water or the shore. Some ground swell waves never break in deep water and appear to just roll along providing gentle slopes to sail down. More dangerous are waves that break over a steep beach or coral shelf that gets shallow fast and over a short distance. They peak up to a maximum height very quickly and then break from top to bottom releasing all their force in one drop. When this happens a tube of water is formed with air in the middle. Some waves don't break along their whole length at exactly the same time (this would be a close-out wave). Instead the wave may break from right to left or vice versa, leaving a defined line of whitewater between the unbroken and breaking wave. The unbroken wave section is called the shoulder and the area where the unbroken and breaking section meet is called the critical section. If you look at a breaking wave and see the whitewater on the right with the unbroken wave section to the left, then the wave is said to be breaking right, or that it is a "right".

Winds can also affect how a wave breaks. Offshore winds blowing into the face of a wave make it stand higher and longer before it breaks in a hollow fashion. Onshore winds tend to do the opposite and push the wave down and flatten it out which will make it break easier and more gently.

WAVES

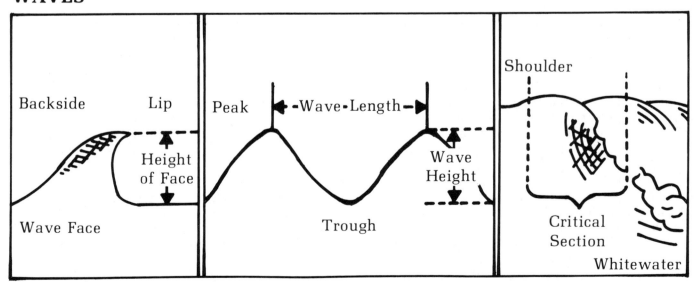

CHAPTER VII

INTRODUCTION TO PRE-SEASON CONDITIONING PROGRAM

Boardsailing is a sport that combines the intermittent movements of holding the sail on a specific tack with the more rapid movements of tacking and jibing. Sailboards are relatively small which decreases potential body movements and can create the potential for stiff muscles and joints and reduce muscle responsiveness. Boardsailing involves movements one hopes to adjust to both spontaneously and effortlessly. A good conditioning program will keep us limber, keep the muscles and joints functioning properly and reduce the potential for a stiff back or shoulders as well as a sore neck or arms muscles. Conditioning will prevent these and increse our quickness and the ease with which we execute maneuvers. It is never too soon to begin a conditioning program but by the same token, getting in shape is not accomplished overnight. However, the rewards of being in good shape include improved strength and endurance as well a a better physiological and psychological well-being and personal satisfaction as you master the basic boardsailing techniques. In climates that don't permit you the luxury of year-round boardsailing, a conditioning program supplemented by other sports activities and exercises will help you maintain a happy, healthy and strong feeling all year long.

PRE-SEASON CONDITIONING PROGRAM

The pre-season or off-season program given to the class by the instructor should have the following objectives:
After the program the boardsailor:

1. ...should look better and work more efficiently.
2. ...increase efficiency of the heart and lungs, the circulatory and respiratory system.
3. ...lessen susceptibility to stress and tension.
4. ...increase strength, endurance and flexibility.
5. ...increase ability to endure harder and longer activity.

Every exercise period in the conditioning program should be preceded by a warm-up, progress to the fast effort or main target of the work out and end with a cool-down period. The main effort is designed to strengthen the muscles and increase stamina.

The theory is that muscles need to be stretched and made more flexible before more rigorous demands are made on them. Once the hard work out is completed the muscles begin to contract. If done too quickly soreness and injury may result, therefore a cool-down activity is needed.

A sample conditioning program used for general conditioning contains the following:

BODY CONDITIONING EXERCISES

Every exercise session should be started with a general warm up or excercise to "Wake up" the body. The general warm up will increase the circulation and respiration, this will stimulate the flow of blood and increase the oxygen supply to the muscle groups. The exercise session may be divided into three areas: warm up, work out or body of the session and the cool-down period.

Circulatory endurance activities such as running, jogging, brisk walking, swimming, rope skipping, or bench stepping should be included in the training program. A conditioning program for the board sailor should include exercises and static exercises. A regular program should be followed. In every lesson, exercises should be performed. Warm up programs will be suggested later in the text.

SUGGESTED WEEKLY PROGRAM

FIRST WEEK

MONDAY	TUESDAY	WEDNESDAY	THURSDAY	FRIDAY
Run 3/4 mile	Run 3/4 mile	Run 1 mile	Run 1 mile	Run 1 1/2 miles
Leg Exercises	Streching Exercises	Strength Exercises	Streching Exercises	Leg Exercises
Arm Exercises	Sprint 5x40 yds.	Cool Down - Stretch	Sprint 5x40 yds.	Arm Exercises
Trunk Exercise	Sprint 5x20 yds.		Sprint 5x20 yds.	Mild Stretching
Cool Down	Cool Down	Cool Down	Sprint 3x40 yds	
				Cool Down

SECOND WEEK

MONDAY	TUESDAY	WEDNESDAY	THURSDAY	FRIDAY
Run 1 1/2 miles	Run 1 mile miles	Run 1 1/2	Run 1 mile	Run 1 3/4 miles
Strength Exercises with equipment	Stretching	Strength Exercises	Stretching	Leg Exercises
Cool Down	Sprint 5x60 yds.	Cool Down	Sprint 5x60 yds.	Arm Exercises
	Sprint 5x30 yds.		Sprint 5x30 yds.	Trunk Exercises
	Cool Down		Cool Down	Sprint 3x60 yds
				Cool Down Stretches

Increase reps, weights, and distance in additional weeks.

You may substitute rope jumping or swimming for runs in later weeks.

STRENGTH

This may be defined as the contractile pull of a muscle or group of muscles to perform a movement against resistance. Individuals may vary as to the degree of strength depending upon the muscle group tested. The key to strength building is to start slowly and gradually and then increase weight and resistance as one shows progress.

Boardsailors are encouraged to follow the exercises outlined in the strength area. One develops strength through exercise against gradual increased resistance, based on the overload principle. Better tonal and muscle elasticity will be a direct result of a good strength program needed by the boardsailor.

SIDE ROLL

Roll out on right side, repeat on left side.

JACK-KNIFE SIT

Lie flat on floor, hands at side. Then sit on floor, bend slightly at the waist, legs together, knees bent and arms straight out in a Jack-Knife position.

CRUNCH SIT UP

Lie on the floor on your back, arms at your sides, and bend your knees, feet flat about 10" apart. Tighten your abdominal muscles, pressing your lower back to the floor. Hold. Now slowly pull your head, neck, shoulders and arms off the floor, chin to the chest. Hold again and return to your original position.

SQUAT THRUST

Stand at attention. Now bend knees and place hands on floor in front of feet. Then thrust legs back far enough so that body straightens out. Return to squat position, or starting position.

LEG RAISER

Lie on back, hands clasped across chest or at your side, legs straight out about 6" off floor. Spread legs as far as possible. Return to original position and repeat.

PRESS UPS

SIT UPS

Lie on back with legs straight or bent, about a foot apart, fingers interlaced behind neck. Sit up, touch elbows to knees. Return to starting position.

COSSACK DANCING

INNER-THIGH STRENGTHENER

Stand with your back to a wall and lower yourself into a sitting position - legs and body form a 90° angle.

ISOMETRIC EXERCISES TO BUILD YOUR STRENGTH

PRESS IN DOORWAY
Stand in doorway, bend arms, lock knees and hips. Push with maximum effort for 6 seconds against top of doorway (use box or stool if necessary)

PULL DOWN
Place hands on top of door frame. Keep arms and legs straight. Pull down as hard as you can.

NECK DEVELOPER
Place folded towel between your head and door jam. Press the front or back of head against door jam. Also use towel this way - push back with head - pull to front with towel.

ARM DEVELOPER
To develop the pushing muscles of the arm and shoulder, rest one elbow against the door jam - then press against it as hard as you can with the opposite arm. Repeat to opposite side.

SIDE PRESS
Place one hand on each side of the door frame. Push outward with both arms.

LATERAL RAISE
Place back of your hands against door jam. Push outward with both hands with maximum effort to develop shoulders.

LEG PRESS

Get in door frame as shown. Press back against one side of door frame as your legs press against the other side.

ANKLE BOUNCE

Stand at attention. Bounce up into the air using only your ankle and calf muscles.

"L" STRETCH

Lie on the floor on your back, with your hands behind your head. Pull your knees up to your chest. Lift your head, neck and shoulders while you try to touch your elbows together. Then straighten the legs up towards the ceiling. Return to starting position.

SPECIAL NECK STRENGTHENING EXERCISES

A combination of isometric and isotonic exercises will add strength to your neck, safely. Get ready by rotating your neck in circles, alternating direction after several circles.

Use ISOMETRIC pressure in these 4 positions....for 6 seconds each.

FORWARD, BACK, RIGHT SIDE, LEFT SIDE

Isometric is a static exercise where you push against your hand with complete resistance - no motion.

CALF AND FRONT-OF-THIGH STRENGTHENER

Stand with feet shoulders width apart, weight centered, legs turned out from the hips. Keeping back straight, slowly bend knees as much as you comfortably can without lifting heels off the floor. From this position, roll up on toes. Then roll down on heels. Return to starting position.

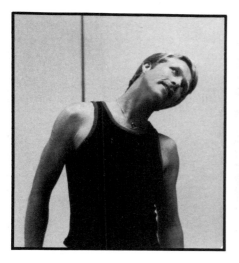  

EXERCISES WITH EQUIPMENT

MID-SECTION ON THE BOARD

Lie on the board with feet hooked under strap. Head at the lowest point. Bend at the knees, hands clasped behind the head. Put the chin on your chest, round the back and curl up, touching chin to knees. Roll back slowly. Uncurl. Repeat.

UPPER AND LOWER BACK ON THE BOARD

Lie on stomach. Feet under straps. Hands behind back. Raise your head and upper back, keeping the waistline on the board. Return slowly to starting position.

ABDOMINAL WORKOUT

Lie on board with head at the highest point. Hood hands under strap. Bring knees up to chest. Straighten legs with toes pointed to ceiling. Lower legs slowly, holding them slightly above the board. Open and close and bring them down onto board. Repeat.

 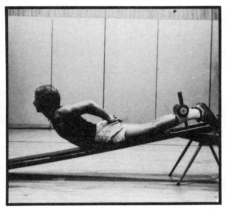 

EXERCISE WHEEL

Thighs, Back, Arms, Hips

Place the Exercise Wheel one foot from a wall. While in a kneeling position, with arms straight, grasp the Exercise Wheel handles. With your weight on the Exercise Wheel, move forward against the wall, at the same time, raise your hips and back until your arms are straight. Return to your original position.

Hips, Waist, Stomach

While in a kneeling position, with arms straight, grasp the Exercise Wheel handles. Keep your head up and back slightly arched. Inhale and tighten your stomach muscles. Hold. Roll Exercise Wheel as far forward as you can reach. Exhale. Return to original position.

SITTING EXERCISE (For Back, Chest and Stomach)

Start with back erect and wheel drawn between legs. Extend keeping back and arms straight. Return to Start position.

PRONE EXERCISE (For Upper Arms)

With arms and legs spread, roll wheel in an arc with arm fully extended moving that arm only. Repeat with other arm.

DOUBLE LEG RAISE

Lie flat on your back, arms extended over head. Raise both legs straight up to 90° while keeping your legs straight and feet together. Exhale as you raise your legs. Slowly lower both legs to the floor, while inhailing.

LOWER BACK EXTENSION

Lie flat on your stomach. Extend your arms with palms facing down. While keeping both legs straight, raise your legs upward as high as possible. Inhale as you raise your legs. Return to the starting position, while exhaling.

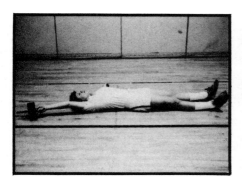  

UPPER BODY

UPPER BODY ON THE BOARD

Lie on the board with feet hooked under strap. Head at the lowest point on the board. Use a 3 lb. weight in each hand and alternate arms forward and backward in a slow controlled manner.

CROSS BODY CURLS

Stand relaxed, feet apart, weight in right hand, right elbow pressed into side to stabilize upper arm. Raise forearm toward opposite shoulder. Return to starting position and repeat.

UPPER ARM TONER

Stand with feet apart, knees bent, leaning forward slightly. Left hand rests on thigh. Right hand grips weight, with elbow bent back behind you. Keeping upper arm still, extend right forearm back, straightening arm. Return to start. Switch arms, repeat.

BENCH PRESS
Lie on floor with knees bent, feet flat. Grasp a 3 lb. weight in each hand and raise arms straight up toward ceiling. Inhale and lower arms. Exhale and again raise arms toward ceiling.

SIDE SWING UP
Lie on floor with knees bent, feet flat. Grasp a 3 lb. weight in each hand and raise arms straight up toward ceiling. Turn palms in and let weights touch each other. Inhale and lower weights slowly out to sides; exhale and bring arms back.

PULLOVER
Lie on floor with knees bent, feet flat and arms next to body. Grasp a 3 lb. weight in each hand and raise arms toward ceiling, palms forward. Inhale as you lower weights slowly behind your head. Lock elbows and keep arms about 26" apart until you touch the floor behind you. Exhale slowly; bring weights back to sides.

WEIGHT TRAINING EXERCISES
UPRIGHT ROW
Grasp bar with overhand grip, hands 4"-6" apart. Keep bar as close to body as possible and lift to chin. Elbows remain elevated throughout.

FRONT ARM CURL
Take underhand grip on bar, keeping elbows next to body to determine position of hands. Lift bar to shoulder area.

BENT-OVER ROW
With overhand grip, hands shoulder-width apart and body parallel to floor, extend arms and lift bar to chest. Upper body remains parallel to floor; knees remain in fixed position.

EXERCISES WITH BROOM OR WAND

STICK HOP

Stand on one foot, hold stick under bent opposite knee with both hands. Hop on straight leg. Reverse sides and repeat.

STICK TWISTER

Sit on floor with broom across your shoulders, arms draped over the stick, left knee bent. Twist at waist, reaching for left knee with right hand. Repeat, twisting right.

STICK STRETCH
(Tones Hips and Thighs)

Sit on floor, holding broom out at arm's length at shoulder level. Rest right foot on stick. Bend right knee and pull it toward you; then lift stick, stretching leg forward. Return to starting position.

BICEPS CURL

Kneel, facing each other, sitting on your heels. Backs straight, hold towel in each hand. Each has the left arm straight in front, right elbow bent so forearm is "Curled" toward shoulder. Only the forearms move -upper arms are stationary.

BACK STRENGTHENER

Kneel upright, seated on your heels, while your partner stands close behind you, his feet 2' apart. Grasp the bottom ends of the towel while he holds the tops. He pulls towel up until his upper arms are parallel to the floor, elbows winging out. You pull towel ends back down. Switch positions and repeat.

TRICEPS-TONER
(Back to Back Pull)

Face in opposite directions, kneeling on the left knee and bending the right leg in front, right foot firmly planted. Hold a towel end taut in each hand. Begin with your elbows bent while your partner's are straight behind. Inhaling, resist as he exhales and pulls the towel ends, bringing his forearms toward his chest, straightening your arms back. Concentrate on moving forearms only, keeping upper arms perfectly still. Pull back and forth smoothly.

ARM AND SHOULDER SQUEEZE

Position your bottom between your partner's feet as you both sit, with knees bent, feet spread and firmly planted. Your partner will keep tension on the towel, holding it with raised, open arms. Grab your towel ends, raise arms to sides and bend elbows so upper arms are parallel to floor, forearms are flush against towel. Slowly bring forearms together. Slowly return to position. Switch positions and repeat.

PULL-UPS

Grasp overhead bar with palms facing forward, hanging with arms and legs straight, feet off floor. Pull up until chin covers over bar, then return to starting hang position. Don't pull with a snap movement, raise knees, kick legs or sway body.

SAILORS LEAN

Bend and stretch holding onto doorknob or bar.

ROLL-UP BUCKET

Sand or water filled. Grasp bar with both hands. Roll the bar up, bringing bucket up to shoulder height. Lower and repeat. Improves strength of fingers, wrist and forearm. Once raised you may attempt a half knee bend and return.

STRETCH ROPE

The stretch rope anchored to a board and pulled offers resistance to the muscles of the upper body when stretching to a hands over head position. Difficult positions using the rope could strengthen other muscle groups. A stretch rope alone may also be used to strenghten the muscles of the arms, chest and upper back.

WRIST WEIGHTS

Wrist weights (2 1/2 lbs. and up) are used to develop the strength of the muscles in the forearms, upper arms and shoulder area due to weight resistance. They may also be used as ankle weights. You may walk, jog, climb or jump with the weights on.

PULL-UP AND JUMP USING HANGING ROPE OR BAR

Reach up and grasp rope or bar. Pull-up with legs together. Jump to other side. Repeat.

STALL BAR LEAN

Stall bar lean strengthens the arms and legs for the sailing position.

STALL BAR HANG

Stall bar hanging with the legs straight, toes pointed and held at an "L" position develops the muscles of the abdomen, legs and lower back.

FLEXIBILITY

May be defined as the ability to move through the full range or motion of each joint in normal movement without restriction. Flexibility in the body joints is a by-product of good stretching programs. These exercises are designed to loosen, stretch and increase the flexibility of all major muscle groups. Do these at a comfortable pace to develop grace and fluidity of movement.

FLEXIBILITY EXERCISES

Flexibility is a specific to each joint and the ligaments, tendons and muscles. The stretching process has to be done gradually, stretching the muscle beyond its resting length, holding the position of maximum stretch pain for several seconds, returning the muscle to resting length, and repeating the process. Don't stretch too hard or too fast.

LEG RAISE

Lie on your back, arms at your sides, extend your legs straight up. Contract your abdominal muscles as you slowly lower one leg to about ten inches from the floor. Raise it again and do the same with the other leg.

LEGS OVER
(Hips-Abdomen-Shoulders)

Lying on back - fully extended hips. Pull legs over the head and touch toes to floor. Keep legs straight. Return to lying position on back - slowly.

SHADOW BOXING

Use to develop timing, coordination, foot paterns and balance.

JACK-KNIFE ROLL -UP

Lie on back, raise legs and arms with palms forward. Grasp ankles. Point chin to chest. Lift upper back off floor and hold.

PALM PRESS

Stand with legs apart. Bend forward. Press palms into floor, fingers straight ahead. Keep arms and knees as straight as possible. Inhale. Bend knees out. Lower buttocks - Bend the knees, keep the arms straight. Return to starting position.

SQUAT FLEX

Get into squatting position, raise up on balls of feet, lean forward on palms. Face heels toward each other. Stretch right leg out as far as possible. Shift weight to right, press left heel down. Pull in and stretch. Bend right knee, extend left leg. Repeat.

MODIFIED WRESTLER'S BRIDGE

Sit down, bring knees up keeping legs together and feet flat on floor. Place hands on floor behind buttocks. Raise chest midsection and buttocks off and parallel with the floor. Return to starting position.

LOWER BACK FLEXOR

Stand. Place right foot about 12" in front of left. Back leg at right angles to front leg. Clasp hands behind your back. Stretch arms up, bend at the waist. Try to touch chin to knee. Repeat to other side.

GRAB ANKLES
(Hamstring-Lower Back)
Standing position - legs straight. Pull chin to knees. Place hands back of ankles.

SPLIT
(Hamstring-Groin)
Standing position. Spread legs slowly going out as far as possible.

BENT OVER WINDMILL
Stand with feet wider apart than shoulders. Tighten buttocks and abdomen. Stretch arms out to sides at shoulder level, fingers spread. Bend forward from the hips. Inhale. Bend right knee. Swing left arm diagonally down. Raise right arm. Repeat exercise with right side.

TWIST AND STRETCH
Lying on the floor, place your left leg over the right one and then use your left leg to pull your right leg toward the floor. Pull down until you feel a good stretch. Do not touch the floor with your right knee; only stretch within your limits. Keep your upper back, shoulders and elbows on the floor and hold position. Repeat the stretch on the other leg.

TWISTER
Lie on your back, arms extended over head. Bring both knees to your chest. Roll both knees to one side, touching the floor, exhaling. Repeat the movement to the opposite side. Return knees to the starting position, inhaling.

WINDMILL
(Hamstring-Groin-Hips)
Lying on back. Touch toes to hand with arms extended to side. Alternate.

ARM CIRCLES

Stand with arms out at shoulder level. Rotate arms, first in small circles, then in larger and larger ones. Continue until upper arms and chest feel warm and arms are tired. Also practice fast arm circling, backwards and forwards over the head.

FOR NECK AND LOWER BACK

Lying on your back and using the power of your arms, slowly bring your head, neck and shoulders forward until you feel a slight stretch. Hold and repeat. Do not overstretch.

FOR LEGS AND GROIN

Sitting with your left leg straight, put your right foot flat on the ground on the other side of your left knee. Reach over your right leg with your left arm so your elbow is on the outside of the right leg. Slowly turn your head, and at the same time, turn your upper body, not your hips. Bending your left elbow creates and stabilizes the stretch. Repeat on the other side.

THE INCLINE BOARD

INVERTED BICYCLING

Lie on the board, head at the lowest point. Grasp the sides of the board. Lift both legs overhead. Raise up as far as you can. Point your toes and begin pedaling the imaginary bicycle.

HAND EXERCISERS

Hand exercisers plus silly putty, play-dough and tennis balls may be used for finger flexibility and hand strength.

DYNABEE

Dynabee - is a commercial piece of apparatus and is used to help strengthen the hands, wrists and forearms.

  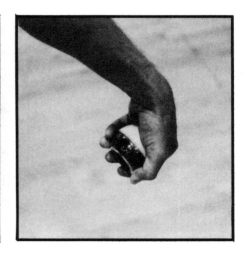

STRETCHING EXERCISES

Swimming is one of the most complete exercises in which the boardsailor can engage. The activity takes off the stress that would normally be placed on the body during running, jogging or some other exercises. The body gets good stretching exercises through swimming. Stretching should be done at the beginning and the end of all programs. The exercises for stretching should be done slowly, gradually, and when you are warmed up. Stretch easily. You do not have to work hard at stretching. The exercises are designed for you to learn to let go of all the tensions in your muscles. So relax and breathe easily. Proper stretching aids in the strength building by maintaining long, supple, low-tension, elastic muscles. Good stretching programs are a definite part for a balanced program of boardsailing exercises.

LEG "V"
(Hamstring-Groin-Shoulders)

Seated position. Legs straddled and straight. Place hands back of ankle. Slowly pull chin to knee. Alternate legs.

INNER-THIGH STRETCH

Sit and spread legs as far apart as you comfortably can. Keep knees straight, toes pointed. Lift arms overhead and turn torso to the right. Bend upper body over right leg, head down, and reach for toes. Lift torso up sideways, arms still stretched over leg. Return to starting position.

LOWER TORSO - LOWER BACK - HAMSTRINGS

Sit on the floor with your legs extended and reach forward. Reach as far as possible and hold this static stretching position.

ABDOMINAL STRETCH

From a prone position and with your hands just outside your shoulders, slowly raise your upper body off the floor until you feel a stretch in the abdominals. Keep your eyes forward and the front of your hips on the floor. Relax to the starting position and repeat.

SHOULDER STRETCH
(Shoulders)

Seated position. Stretch arms out behind you as far as you can.

LOWER BACK STRETCH

Lie on your back with legs extended, draw one knee toward your chest and hold, then draw up the other and hold.

KNEEL STRETCH
(Thigh)

Kneeling position. Put hands on buttocks, push hips forward and arch the back. Slowly lean head and shoulders back as far as possible. Repeat from a standing position.

SIT UP

Sit up, legs spread apart. Extend arms in front at shoulder level, palms down. Flex feet. Pull in and stretch up. Inhale. Point feet to floor. Bend elbows close to body and bring fists to chest. Lower torso to floor and pull in.

LEG LIFT
(Hamstring)

Lying position. Elevate straight leg with toes pointed toward ceiling. Hold. Alternate legs.

POST EXERCISES

CALF STRETCHER

To stretch your calf, stand a short distance away from a solid support and lean against it with your forearms. Rest your head on your hands, bend one leg, and place that foot on the ground in front. Leave the other leg straight, and slowly move your hips forward until you feel a stretch in the calf of your straight leg. Keep the heel of the straight leg on the ground and toes pointed straight ahead. Hold.

SHOULDER STRETCH

Sitting or standing, interlace your fingers above your head, push your arms slightly back and up. Hold this stretch, but do not hold your breath. Then push to left and repeat to right. This stretch is excellent for slumping shoulders.

UPPER ARM STRETCH

With your arms overhead, hold the elbow of one arm with the hand of the other. Gently pull your elbow behind your head, and hold an easy stretch. Do both sides. This stretch can be done from a standing or sitting position.

NECK, SHOULDERS AND ARMS STRETCH

To take the kinks out of a tired back, bend at the waist and keep your knees slightly bent. To change the area of the stretch, bend your knees just a bit, and place your hands at different heights. You can use the mast or boom, and do this exercise standing or kneeling. Hold the stretch.

CALF AND ACHILLES TENDON STRETCH

Face the wall with your arms extended and hands flat against the wall. You should be flat-footed with your feet 3-4' feet away from the wall (leaning position). To apply the stretch, lean toward the wall, keeping your feet flat.

TOE TOUCH

Start with back straight, arms at your side. Bend down and touch the toes. Stand back up straight again, breath deeply. Sweep the arms up and stretch the back muscles. Repeat.

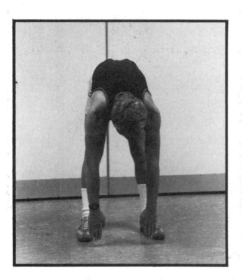

WISH-BONE
(Groin)

Seated position. Pull feet to crotch. Place hands on knees. Push slowly downward.

YOGA STRETCH

Sit down with legs crossed. (To modify, keeps legs straight out.) Tighten abdomen and buttocks, relax arms at sides. Stretch spine, raise arms straight overhead. Then, bend forward at waist, bring arms to shoulder level and lower head. Relax neck and face. Repeat.

BUTTERFLY STRETCH

Sit comfortably with the soles of the feet together, grasp the inside of each ankle (right hand to right ankle and left hand to left ankle), and place your left elbow on the inside of your left knee and your right elbow on the inside of your right knee. Apply pressure to your knees and attempt to push them toward the floor. Hold the push phase for an appropriate static stretch.

CROUCH AND JUMP

Crouch down and jump up, stretching the body.

THE LEG STRETCH

Holding towel around right foot, raise leg straight, pulling on towel while pushing with foot. Hold that position for a count of five; do once each leg.

TOWEL DROP

Do this one as fast as possible. Place towel between feet. Bending knees, reach behind you with left hand to pick up towel. Second part; keeping legs straight, bend down, and place towel between feet. Pick up towel as before, using right hand.

TOWEL STRETCH

Hold towel taut over head, arms wide apart. Keeping towel taut, bend to one side. Return to original position. Bend to opposite side.

ONE ARM TUG

Sit facing each other, legs slightly apart, balls of feet pressed together. Grasp opposite ends of a towel with both hands. Sit upright; your partner curls back while you pull on the towel and resist. As you pull him up, slowly roll down into a half-sit-up. Seesaw back and forth smoothly, evenly.

TORSO-TONER FOR TWO

With feet firmly planted about 2' apart, crouch facing each other, about 3' apart. Each grabs to opposite end of a towel with the right hand. Bend knees, resting left arm on left leg. Draw your right elbow into your side, straightening his right arm. Switch hands and repeat.

STATIC EXERCISES OR ISOMETRIC EXERCISES

Another method of training used for gaining strength is the use of isometric or "Static" exercises. In doing static exercise, the idea is to push, pull or lift against an object that does not move. There is a time element involved in the static exercise program. It is suggested to go with an all out effort and hold it for approximately six seconds. Since the isometric program of exercises may be defined as the contractile pull of a muscle or group of muscles against a relatively immovable object, the program may be performed without the use of strength equipment.

STATIC STRETCHES

Several exercises can be helpful in stretching important areas of the body. Hold each position 45-60 seconds, but do not bounce. All exercises must be done properly to be helpful in a conditioning program.

It is possible to stretch the same muscle group from several different body positions. Floor-supported stretches are the easiest to do correctly and are just as effective as standing, or supported positions.

A sit-up done as shown greatly increases the flexibility of the back area and also strengthens your center of effort area. Exhale when flat on the floor, inhale when rolling up.

Sitting with legs together, knees bent, arms out to the side rotate the upper body about 45° Do not strain, and turn only as much as seems comfortable. Stretch out on right side, repeat on left side.

Lie on your back with arms crossed and hold that position. This relaxes the lower back and spine. Turn onto your stomach and place a pair of books or a cushion under your crossed arms to raise the upper part of your body from the floor. Hold. This relaxes the abdomon area.

AQUACISE

BOARDSAILING EXERCISES IN THE POOL

The exercises can be done in the pool area in the beginning of the period and at any time during the class. In large classes it may be advantageous to use a station approach with small groups at each station and a workable rotation. This will make it possible for everyone to experience the whole circuit of pool exercises and skills on the board. The basic requirements of the boardsailor are to have good balance, reasonable agility and to be physically fit. The fitness refers to the stamina or the ability to resist fatigue and to have good overall body strength.

The resistance of water to body movements offers the same strengthening effects as does working with weights, without the stress of weight training. 90% of the body weight is lost under water.

STATIONARY CRAWL
Stand in chest deep water, reach out with right hand and press downward and pull bringing arm to side of hip in crawl stroke motion. Do same with left hand.

FIGURE "8"
Standing in chest-deep water, extend straight arms and cup hands. Push water in a large figure 8 motion in front of and along body.

DOUBLE LEG BOUNCES
Stand in waist to chest deep water with hands at side. Jump out of the water pushing off with the balls of your feet and jumping as high as you can.

WATER JUMPING JACKS (Legs Only)

Stand in waist to chest deep water with hands on hips. Jump to a side-straddle jumping jack position with feet about 2' apart. Return to position with the feet together. Variation: Hopping and jumping forward. These strengthen the lower half of the body.

KICK BOARD
In water deep enough so that the feet will not touch the bottom, grasp the kick board with both hands held out in front of the body. Kick flutter style with toes pointed back. The entire leg acts as a whip. To strengthen stomach and shoulders, hold a kick board with straight arms and bend forward to touch the water, then bend back to touch the water.

LEG EXTENSIONS

Stand in chest deep water and raise right knee to chest, straighten out lower leg, stretch, hold and return leg to standing position. Repeat with left leg. Variation: To tone leg muscles, hold onto the side of the pool, keep leg straight, kick it out of the water. Variation: Stand in chest-high water, left arm resting on side of pool, right arm outstretched. Bend right knee, bringing it toward body; then kick it to the side in a wide circle, straightening legs at the same time. Now turn around and repeat exercise with left leg.

KNEE-CHEST PULLS

Stand in chest deep water and raise right leg up toward chest and grasp lower leg with both hands pulling leg tightly to chest. Hold leg three counts and return. Repeat with left leg.

WATER-WALK WARM UP

The student is in the pool at waist to chest depth with palms extended and does a five minute non-stop water walk (keep feet flat) back and forth across the pool area. This is good for hips, stomach and leg muscles. Variations: Walk with legs spread apart. Walk through hip-high water with an exaggerated marching step, raising each knee as high as you can. Cross pool several times, keeping feet flat as they touch bottom.

TREADING WATER

In water deep enough so that the feet will not touch the bottom in a vertical position, move your feet and legs in a scissor kick, while keeping your hands out of the water. Keep your head above the water. Repeat using hands and feet.

JACK-KNIFE STRETCH

Face side of pool, holding on with both hands. Bring knees up to chest, hold, then place feet against the wall. Straighten the legs to a jack-knife position.

PUSH AND PULL

Standing in chest-deep water, extend arms and cup hands. Push water backward and outward, then pull arms back to starting position through the water.

ELEMENTARY BOBBING

Standing chest-high in water, the student;
1. Takes a breath.
2. Submerges in a tuck position with feet on the pool bottom in shallow water.
3. Shoves up off the bottom and regains a standing position.

4. Inhales with head out of water.
The student should be in shoulder depth or above and begin to swim 50 yard laps and increase these distances until he can successfully complete a 200 yard non-stop distance. This will give him confidence in his ability to handle any problems in the water.

ENDURANCE

Endurance may be defined as the physiological condition manifested by the length of time one can persist at an activity. Endurance may also be specific to the type of activity, the style used in the activity and the rate of performance in the activity. Boardsailing is an activity that requires considerable work on endurance conditioning. The human body will adapt to various stresses placed upon it by training and conditioning programs. Over an extended period of time, cardio-respiratory improvement will take place. Endurance transfer depends upon the amount of work and the willingness to push oneself into the overload principle, which will necessitate raising the threshold of resistance against the distress of the fatigue syndrome. In the overload principle, the stress is placed against the present level of development by utilizing Rate, Resistance and Repititions. Sample Cardio-respiratory activities include the following:

ROPE SKIPPING

Skipping is a great leg developer, but more important, Rope Skipping promotes endurance and energy in the leg muscles. Muscles must have endurance in order to be strong.

RUNNING

Run in place at top speed, pump arms vigorously, raise knees high and stay on the balls of the feet.

Running (Jogging) up and down a stairwell can be used for cardio-vascular conditioning and for total leg strengthening. (Ankle weights and wrist weights would increase the difficulty.)

HARVARD STEP

The "Harvard-Step" type exercise is used for agility and developing the strength of the lower leg. Ankle weights and wrist weights would increase the difficulty. Extended periods of this exercise would increase cardio-vascular efficiency.

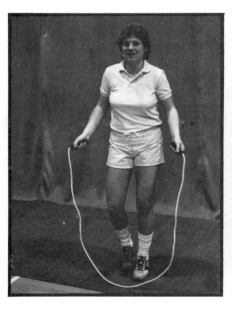

BALANCE

HORIZONTAL BAR
A horizontally positioned bar may be used to simulate bringing the center of gravity in over the board by bending the knees, swinging in and under the bar.

SQUARE BALANCE
The home-made square balance board can be used for side to side or front to back balance maneuvers.

BONGO BOARD
The bongo board is a commercial piece of apparatus and is used to develop side to side lateral balance.

WONDERGYM
The Wondergym was designed for boardsailors and is totally effective because it reproduces the physical stresses of sailing. Using this physical conditioning program will dramatically increase your endurance and strengthen the muscles you use in sailing.

Select a location that has an unobstructed area around it. The Wondergym may be hooked up to a door that opens away from you. First test the strength of the door knob on the other side of the door by pushing down and pulling up on it. If it is firm, pass the rope over the top of the door and around the knob and hook the rope to itself with the small 'S' hook. Alternately, it may be attached to a tree or post by simply wrapping the rope around at the height of 7' and hooking it to itself. If the rope slips, wrap around twice, then hook. Keeping one foot placed behind you, test the strength of your installation. When adjusting the rope length, always make sure that the knotted end goes under the rope between the holes, or else the rope will slip.

The Wondergym is designed for a maximum user weight of 225 lbs. Never use it in tandem with another person or as a chin-up bar, trapeze, swing or in any other way in which your entire body weight is hanging on it.

BOARDSAILOR'S HIGH WIND WORKOUT

Biceps, forearms, grip, upper back, shoulders. Medium spring. Hands well apart and arms bent. Oscillate using slight arm flexure while holding arms in bent position. Do 25 reps palms down. 25 with palms up. Repeat.

PECTORAL BUILDER

Pectorals, biceps, hamstring stretch. Medium spring. Long rope. Hold boom behind you at ends, palms down. Feet well back. Arms bent at elbows. Oscillate by flexing biceps.

ARM AND SHOULDER STRENGTH

Using very light spring tension, hold the boom in front of you with your palms down and arms slightly bent. Pull the boom toward you and release and repeat this rapidly and continuously. The frequency should be 3 or 4 times per second. The faster you pull and release, the further back you'll have to lean to balance the inertia of the spring. Repeat with palms up.

SIDE STRETCHES

Lastissimus dorsi, deltoids, biceps. Short rope. Medium spring. Wind boom up and hold at each end. Feet heel to toe and near wall. Allow body to bend. Oscillate by pulling on lower end of boom. Alternate sides by turning on heels.

PECTORALS, TRICEPS, ABDOMEN

Medium spring. Long rope. Oscillate by combined movement of shoulders and arms flexing. Alternate palms up and down.

HAMSTRING STRETCHER

Spring tension to suit your strength. Back against the wall and grasp base of spring with both hands. Place arch of foot in boom and straighten your leg. Adjust the rope until boom holds your leg at the highest possible point when straight. Then shorten the rope 3". Push the boom down with your leg and allow the spring to pull your leg back up while you control the amount of rise with your hand on spring. Mark the rope setting and shorten it over time.

AEROBIC

An aerobic routine to lively popular music will increase cardio -respiratory efficiency because it is continuous and nonstop. Some of the basic steps that may be used in the routine include:

EXERCISES

SHOULDER SHRUG

1. Starting Position: Stand, hands on hips, elbows drawn back.
2. Alternate rolling shoulders up, back and around (clockwise).

DIG

Starting Position: Stand.
1. Step left foot forward to the left, swinging both arms forward as though using a digging motion.
2. Bring hands back while stepping weight on right behind left.
3. Repeat Step 1. (Hold 1 beat)
4. Repeat opposite side.

POLKA STEP

Starting Position: Stand, hands on hips.
1. Put right foot forward and then put left foot alongside or behind right heel.
2. Step forward with right foot. Wait one beat.
3. Repeat on left foot.

DOUBLE HIP BUMPS

Starting Position: Stand, hands on hips. When rocking to right, right leg is straight and left leg is bent slightly at knee.
1. Rock right hip to right twice.
2. Rock left hip to left twice.

SIDE ARM MOVES

Starting Position: Stand.
1. Walk in place, and extend the arms forward in front of the body.
2. Continue walking and bring arms in so hands touch shoulders.

BOW STEP

Starting Position: Stand, hands on hips.
1. Touch right toe about 12" to right.
2. Touch right toe in front of left toe.
3. Repeat Step 1.
4. Bend right leg and touch right toe against and behind left knee.
5. Repeat Step 1.
6. Bring right leg back alongside left and shift weight to right foot.
7. Walk forward with left and then right foot.
8. Repeat pattern on left side.

SNAP AND MOVE

Starting Position: Stand.
1. While walking in place, snap fingers.
2. Continue walking, and bring arms up so hands touch shoulders.

BACK TIPPER

Starting Position: Stand with arms extended overhead, hands clasped.
1. Raise the left knee while leaning backwards.
2. Drop leg, but keep arms extended.
3. Do Step 1 with the right leg.
4. Repeat Step 2.

MOVIN' AND WALKIN' 1

Starting Position: Stand.
1. Walk in place, and extend the arms out to the sides.
2. Continue walking, and bring arms in so hands touch shoulders.

MOVIN' AND WALKIN' 2

Starting Position: Stand.
1. Walk in place and extend the arms above the head.
2. Continue walking a bring arms in so hands touch shoulders.

TOUCHBACK

Starting Position: Stand.
1. Touch right toes behing left leg. Raise arms and snap fingers.
2. Bring right foot even with left foot about shoulder's width apart.
3. Repeat on other side.

CARDIO-RESPIRATORY ACTIVITY

Perform for at least 15 minutes every other day or at least 3 times a week for two weeks any one of the following activities at a pace that will increase heart and breathing rate:

1. Running; 2. Jogging; 3. Swimming; 4. Rope Jumping; 5. Calisthenics; 6. Bench Stepping.

Other activities may be substituted provided heart and breathing rate can be increased and maintained at a rate of at least 140 beats per minute for at least 15 minutes.

EXERCISES

WALKING

Walk 1/4 mile, maintaining a pace of 120 steps per minute while swinging arms and breathing deeply. Repeat for each of the following:
1. 1/2 mile
2. 1 mile

RUNNING IN PLACE

Complete 2 sets of running in place while bringing each foot at least 4" inches off the floor and counting each time the left foot touches the floor for each of the following:

1. Run 50 counts and straddle hop (jumping jacks) 10 for each set.
2. Run 60 counts and straddle hop 10 for each set.

600 YARD WALK-RUN

1. Perform the 600 yard walk.
2. Perform the one mile run in at least 9 minutes.

WALK - JOG

While swinging arms and breathing deeply alternately jog and walk for each of the following:

1. Jog 50 steps and walk 50 steps for 1/2 mile.
2. Jog 50 steps and walk 50 steps 1/4 mile; jog 100 steps and walk 100 steps 1/4 mile.
3. Jog 50 steps and walk 50 steps 1/4 mile for a total of 3/4 miles.
4. Jog 100 steps and walk 100 steps for 1 mile.

JOGGING

1. At a pace of not less than 110 yards in 35 seconds, jog a distance of 2 miles in at least 18 minutes.
2. Run for 12 minutes measuring distance covered.

ROPE JUMPING

1. Jump continuously for 2 sets of 30 seconds jumping and 60 seconds resting on each set and complete each of the following:
   A. Jog step.
   B. Two Foot Hop.
2. Jump continuously for 2 sets of 30 seconds jumping and 30 seconds resting on each set completing each of the following:
   A. Jog step.
   B. Two Foot Hop.
3. Complete 3 sets of continuous jumping for 1 minute with a 1 minute rest in each set.
4. Complete 3 sets of continuous jumping for 2 minutes alternating between the jog step and the two foot hop with one minute rest between sets.

CHAPTER VIII

ORGANIZATIONAL HELPS

THE TRUTH ABOUT BOARDSAILING PROGRAMS

Many colleges and high schools throughout the country currently offer boardsailing classes and club programs that do everything from teaching newcomers the introductory techniques of boardsailing to participating in regattas and competitions. These schools are located in both warm and cold climates where there may be severely cold winters. Many schools contemplating starting a boardsailing program are often concerned that they need to be located on the water, in a warm climate and have one sailboard per student to start the class. This is not true. By using the techniques outlined in this book, a successful class can be run with as few as two sailboards and a simulator, as long as there is the capability of renting additional sailboards on an hourly basis during the final few weeks of class for the open water sailing and final exam. The techniques outlined show you how to master 90% of the basic boardsailing techniques right on campus, using only a swimming pool and a simulator.

STRUCTURING A BOARDSAILING PROGRAM

Because every school situation is slightly different you will have to tailor the program to fit the individual schools needs.The programs are structured for the average three hours per week format:

Semester Program - 15 weeks.

Trimester Program - 5 weeks.

1/2 Semester Program - 8 weeks.

Summer School Program - 6 or 9 weeks.

OPTIONS:

Once a week for 3 hours.

Twice a week for 1½ hours

Three times a week for 1 hour.

The Basic Program includes the following basic sections:

   1. Theory - parts of craft - safety and classroom discussions.

   2. Exercises.

   3. Practical rigging and derigging of the sailboard, knots.

   4. Swimming pool activities.

   5. Simulator activities.

   6. Open water activities.

You may find that you want to mix and match class times to meet that days activities. For example, theory, exercises and rigging could easily be taught in the classroom or gym in 1, 1½ or 3 hour blocks. However, when you are in the swimming pool or on the simulator, which requires set up and breakdown time, you may prefer the longer 1½ or 3 hour class block for time efficiency. When you do the open water activities, you may have to travel off campus to reach the sailing site and a 3 hour time slot would be preferred to allow the students maximum time on the water. Let's take an example of a 15 week program in a cold climate. There is snow on the ground in week 1 and warm weather by week 15.

Weeks 1 - 4: Theory, parts of craft, safety, classroom discussion and exercises.
Weeks 5 - 6: Practical rigging and derigging of the sailboard, knots.
Weeks 7 - 9: Swimming pool activities.
Weeks 10: Simulator Activities.
Weeks 11 - 15: Open water activities.

The first 10 weeks are spent on campus with the first 8 weeks spent indoors. Weeks 9 & 10 spent outdoors fully clothed in warm-ups. Finally during the five warmest weeks, Weeks 11 - 15, you travel off campus to the open water site (wetsuits can be worn if still cool) to complete the requisites of the course.

Now let's suppose your school was located where there was warm weather all year round or you were running a summer or camp program. Here you may mix and match any of the first 5 sections to keep the program moving smoothly and the students interested. Leave the open water activities until the end of the program when the student is fully prepared for sailing.

Class size is a variable to consider. The class may only have 5 students or possibly 20 or maybe even 35 students. If it is a large class, you may want to break the class up into smaller, more manageable groups which spend an equal amount of time at selected stations. A good example in the swimming pool and a class of 35 students with 2 boards is:
Divide the class into 5 groups with 7 students per group.
Group 1 - mounting and balance of the anchored board (in pool).
Group 2 - pulling up the sail on the tethered board in pool.
Group 3 - on land rigging/derigging and furling the anchored boards sail assembly.
Group 4 - on land exercises.
Group 5 - water exercises (in pool).
A large group can be handled very effectively in this manner and should have at least 1 instructor to lead the class and a knowledgeable assistant for each group. Fewer stations can be used with more students per group. Later in this section you will find a variety of proven sample course programs for schools located in both warm and cold climates.

THE COSTS OF STARTING A BOARDSAILING PROGRAM
Running a boardsailing program need not require a large budget. The basic minimum requirements for starting a class consist of having access to 2 complete sailboards (at least one with a small sail), a simulator, 2 personal floatation devises (PFD's), lines and a budget to rent additional sailboards for the final open water classes and to provide transportation to the water site.
2 SAILBOARDS - 1 good quality sailboard and a wetsuit can easily be purchased for under $1,000. If you shop around or go to boat shows you will find new recreational

sailboards for as little as $500-$600. Another route would be to look for a used board which could be less expensive for class use. Quantity and institutional purchase could further reduce costs.

There is nothing that says you have to purchase two sailboards. To begin, a rental option from a local dealer may provide boards only on the days the class meets. The options are numerous. In the long run it is better to own the boards for accessibility.
1 SIMULATOR- manufactured simulators range in price from $150-$300 while home made ones can be assembled for under $50 (see section on simulators for how to make your own).
PERSONAL FLOATATION DEVICES (PFD's) - One for each board.
LINES - these include 60 feet of shock cord or stretch rope for tying off the board in the pool, 20 feet of line for tying the anchored board to a weighted object and a tether line around 100-150 feet long to hold the student while boardsailing on the open water.
FIRST AID KIT - a complete first aid kit should be present at all times.
TEXTBOOK - students should own a text book to help speed up the learning process and to show them how to correct mistakes and increase their enjoyment of the sport of boardsailing.
MONEY TO RENT BOARDS - sailboards can be rented for around $25 a half-day. You can figure 2 to 3 students will share 1 board during the class or approximately $8-$12 per student/per open water class. So if you had 3 open water classes you should budget $25-$35 per student for this charge.
TRANSPORTATION - the relationship of the open water site to the school will largely affect this budget.

NECESSARY EQUIPMENT TO INCLUDE IN BUDGET:
FIXED COSTS - to get started it could look like this:
2 Sailboards - Shop around - $600 and up each.
1 Simulator
2 Personal Floatation Devices (PFD's) - 1 for each board.
All Lines - as described earlier.
First aid kit.

VARIABLE COSTS
Those are per student costs and may change depending on the number of students and the local rental rates.
Student textbook.
Rental of Sailboards.
Transportation.

A well equipped school

THE SIMULATOR

The simulator is a useful dry land teaching and training aid designed to allow you to simulate the movements and actions of boardsailing. While the mechanics of the sport are being demonstrated and practiced on the simulator, the basic terminology can be explained and outlined in a controlled class situation. The simulator works on the lazy-susan principle allowing the board to rotate 360° in either direction. Here the student can go through the basic techniques on land where the instructor can easily correct any mistakes as well as reinforce the basic instructional terminology. There are a variety of manufactured simulators on the market that vary in both quality and price. Some use hydraulic shocks to control the speed of the boards rotation, while others work on a friction principle. Some require you to strap your complete board and sail assembly on top of it (it is advisable to remove the skeg), while others come equipped with a shortened sailboard (one with the nose and tail cut off) on it and you just add your sail assembly. Others use a rectangular shaped piece of wood or plastic as a base into which sail assembly is placed.
Note:
1. Always lay the simulator on flat level ground.
2. There are cases where you mount a complete sailboard on top of the top piece of wood. If the two universal connections are over each other then the simulator should turn freely - however, if you move the universal connection much further forward or aft of this point, the simulator may not function properly and appear difficult to move through certain points of sail or possibly move very fast through other points of sail.

HAND HELD TETHER LINE

A hand held line called a tether line can be attached to the hull of the sailboard to enable the instructor to control one student at a time. This line is usually attached to the daggerboard handle or strap and then run down through the daggerboard well and back to the instructor. 100-150 feet of line should keep the student within hearing range of the instructor. If the student drifts downwind or can only sail on one tack, the instructor can pull the student back upwind, correct the mistake and let the student start over again. The instructor can also make a fixed tether by tying the tether line off to a fixed object on or off shore and work with another student if he seems to be spending too much of his time with one student. This is an excellent method of keeping control of your class when not all of your attention can be devoted to one student. Fixed tethers can be shorter lines (50-75 feet) when tied off to a floating buoy or anchoring system off shore enabling the student to sail in a circular area with a 50-75 foot radius. This allows more students to be on the water at the same time while still giving the instructor the capabilities of handling the class effectively and not spending the would period trying to bring students back upwind. If you make your own anchored tether system you can use anything that will stay on the bottom from a real anchor to concrete blocks to milk cartons filled with rocks to old tires filled with rocks or concrete. Tie a heavy line from the anchor to a floating buoy or milk carton on the surface which marks where the anchor is and have the 50-75 foot tether line extend from this buoy.

INSURANCE

The school should check it's insurance coverage to make sure its adequate for this type of water sport.

ADDITIONAL EQUIPMENT

As more money becomes available the following purchases could be made in the following order of priority. These aids may help make learning to boardsail easier and more enjoyable for both the instructor and the student and increase the overall effectiveness of the program.

CUT OFF SAILBOARD

For the simulator, only in situations where your simulator requires you to attach the complete sailboard to it. By purchasing an inexpensive cut off board, one with the bow and stern missing, the instructor can stand closer to the student. The hull that was once used, can be used in the swimming pool without a rig to practice mounting and balance.

POINTS OF SAIL TEACHING AID

Visual aids such as sketches, charts, wind clock and a chalk board will be helpful in explaining the various points of sail, wind direction, sail trim, tacking and jibing to the students.

DIRECTIONAL CONES

Markers can be very helpful when used as reference points around the simulator to help the student remember the various points of sail. 4 cones placed 10 ft. from the simulator at 12 o'clock - the eye of the wind, 3 and 9 o'clock - beam reach and 6 o'clock - downwind, will serve this purpose.

HIGH WIND OR TRAINING SAIL

To make it easier for beginners to pull up the sail or get underway.

COMPLETE SAIL ASSEMBLY

(This way both complete sailboards can be used in the pool to practice the sailing techniques while the spare rig can be used on the simulator). Children's rigs are available. They have smaller masts, lighter and shorter booms and smaller sails. They also have lower inhaul attachments which are very helpful for younger and smaller students or even for beginning adults in stronger winds.

WETSUITS

Since most students are different sizes, you might purchase a variety of large and small farmer johns or wetsuit tops with fabric sleeves. The students could use one or the other on cold days when the air or water temperature drops below 70° to help prevent hypothermia.

EXERCISE EQUIPMENT

A Wondergym, exercise wheel, sit up bar, dumb bells, wrist exerciser or hand strengtheners.

VARIOUS SIZED SAILS

Additional sails of various sizes could be made available for every level of ability or wind strength. Very light winds may warrant a beginner using a full sized sail (60 sq. ft./5.5sq. m.) whereas in very strong winds a mini sail (35 sq.ft./3.2sq. m.) may allow you to keep teaching where conditions would otherwise force you to cancel the class. Sails without battens are better for a class as they are easier to set up and breakdown.

BULLHORN

This will help the students hear the instructor's voice while they are out on the water.

134

TOOL KIT

A well stocked tool kit will help insure that all your equipment stays in good working order and on the water. The kit should include duct tape, rip stop tape and a piece of sailcloth, screwdrivers and allen wrenches, extra inhaul and outhaul lines, knife, lighter or matches, pliers, file or rasp, sandpaper, wax and some bio-degradable soap (for washing suntan oil off students and boards).

EXTRA LONG DAGGERBOARDS

These can be very helpful for large students as they help increase the stability of the board. A 45 inch daggerboard is good for this purpose.

FILMS AND VIDEO TAPES

On boardsailing will help stimulate the students and show them some of the other aspects of the sport. These may include wave jumping and surfing, racing, freestyle and slalom.

BOUYS

With anchor weights and lines can be used to mark the perimeters of your designated class area. They may also be used as visual reference points for students to sail to or practice tacking and jibing around.

PLAYPEN

This is the name given to a designated teaching area located within a larger body of water. Long ropes floated by buoys approximately 10 feet apart form the boundaries of a square or rectangular teaching area. A good teaching area should be approximately 150 ft. x 200 ft. Anchors at each corner will help hold the shape of the area. While beginners can self rescue back upwind if they drift down to the ropes, more advanced sailors can simply lift their daggerboards and sail over the line to get outside the boundaries of the playpen.

FLOATING DOCK

This makes teaching easier in areas where the shoreline is unsuitable for wading due to rocks, steep dropoffs or potentially dangerous bottoms. In areas where the wind gets blocked by trees or buildings, a floating dock will provide a teaching station out in deeper waters with cleaner, steadier wind. The student has more area to maneuver in and with a hand held tether attached, it makes returning to the dock easy. Obviously a floating dock is not an item to purchase for your class if you are renting boards and going to a variety of different open water sites.

However, if you have a choice of 2 or 3 sites at which to teach and one has a floating dock, then consider that as a preferred site Also, if your school has a body of water on campus, and a well equipped sailboard school, you may consider purchasing or building one sometime down the line. A floating dock doesn't have to be permanently anchored offshore. The dock, with the students aboard, can be pulled out to deep water with a line attached to an anchor offshore.

TRAILER

Two boards can easily be carried on most cars with a roof rack or even placed in a van or bus. A trailer with lockable compartments can be built to carry wetsuits, PFD's, daggerboards and universals. Racks can be built to hold the boards, rigs and simulator while a chain with a lock can be run through the daggerboard wells, booms and simulator to keep them locked to the trailer. This will expedite the set up and breakdown time needed to get off campus.

There are no rules or absolutes when setting up a school or class program about the amount of equipment needed, number of students in the class, how much credit should be given for the course, how much of the costs should be passed onto the students or how many times or hours you should meet during the course. The preceeding guidelines and organizational helps are for the benefit of those schools that have never been introduced to boardsailing and for those who may already have a club at school but didn't know how to turn it into an official course. Remember that many variables need to be considered including climate, financing, assessability to open water and the availability of rental boards or boardsailing equipment in your area. The information in this section should allow you to make a decision on the feasibility of organizing a boardsailing class at your school.

BUILDING A SIMULATOR

Although manufactured simulators can cost between $150 and $300, you can build a simulator at home or at school for under $50. The following diagrams and plans show you how to build a simulator.

SIMULATOR

Equipment needed:

1 4'x4' piece of 3/4 inch thick wood or plywood.
1 2'x3' piece of 3/4 inch thick wood or plywood.
4 sets of wheels from a skateboard or pair of roller skates (4 wheels per set)
2 4" pieces of metal pipe with end fittings for mounting it to a flat piece of wood. The pipes should have different diameters so that one can fit inside the other and rotate freely.
1 female universal insert or modification to allow the sail assemblies universal to be attached to 2'x3' piece of wood.

INSTRUCTIONS

Step 1.: Lay the 4'x4' piece of wood on the ground, find the centerpoint and mount the piece of pipe of smaller diameter here.
Step 2.: On the underside of the 2'x3' piece of wood, find the centerpoint and mount the piece of pipe with the larger diameter.
Step 3.: On the underside of the 2'x3' piece of wood mount 1 set of roller skate wheels along and perpendicular to an imaginary corner to opposite corner line about 6" in from each of the four corners.
Step 4.: On the top side of the 2'x3' piece of wood, place or mount the female universal insert approximately 6" forward of the center point along the corner line.

Step 5.: Take the top piece with wheels down and put it on top of the bottom piece so that the top pipe fits over the bottom pipe. You may have to shorten both pieces of pipe depending on how high your wheels are so that the weight of the wood is on the wheels and not the pipes. The pipes assure that the top piece remains centered, and it should be able to rotate freely through 360° around this point.
Step 6.: The sail assembly may now be attached to the wood and used as is. An alternate method here is to strap a complete sailboard hull right onto the top piece of wood making sure that most of the sailors weight will be over the centerpoint and that the two universal connections are over each other. Remember to remove the skeg from the sailboard hull.

CREDIT FOR THE CLASS

Class credit will be an institutional decision based on individual curriculum.

INSTRUCTORS RESPONSIBILITY

To run a successful course on boardsailing, an instructor must be proficient at executing the basic boardsailing techniques and also be able to explain the techniques thoroughly and correctly to his students. He is a representative of the sport. Novices will evaluate their introduction to the sport based on his performance and teaching ability. Patience is important since many of the students will be making some basic mistakes. The instructor should use good teaching methods for correcting performance. The instructors job is to provide a structure for learning and at the same time evaluate student progress.

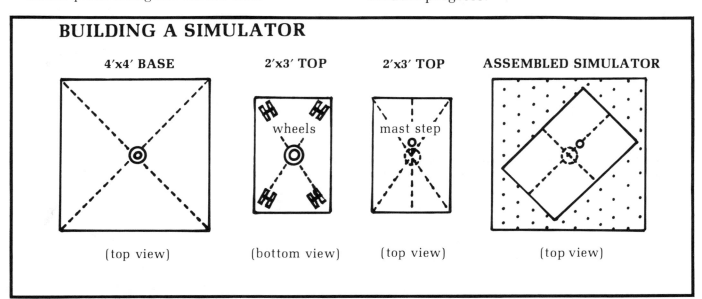

BUILDING A SIMULATOR

4'x4' BASE

(top view)

2'x3' TOP

wheels

(bottom view)

2'x3' TOP

mast step

(top view)

ASSEMBLED SIMULATOR

(top view)

A good instructor will be thorough with his instruction of the techniques

INSTRUCTOR TRAINING

Any good boardsailor, with a text and some guidelines should be able to organize and run a successful Boardsailing class at your college or school. The intention is to offer the students a top quality program. It is recommended that the head instructor or physical education teacher that plans to offer the program attend one of the many Boardsailing Instructor Seminars and courses taught periodically around the country. There are independent groups such as B.I.G. (Boardsailing Instructors Group) and manufacturer supported groups such as the IWSS (International Windsurfer Sailing School), M.B.A. (Mistral Boardsailing Academy) and Connelly as well as others that provide potential instructors with the knowledge needed to run a professional and successful program. In the open water class, the head instructor should not attempt to handle any more than 5 students at one time.

CLASS SAFETY

Ultimately you are responsible for the safety of the students so you should outline the safety procedures to them before you allow them out on the water. **NEVER LEAVE THE BOARD** is the most important rule to emphasize. Some students may want to abandon the sailboard and swim to shore. It could be they broke a piece of equipment, got tired and frustrated, or just wanted to take a swim. To insure the safety of the class, you can't allow this to happen.
Two important points before going out on the water:

1. Self rescue; know how to furl the sail assembly properly and be able to paddle both the board and sail assembly back to shore.
2. Emergency Hand Signals; "HELP or SOS!" — Both arms waving up and down from your head to your sides. "I'm O.K." — Arms hooped overhead.

RETRIEVING A STUDENT

As an instructor, the safety of your students is your primary concern. Sometimes, either due to a lack of sailing ability and a difficulty in executing a self rescue on the part of the student or due to an unforeseen emergency, it may be necessary to rescue or retrieve a student off the water as fast as possible. The following are sample solutions to various situations you may encounter.

Rescue Due To Lack Of Ability:

1. Sail out on a board rigged with a smaller sail than the one the student is currently using and trade the big sail for the small one.
2. Sail out to the student, tell him to roll up his sail and get in the self rescue position and lie on top of his board and rig and pull along side next to you and grab your daggerboard strap and you tow him to shore with your sailboard.
3. Sail out to the student, tell him to roll up his sail and get in the self rescue position and kneel on top of his board and rig and then throw him a towline which he will hold while the other end is tied off at your universal and you will tow him to shore with your sailboard.

137

4. If a student is already in the self rescue position but is having difficulty paddling upwind or the rig keeps sliding off, you may want to paddle out to the student and trade, letting him paddle the hull in while you paddle his hull and rig in.

5. At some locations you may have access to a powerboat or rowboat which you can use to reach the student. Depending on the size or type of boat, tow the student back, or put the board and rig in the boat or even bring a qualified student with you who can trade positions with the student having difficulty.

Emergencies tend to be one of a kind unique situations that happen when you least expect them. They are usually due to uncontrollable circumstances and most often require immediate action and attention. A list of potential emergencies is impossible to formulate but the following accidents could happen and an instructor should be able to recognize these situations and take immediate action.

1. Student receives an injury from a collision with another vessel.
    a. powerboat.
    b. jet ski.
    c. sailboat.
    d. another sailboard.

2. Student receives an injury on his own sailboard.

3. Student swallows large quantities of water.

4. Student gets hypothermia.

5. Student gets caught in a hazardous area or situation.

6. Student gets sunstroke.

7. Student panics.

In all of these situations, get the student off the water as quickly as possible and once on shore take the appropriate action.

Rescue Due to Emergency:

To rescue a student immediately:

1. With a powerboat, this is the fastest way to get offshore and if necessary, leave the student's sailboard floating and have a qualified student paddle out on his board and retrieve it.

2. With a rowboat.

3. With a sailboat or sailboard.

4. With a sailboard hull.

5. With anything that floats.

6. Do not attempt a swimming water rescue unless you are close to shore and do not have any other means of reaching the student.

ORGANIZING THE OPEN WATER CLASS

CHOOSING A LOCATION

When choosing a location to teach your class, the prime concern is that it will be safe. You are responsible for the safety of your students. You should be safety conscious at all times, know all the safety rules and convey their importance to the students. Always try to get the students to learn to sail upwind first, since anyone can drift downwind just by sitting on a board. It also offers reference points for the beginner to determine his position more easily. You should also make anyone that sails or drifts out of the sailing area or into a hazardous area, immediately stop sailing and do a self rescue and return to the area. The limits should include a downwind boundary, a maximum distance from the launch site, and not go into any hazardous areas.

DEALING WITH LOCAL AUTHORITIES

If your program rents boards or sails at an established boardsailing school site, the conditions and local restrictions will have already been established. If utilizing other areas for open water classes it is best to consult local authorities and/or private owners to clarify local ordinances and gain necessary permissions. This will make your sailing more enjoyable and enlist local support for the sport.

INTRODUCTION TO THE WATER, POTENTIAL HAZARDS

When running a class, it is your responsibility to be aware of any hazards or potentially hazardous areas that may be at your teaching site or location. You should then tell the students of these hazards and mark off any hazardous areas. Hazards can include currents, channels, excessive boat traffic, docks, submerged pilings, logs, fallen trees or branches, rocks and a variety of other submerged articles that one might find on the bottom such as shells, oyster beds, broken bottles and an assortment of sharp-edged or cutting objects. Hazardous areas could be oceans, maybe with a shorebreak, or channels or areas with fallen logs or trees just below the water surface, or areas with strong currents. Again, the instructor should be aware of any of these hazards and obstacles at the teaching site and pass this information on the the beginning boardsailor.

You want to introduce the student to the open water with conditions as close to ideal as possible. A nice, calm, five mile an hour wind, with no waves on a body of water 3 to 4 feet deep with no boat traffic, shore currents, rip tides or surrounding houses or trees to break up the wind would be ideal. The more confident and relaxed that the student is that he can return to shore, the quicker and easier he will be to teach. In any case, remember that safety is the prime concern and plan ahead. If the water is too cold, insist on wetsuits and if you don't have any, postpone the class. As a reference, in water temperatures below 70° all students should wear some form of a wetsuit and if the water temperature is as low as 50° than full coverage wetsuits are a must for all students. If you have some weak swimmers, insist on them wearing PFD's even if the law doesn't require it. Let's help keep boardsailing's safety record clean.

PROPER WEATHER FOR RUNNING A CLASS

When running a class, you should become familiar with local weather patterns and plan your classes accordingly. The weather is your main factor in determining whether or not to hold the class. If you know that the winds are generally light in the morning but blow harder in the afternoon, then obviously try for the morning class. If you have the choice of two locations, check that morning to see if there is a big shorebreak that day at one site and not the other, or if one has an offshore wind and the other an onshore wind. The reason, of course, is to pick the overall best location where teaching will be the easiest. The morning of the class, listen to the radio, watch the TV and get the weather forecast if possible. Then check your location(s) and if it's all O.K., go for it. If something isn't right and you can't find an alternate teaching site that is suitable, then cancel and reschedule your class for another day.

RUNNING THE OPEN WATER CLASS

The studying of this text, accompanied by practice in the school's swimming pool and on the simulator should have taught each student 90% of the basic boardsailing techniques. In order to complete your training you must go out and physically experience boardsailing on a body of water with some wind. Once a location has been chosen and the necessary arrangements such as permits, equipment availability and transportation of the students to the site is secured, you are ready to begin Lesson 1 on the water.

In Lesson 1 we will take you through:
1. Board paddling and balance.
2. Launch technique.
3. Students first attempt on the water using a tether.

If you have a small class or enough boards so that each student can have his own board, then assign each student a board and you are ready to begin. However, if you have a large class and many more students than boards, then you may find it helpful to break up into smaller groups of workable numbers that can be taken through separate stations. Divide the class into 3 equal groups and have each group spend 1/3 of the class time at each station before moving on to the next one. Give each station an equal amount of available boards. However, if there are twice as many students as boards, you may want to break up into 2 stations only. Combine the board paddling and balance with the launching technique so that the students will have a longer time at that station before moving on to the second station.

Before you put the students out on the water, the instructor should explain the advantages of the tether leash and give an on the water demonstration of what he expects the class to do. He should stay close enough to the class so that they will all be able to see and hear him clearly.

LESSON 1

1. Board Paddling and Balance:
a. The student should get the feel of paddling the board from both a lying down and kneeling position. This will be useful later when he executes a self rescue. Practice turning the board as well as flipping it over and righting it again and practice how to get back on it from the water.

b. The student may practice balancing the board without the rig and also experiment with its instability. Then with the full assembly he can concentrate on hand positions when he tries sailing. This exercise should include transferring your weight from side to side and from fore to aft. Try everything from kneeling and standing to walking and jumping as well as getting on and off the board while in the water.

2. Launch Technique:

Review the various launch techniques remembering to attach the safety leash and checking to make sure there is deep enough water for the daggerboard to be inserted all the way. The daggerboard provides lateral stability.

3. Tether Instruction:

a. Explain how you will attach a tether line (a long rope) to the board and how this is a useful teaching aid. The tether line will either be hand held or tied off to a floating raft or a buoy or a stable object on shore.

b. The tether will give the student the freedom to sail away from the start position for the length of the line. This will give the student the feel of the equipment on the water without the fear of being taken downwind and not being able to sail back. If he reaches the end of his rope, he can turn around and sail back or if this is too difficult, pull himself in hand over hand or be pulled in by whomever is holding the tether.

c. The tether will also keep each student within hearing range of the instructor and force him to execute the various maneuvers of tacking and jibing without sailing off into the horizon on one long tack.

4. Instructor's Demonstration on Water:

The instructor should now demonstrate to the class how to boardsail. He should stay close to the class so they can hear him and review the steps aloud as he does them.

a. Demonstrate a launching technique.

b. Get into the ready position and review the checklist.

c. Point out the various points of sail in relation to this ready position.

d. Check the foot positions.

e. Talk your way through each step from getting the uphaul to pulling the sail out of the water to filling the sail with air.

f. Show how to steer the board.

g. Demonstrate a tack and a jibe, talking your way through each step before sailing back to the students.

5. Students First Attempt on the Water:

The students will now attempt to boardsail. This initial trial should be done by one student at a time while the others watch and mentally run through the procedure. Let the students you feel capable of sailing best get underway first, as this will help to boost the confidence of the weaker and more shy students.

a. Start the student in waist deep water or from a floating dock offshore after making sure the tether line is attached.

b. Talk the student into the ready position and review the checklist.

c. Have the student check his foot position.

d. Tell the student to retrieve the uphaul and pull the sail out of the water.

e. Once the sail is out of the water have the student walk through a tack and then a jibe and point out the courses and points of sail between these positions.

f. Have the student sail towards a particular point.

g. Try to point out any mistakes and the necessary corrections as they develop and before the student falls. If the student is totally confused and twisted it may be easier to have him take hold of the uphaul or mast and return to the start position and begin again.

h. Have the student tack and return to launch position.

i. Send the student out once more and have him jibe and return once again.

j. Repeat steps 'a' - 'i' with the remaining students.

If you find you have some students that are naturals and are ready for the water, you can tie them off on tether lines or let them sail in a confined area while you run through the basics with the remaining students. Once all of the students have gone through the basics you can let them out on the water and sail over and work with them individually from your board, boat or dock. In order to avoid confusion, make individual corrections on the water using name, sail number or color. Some students may also execute slightly different maneuvers which give the same end result. When correcting a student, don't over correct. Instead, offer criticism on moves that may lead to bad habits later down the line. When the student has returned to the dock offer positive encouragement for the first attempt before explaining all the mistakes he made and how to correct them.

LESSON 2

In Lesson 1 students took turns learning the basic techniques of boardsailing while sharing a small number of sailboards. In Lesson 2, the ideal situation is to have one sailboard per student, each complete with a training sail and a tether line or confined to a safe teaching site with boundaries marked off.

If you have a large class and not enough boards for each student to have his own, then it is recommended to divide the class into groups of workable numbers that can be taken through separate stations. Each station can then be given one board, except for the water sailing station which would ideally have one board for each student in that group. The time allowed for your class should be divided by the number of stations to determine how long each group spends at that spot. When the time limit is up, each group moves along to the next station. Depending on the number of students in your class and the number of boards you have available and the amount of time you have to conduct the class, will determine just how many stations into which you should divide. Examples of circuit stations can include;

1. **Rigging.**
2. **Launching.**
3. **Self-Rescue.**
4. **On land review of techniques.**
5. **On the water sailing.**

RIGGING:

Here the group of students practice the technique to rig/derig/rig and disassemble the sail assembly (described in detail earlier). This group should have one sail assembly or complete sailboard and should practice the following maneuvers.

1. Lay all the parts of the sail assembly on the ground (mast, booms, sail, inhaul, outhaul, downhaul and universal).

2. Assemble the parts correctly so that you have a fully rigged sail assembly. Connect the rig to the board.

3. Separate the rig from the board, uncleat the outhaul and furl the sail as you would for carrying, transport or cartopping.

4. Unfurl the sail assembly, recleat the outhaul and rig it as if you were going sailing. Again connect the rig to the board.

5. Uncleat the outhaul, totally disassemble the sail assembly, refold the sail and lay all the parts on the ground again. This will help confirm the students knowledge of how to rig and derig a sailboard.

LAUNCHING:

The students practice launching a sailboard (described in detail earlier). This group should have one complete sailboard and should practice one of the following methods:
METHOD 1.:
Put the rig into the water first. Then carry the hull into waist deep water and put the daggerboard all the way in. Connect the rig to the board and attach the safety leash.

METHOD 2.:
On soft sand or grass, fully rig the board and then stand between the board and the mast and lift the board up onto its side. Then take hold of the nose of the board under one arm and grab the uphaul with the other hand before dragging the board into waist deep water so you can insert the daggerboard.

SELF RESCUE:

The students practice the various methods of self rescue (described in detail earlier). This group should have one complete sailboard and should practice one or more of the following methods:

1. Derig and paddle with hands.
2. Derig and paddle with daggerboard.
3. Derig and paddle with mast.

ON LAND REVIEW:

The students line up on the beach with their backs to the wind and go through the fundamental techniques of starting, steering and posture without a board. During this exercise, the instructor talks the students through the various steps in the hopes of answering any last minute questions before the student sails away. No boards or rigs are needed for this exercise.

1. The students should all stand in a line with their backs to the wind.

2. Everyone should now grasp an imaginary uphaul line and check to see that their feet are properly positioned on the centerline of their imaginary board.

3. Depending on whether you are explaining the mast hand technique or the cross over technique, talk the students through the starting position until their sails are filled with wind.

4. Check their posture, sail, and mast positions.

5. Go over the fundamentals of steering and demonstrate heading off or bearing away from the wind. Check to see that the front arms are extended forward and the back arms are pulled in, since some students have a tendency to keep the arms fixed and tilt the whole upper body forward instead of the sail.

6. Demonstrate heading up or turning into the wind and ask the students to repeat the same by raking the mast back.

7. Steps 2-6 should be repeated, only this time in the opposite direction to get the feel of sailing on the other tack.

ON THE WATER SAILING

The students practice actual boardsailing techniques on the water. Instead of the instructor telling the student how to execute a maneuver, the student should be familiar enough with the techniques enabling him to execute any maneuver the instructor asks him to carry out. Ideally each student should have his own board in this group. If this is impossible, divide the number of people by the number of boards to give you the students per board ratio. Then divide the time allotted to this group by that same number to determine how many minutes each student should get on the board. The number of boards you have available should determine the number of stations in your circuit. For instance, if you have one board for every 3 students, the students will have more fun if you only break into 3 groups and stations instead of 5. Since the sailing station is the most fun for the students, it should never be combined with another board station since sailors want to spend as much time on the water as they can get. So if you have 3 groups, give one board and try combining rigging and on land review of techniques together since you stay dry doing both of these. Also combine launching with self rescue and give them 2 boards since you will get wet here. On the water sailing should remain as its own group and be given the rest of the boards so the students can get the maximum time on the water.

1. Before going out on his own board, each student should sail out and back once on a tether attached board and show that he can successfully sail upwind.

2. Correct any mistakes and offer any constructive criticism before setting the student out on his own board. If you feel the student can't sail upwind or will have trouble staying within the designated area then attach a tether line to his board or tell him to execute a self rescue back to the starting position any time he leaves the designated sailing area. Once the student can stay upwind of the launch area he can be released from the tether.

3. Once all the students are out on the water, sail out and circulate among them. Try to correct mistakes and offer encouragement to them as well as giving equal attention to everyone. Remember to call out the students name, sail number or sail color when correcting mistakes so as not to confuse the others.

4. Try to keep the students upwind of the launching area and have them practice heading up and heading off as well as tacking. If a student goes too far downwind, then tell the rest of the class to remain sailing upwind while the instructor sails downwind and tries to talk this student back upwind. If

the student doesn't make any upwind progress, the instructor should have that student self rescue back to the launch area and either get a smaller sail or attach his board to a tether. Remember to divide your time equally among the students.

5. Once the students have mastered upwind sailing, you should let them try downwind sailing and jibing. Demonstrate the heading off process of tipping the mast forward and to windward while pulling in on the back hand so that the front of the board turns away from the wind. As the board heads downwind, the mast is brought across the centerplane and pulled in slightly with the back hand so that the new sail position has the rig perpendicular to the centerline of the hull. The feet are moved back away from the mast and placed on either side of the centerline about shoulders width apart. Steering on a run is accomplished by tilting the mast to the right to turn left and tilting the mast to the left to turn right. The student should practice his steering and then execute a jibe and start heading back upwind.

6. If most of the students seem to be sailing, tacking and jibing, then you may try to get them to play a game of follow the leader and have them sail in a circular pattern. Start with everyone sailing upwind on a close hauled course. Then have them tilt the mast forward and to windward and pull in the back hand so that they start to head off. Head off first through a beam reach and then a broad reach until you are sailing downwind. Then execute a jibe and start to rake the mast back until you are heading back upwind on a close hauled course. Once you are back upwind, tack and repeat the maneuver or try reversing the direction of the circle.

INTRODUCTION TO LESSONS

The following six lessons contain material to be taught in a pool or in calm waters where the boards may be anchored, tethered, or restricted. No time limit is given, since each student will need practice time to become skilled on each one of the essential boardsailing techniques. The instructor will try to cover each lesson area and allow time for the pupil's "hands on" experience, observation and practice.

These skills are arranged in a sequence to insure logical progression to build a strong skill foundation. How capably the instructor can move through these lessons depends on class size, age, ability and length of class sessions.

These organizational helps and educational techniques will help insure the success of the novice prior to the actual open water boardsailing experiences.

The instructor should allow time in the activity sessions for teaching new skills and for repeating previously taught ones.

CLASS ORGANIZATION
The following organizational structure may be used for all lessons in the pool; mounting the board, getting the sail up, moving the sail, positioning the feet, basic sailing position, tacking and jibing.

30 students or less
2 sailboards (minimum) in the water and 'tied off' and 'anchored'.

The class will be divided into two groups for the lessons in the pool. All of the lessons after general warm-ups will be conducted in the water.

One sailboard will be tethered by stabilizing the board with stretch ropes secured at poolside. The other board will be tethered by a rope and anchor or weight to the pool bottom, allowing the board to turn a full 360°.

Three lines of five students will be at each end of the pool facing the sailboards so they can observe each student sailor. On command, one student will move up to each board and practice the technique for each skill in the lesson.

After completing the skill, the student will jump off the board and move to the far right of the pool, using the approach stroke in the open lane to get to the formation at the opposite end of the pool (see diagram).

TEACHING IN A SWIMMING POOL

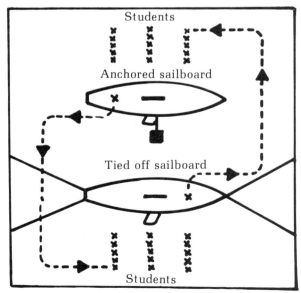

(Students swim to the end of the line at the other sailboard after they have had their turn)

The students should be instructed to stand back clear of the board and mast assembly until it is their turn to perform the skills.

BOARDSAILING IN THE POOL

LESSON #1: RIGGING THE BOARD FOR THE POOL

1. The "tied off" tether and "anchor" tether:
A. The "tied off" tether;
Tie the board off in the pool using the "tied off" tether technique. Placing the board in this position will enable the beginner to work on mast and sail exercises later on. The "tied off" tether method is more stabilized for the beginner. There is enough movement of the board, allowed by the stretch cord, to make it a challenge for the novice to balance. The number of attempts that can be made at getting onto the board, kneeling, standing and balancing as well as foot patterns are dramatically increased by the use of the "tied off" tether. The stretch ropes or shock cord allows for much movement but keeps the board in basically the same position throughout the entire class period. The class will get many more chances to get onto the board and practice balancing because it is tied off and not free floating. The potential safety hazard of a pushed or kicked board hitting a student is eliminated in this method. In large classes more than one student can practice balancing and getting onto the board at one time.
B. The "Anchored" Tether
Tie the board off in the pool using the "anchored" technique. The difference to the "tied off" tether, is the "anchored" tether allows a 360° turn to be accomplished. This method is less stable than the "tied off" tether, therefore the balancing and maneuvering becomes more challenging. It allows for a complete and free moving circular pattern without the board going all over the pool. The "tether" coming from the weight up through the daggerboard well. This also will enable the use of more than one board in the pool. Using the "tied off" and "anchored" tether in the pool make it easier for the novice to grasp the fundamentals of balancing. It is the contention of the authors that success will be insured with the methodical progression used in the pool sequence. The continuous falling off and getting

back on required much energy and perseverance on the part of the novice. Eliminate those negative aspects by utilizing the pool area.

2. Rigging the Board for the Pool:
After the hulls have been tied off in the pool some students may practice the rig/derig/rig and disassemble sail assembly exercise.

3. Exercises:
Some students may practice selected land, equipment and aquacize exercises while others prepare the hull and/or sail assembly.

LESSON #2: MOUNTING THE BOARD

1. Mount with pushoff:
The student can begin to get the 'feel' of the board by standing parallel to and facing the board with the bow to one side and the stern to the other. He can mount the board in two basic ways.

A. He may push off the bottom of the pool to get his stomach down on the board and then get to a kneeling position with his body centrally located on the board.

B. The student may place both hands on the board and spring off the bottom and land immediately on the board on one knee. The other knee is brought up on the board and the student is now in this centrally located position.

2. Mount without using pushoff:
In deeper water the sailor will have to mount the board without the benefit of a push-off from the bottom, so he should begin to practice the arm support-to-stomach mount without using the feet. Being up on both knees, the student rocks the board from side to side and tries to maintain his balance.

3. Mounting the Board:
The novice then attempts to get to his feet and to place them in the correct beginning sailing position with one foot beside or in front of the mast and the other foot on the daggerboard well. Standing up, he can attempt to balance the board from side to side and from front to back by shifting his weight. He experiments by placing his feet in different positions on the board.

The ability to get from a standing position, back to a kneeling position and up again can also be practiced at this time. Keep the class moving by having them take as many "turns" as possible getting up on the board. Rough water may be provided by the class standing around the craft and making waves to increase the difficulty in maintaining balance on the tethered board.

4. Exercises:
Some students may practice selected land, equipment and aquacize exercises while others practice mounting the board.

LESSON #3: PULLING THE SAIL UP

Because there is no wind in the swimming pool, it is best to use the smallest rig you own (i.e., shortest mast and booms on the smallest sail), to help reduce the possibilities of the sail hitting the side of the pool.

1. Scissor mast and board-pull uphaul:
The student gets his body centrally located on the board in a kneeling position. Scissor the mast and board together and reach forward to take hold of the uphaul line. Push the mast back to a right angle position with the board.

2. Pulling the sail up:
Maintain grip on the uphaul line. Get to a standing position with the body centered on the board. The forward foot is in front of the mast, the rear foot is 15-18" behind the front foot centered on the daggerboard, shoulders width apart. Maneuver the board and sail into position for pulling sail out of the water.

Pull on the uphaul line with a steady hand-over-hand motion until the end of the booms are about 2" out of the water.

The sail should remain at a right angle to the sailboard and the sail will be pointed downwind. As the sail is pulled out of the water, the buttocks are in and the shoulders are out. Maintain leverage with legs.

3. Exercises:
A. Have the pupils practice inserting the rig into the mast step by pushing on the base of the universal joint. The entire sail system will now be joined to the hull of the sailboard. The students can practice inserting the rig, either standing or while treading water.

B. Some students may practice selected land, equipment and aquacize exercises while others practice getting the uphaul and pulling the sail up.

LESSON #4: MOVING THE SAIL

1. Moving the sail (Content):
The novice boardsailor will practice the movement of the sail in all directions even though there is no wind available. Tip or lean the sail forward, toward the bow of the board and the board will turn away from the wind. Tip or lean the sail toward the stern of board and the board will turn into the wind.

2. Positioning the feet-while moving the sail:
The pool is the ideal place to practice all the positions of the feet on the board. The

novice boardsailor will find that tense, rigid feet tend to make the board very unstable. Practice with this basic rule in mind, "the wind is always at your back and you are facing the sail". When the feet are relaxed and in proper position, the novice will enjoy successful boardsailing.

3. Pulling the sail up

When pulling the sail out of the water, the novice should straddle the universal joint with the arches of the feet directly over the centerline about shoulders width apart.

4. Exercises:

Some students may practice selected land, equipment and acquacize exercises while others practice moving and pulling the sail up as well as positioning the feet.

LESSON #5: SAILING POSITION

1. Basic Sailing Position:

A. Ready Position:

The basic ready position for the feet is the forward foot beside or slightly in front of the mast, the back foot placed on the daggerboard or shoulders width apart from the front foot. Both feet are on the centerline.

B. The Tack:

To practice the foot positions for tacking, position yourself on one side of the board, then step in front of the mast with both feet straddling the centerline. Then hold on to the uphaul line and step to the opposite side of the board and regrasp the booms; the normal procedure for hand positions should be followed.

C. The Jibe:

To practice the foot positions for the jibe, keep the feet in the side by side, normal sailing position. Lean the sail forward and as the board would turn downwind, step with both feet around to the stern of the board. Place a foot on either side of the centerline. Return to sailing position.

2. Exercises:

Some students may practice selected land, equipment and acquacize exercises while others practice the basic sailing positions, tacking and jibing.

LESSON #6: EMERGENCY PROCEDURES

1. Pack It Up and Paddle In:

Many times the novice may find that it is easy to drift out of shallow water and away from shore. The novice sailor finds that it is impossible to sail back to shore, therefore, the board must be paddled back.

No matter what happens, the sailor does not leave the board. It is imperative that all boardsailors go through the routine of paddling in an emergency situation. The practice in the pool will save the novice boardsailor some trying moments on the water.

There are several points to consider when caught in an emergency situation:

    A. How far away from shore?
    B. Wind direction - currents.
    C. Flat water - waves.
    D. The boardsailor's physical condition.
    E. Stay calm, keep everything together and paddle in .

To prepare for any emergency situation, the class will practice the proper techniques in the pool.

2. Learning how to paddle using the hands:
If the novice boardsailor has drifted too far offshore and the wind has died down to a slight breeze and the water is relatively calm, place the booms on the stern of the board positioned to keep the mast and sail out of the water, kneel straddling the mast, and paddle with your hands. In the pool, start at the low end and go up to the deep end and maneuver the board around and come back down to the low end. Constantly be aware of the sail and mast not dragging in the water.

From the kneeling position, the sailor should go to a flat swimmer's position on the board. In this manner, he is able to use either a crawl stroke or paddle with both hands. Follow the same procedure in starting at the lower end of the pool, going up and coming back.

3. Derig and paddle using the daggerboard:
Release the outhaul, gather the sail to the mast, fold the booms to the top of the mast, place the mast, booms and sail lengthwise on the board. Remove the daggerboard, sit or kneel straddling the rigging and use the daggerboard as a paddle. Getting the sail close to the mast and out of the water should be done facing downwind. Also try to roll the sail up onto the mast, take out the battens, and secure the mast, sail, and booms. This technique is a must for novices to work on in the pool.

4. Derig and use the mast as a paddle:
While in the shallow end of the pool, the novice should roll the sail onto the mast. The next step is to separate the mast from the booms and sail. Leave the daggerboard in, position the sail and booms on the board, and in a standing position, use the mast as a paddle. When there is little wind and the water is flat, this method is the easier method of paddling in. Practice going around the perimeter of the pool.

5. Pack it up and paddle in:

Pack it up and paddle in if you must; however, try not to get into situations that are potentially hazardous. Always be aware of the several points of consideration listed at the beginning:

    A. Distance from shore?

    B. Wind direction currents?

    C. Type of water?

    D. The boardsailor's condition?

Being aware of these points and not over attempting your personal limitations will keep you from getting into a critical situation on the sailboard.

Remember, whatever you do - stay calm - study the situation - don't panic - and stay with your sailboard.

Never put yourself and your board into a situation that can become dangerous. An offshore wind that does not have a lee shore can be a dangerous situation. The boardsailor may be blown far from shore, unable to handle the strong winds coming offshore. In a light wind plus a strong current, the sailor may again find himself in a potentially dangerous situation, being forced to pack it up and paddle in.

The options that you would have in emergency situations like these would be:

1. Paddle in using your hands from a prone or kneeling position.

2. Derig and use the daggerboard as a paddle.

3. Derig and use the mast as a paddle. Remember, whatever you do - stay calm - don't panic - and stay with your sailboard.

6. Exercises

Some students may practice selected land, equipment and aquacize exercises while others practice the emergency procedures of self rescue.

INTRODUCTION TO CIRCUITS

The following 5 circuits consists of various stations to teach and/or reinforce the skills of boardsailing. Circuits are beneficial to provide maximum participation in a short period of time, to utilize limited 'water or deck' space, or to provide equal time on the teaching simulator or boards. The number of stations is dependent upon the size of the class, the space or equipment, and the time needed to practice the skill.

Circuits may be used as a quick review of previously taught lessons, as an entire class period or as a remedial technique to practice a weak skill area. The circuits are samples for the instructor until he/she develops additional task style lessons.

CIRCUITS

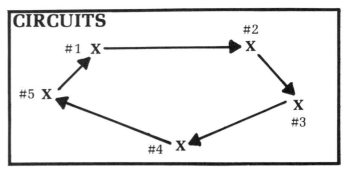

CIRCUIT #1:

Approximately 30 students divided into 5 groups, 6 students at 5 stations.

Minimum Equipment:

2 boards

1 simulator

Rope

Pieces of sail assembly

Station #1

Equipment exercises

Station #2

Tying and practicing knots on rope lengths.

Tying knots on rig pieces.

Station #3

Rigging sail.

Place sail assembly in the board.

Derig.

(leave sail de-rigged for next group)

Station #4 (in water)

Ways of mounting the board.

Balances on board.

Station #5 (on simulator) in pool area.

Pulling sail up.

CIRCUIT #2:

Equipment needed:

Aquacize equipment for exercises;

6 PFD's

2 boards

Ropes for tethering and anchor

Station #1

Aquacize

Treading water practice

Station #2

Tied off tether

Mounting and balance

Pulling sail up

Station #3

Short swim for endurance using approach stroke (crawl with head out of water)

Station #4

Anchor tethered 360° movement.

Turning

Tacking

Jibing

Station #5

Use of PFD (personal floation device)

Jumping in and swimming with PFD short distances

CIRCUIT #3:
Station #1 (pool)
Aquacizes - pool exercise
Arms
Legs
Station #2 (pool)
Pack it up and paddle in
Derig and pack sail on board
Station #3 (pool)
Jump in PFD
(Personal Flotation Device
and swim 25 yards.
Station #4 (deck or land)
Practice distress signals
Stationary paddling -
Hands
Daggerboard
Mast
Station #5 (pool)
On board, paddle length of pool on stomach
with hands, sitting with daggerboard (canoe
action)

CIRCUIT #4: DRY LAND AND SIMULATOR
Station #1
Simulator
Pulling up sail
Tacking
Jibing
Station #2
Knot tying

Station #3
Sail assembly
Rig and derig
Station #4
Balance beam
Low or high
Walking forward, turning with small steps.
Walking forward and backward for balance,
body control.
Station #5
Wondergym
Wall pulley weights or exercise wheel.

CIRCUIT #5: EQUIPMENT CIRCUIT
Station #1
Exercise wheel
Station #2
Hand dumb bells
Station #3
Exercise with free weights
(barbell type)
Station #4
Wondergym
Station #5
Incline board
Station #6
Stretch rope or towels
Station #7
Tennis ball squeeze or spring type handgrip
exercise
Station #8
Jump Rope

SAMPLE COURSES

15 WEEK SEMESTER COURSE
Weeks 1-4 (12 hours)
Place: Classroom, gymnasium or exercise room.
General Objectives:
   A. The student will become aware of the physical aspects affecting the sport; wind, water and temperature.
   B. The student will know and be tested on the existing terminology, signals and rules of open water sailing.
   C. The students will be able to name the parts of and assemble the craft on dry land.
   D. Student will successfully launch and be able to sail to a point and return.
   E. Students will be prepared for common emergencies and first aid procedures.

PERIOD 1	PERIOD 2	PERIOD 3
Week 1		
History and Introduction	Vocabulary	Teaching Vocabulary
Text Book	Selection, Purchase and Care of	Nomenclature
Pre-Season Conditioning	Equipment	Parts of the Craft
Exercise Sheets given to class	Types of Sailboards	Small models, visual aids, charts
	Outstanding Feature	Labeling craft parts on drawings
	Promotional flyers	

147

15 WEEK SEMESTER COURSE

PERIOD 1	PERIOD 2	PERIOD 3
Week 2		

Knots -
   Visual aids
   Overhead Projections
   Knot board
	Knots
	   on individual ropes
	 Pieces of craft
		Loading boards
		 Transporting
		 Launching
		   Land/surf/dock
		 Tools/Repair

Week 3		
Basic Sailing Theory	Wind Direction Beaufort Wind Scale	Points of sail Right-of-Way Rules International Distress Emergency Hand Signals
Week 4		

Safety
   Hypothermia
   Self Rescue
   Injuries
   Personal Floation
     Devices
	Weather
	   Weather Patterns
	   Thunderstorms
	   Personal equipment
	     Wetsuits, harness,
	     etc.
		Evaluation on classroom
		   material

Weeks 5-9 (15 hours)
Place: In Pool
Start out period with over-all conditioning workout
Equipment: At least 2 boards, PFD, Roof racks, possible floor fans

PERIOD 1	PERIOD 2	PERIOD 3
Week 5		

Rigging the board for
   use in the pool
 Tied off position
 Anchored position
	Introduce aquacize -
	   in pool exercise
	 Mounting the board
	   Shallow water -
	     Push off
	   Deep water -
	     without push off
		Review 3 water exercises
		 Teach 3 more in addition
		 Mounting the board
		 Balancing
		 Pulling the sail up

Week 6		

Review water
   exercises
 Teach additional
 Repeat mounting
   the board
 Pulling sail up
	Pool Exercises
	 Moving the sail
	   Position of feet
	   Position of Hands
		Pool exercises - add
		   treading water
		 Approach stroke
		 Proper use of Personal
		   Floatation Device

Week 7		
Circuit #1	Repeat Circuit #1	Aquacize Tacking and Jibing
Week 8		
Teach Circuit #2	Circuit #1 Circuit #2 Shorten time at each station	Aquacize Derig and Pack It Up getting "in"
Week 9		
Paddling Lesson Circuit #3	Pack up and Transport Load and unload Circuit #3	Testing

Week 10 (3 hours)
Place: Inside or outside simulator instruction (fans used inside)

PERIOD 1	PERIOD 2	PERIOD 3
Week 10		
Simulator	Simulator	Simulator
Introduction	Mast Hand Technique	Sheeting In/Out
Similarities to	Tacking	Steering
board	Hands	Sail Adjustment
Differences to	Feet	Falls and Falling
board	Jibing	
Hand Grips/Positions	Hands	
Rig-Derig	Feet	
Mounting the board		
Balancing		
Pulling up the sail		

Weeks 11-15 (15 hours)
Place: Open Water
May be broken down into more frequent smaller time periods, such as weekend trip.
Equipment: 1 board per 2 pupils, PFD's, chase boat
Week 11 (1st trip to area - 3 hours)
Working pairs. "Buddy System" for safety in the water and pairs for reciprocal style teaching - teacher-pupil.
Determine wind and current direction at site. Estimate wind velocity.
Assemble rigging.
Practice various launches.
Get underway.
Tack and Jibe - sail to point and return.
Practice getting underway and return to shore or dock.

Week 12 (2nd trip to area - 3 hours)
Place markers in water (colored plastic jug buoy markers)
Sail to points, change direction, and return to launch site.

Week 13 (3rd trip to area - 3 hours)
Sail to points of a course - set up course with plastic buoys.
Practice course.
Begin competition.

Week 14 (4th trip to area - 3 hours)
Practice sailing on all points of sail including tacking and jibing. Stress execution and control

Week 15 (5th trp to area - 3 hours)
Divide class into two sections:
  Half on water - pupils are evaluated on performance and criteria set by instructor (see evaluation section)
  Half - written test - shown sailboard books/magazines/equipment
Reverse roles

5 Week Course
Weeks 1-5 (2-3 Hour time block)
Equipment: 1 board per 2-4 students, PFD's, Chase boat.
This program is set up for a shorter course with open water and warm weather for boardsailing. The students will be on the sailboards in open water as soon as minimal skills are learned. A brief orientation will be held in an indoor classroom or gymnasium area and this area used for inclement weather.

5 WEEK COURSE

PERIOD 1	PERIOD 2	PERIOD 3
Week 1		
Pre-season Conditioning Introduction	Conditioning Exercises Simulator Demonstration by instructor	Conditioning Exercises Rigging the Simulator Pupils on the Simulator
Introduction & History of Boardsailing	Indoors - Parts of Crafts Rigging	Indoors Mounting the Board Foot Position
Swimming Ability Assessment for Classification of class	Pupils Mount Simulator	Balancing Hand Grips Pulling up the sail
Individual Flotation Devices Explained and Tested (Textbook)		
Week 2		
Water Exercises Swim Simulator outdoors Rig & Derig simulator Mounting the board Pulling up the sail Sailing position Parts of the sailboard Rig and Derig Launching the board Mounting the board Tethered	Land Exercises Carrying the board & sail system to site Rig Boards Konts-demonstration and practice Launching Techniques Beach Dock Discuss water, weather conditions at site Mounting the board Pulling up the sail	Water Exercises Review parts of Craft-Knots Basic Sailing Theory Rigging the board Launching Mounting Pulling up the sail Loading and Transporting Boards Storage
Week 3		
Water Exercises Points of Sail Falls Self-Rescue "Pack It Up and Paddle in"	Conditioning Exercises Right-of-Way Rules Distress Signals Sailing Positions Tacking Demonstration Jibing on Simulator Work on Simulator Outdoors & Jibing	Water Exercises Wind Direction Beaufort Wind Scale Tacking - Hands, Feet Jibing - Hands, Feet
Week 4		
Water Exercises Sail Adjustment Sheeting In/Out Steering a Course	Water Exercises Swim Hypothermia Sailing a Course on Water Simulator Practice Sheeting In/Out	Conditioning Exercises Safety and Repairs Emergency Procedures Modify Circuits to Practice Techniques in open water
Week 5		
Water Exercises Introduce Formation Sailing A sails to indicated point B must sail to join A return to start Place markers in water (colored plastic jugs)	Begin to Evaluate - Rig Derig, Knots, etc Sailing A Course Instructor sets up course Evaluated on accuracy & time	Evaluation Observation and Written Observation Mock Regatta

CAMP PROGRAM

The introduction of boardsailing to a camping program would utilize indoor and outdoor areas and water and land teaching areas. The campers in the beginning may not need to be involved with as much theory, but rather get as much water time as possible. (Craft may be rigged, tethered and/or launched by camp personnel to get campers on the board) The emphasis is placed on the camper becoming familiar quickly with the craft in a very structured and safe environment. The waterfront counselors involved in teaching would be carefully selected as having excellent board knowledge with their assistants chosen for swimming ability.

Camp boardsailing could strive for an integrated approach in the camp setting. Suggestions for integrating:

1. Arts and crafts - Knots and knot tying could be part of a craft project in constructing knot boards. Small model craft could be constructed to learn parts of crafts and rigging.

2. Nature study. Could include wind direction, water currents and safety procedures.

3. Outdoor pursuits. Could include wind direction, water currents and safety procedures.

4. Camera craft - Could take stills, slides and motion pictures of parts of crafts, techniques, and could be displayed in the camp setting.

5. Simulator - Could be used at water front for extra practice area or in the evening as an additional activity.

6. Learning rigging and derigging may be taught and practiced as a night activity to prepare for campers taking over the job of preparing boards themselves.

7. The use of flotation devices may be taught in water safety classes prior to sailing.

SAFETY

1. The site shall be safe, well-marked, and defined so the camper will be secure in learning the new sport.

2. Personal flotation devices should be mandatory in the program for all persons on the boards.

3. Campers should have a screening test of swimming ability and confidence in the water.

4. A buddy system (pairing of campers) and a camp "dog-tag" board would endorse water safety.

5. Wind direction - water currents given by instructors every class or posted for beginner.

BEGINNING LESSONS

Simulator
Tethered - Shallow
         Deep   (or in pool area)

Defined and marked beginners area. Placement of instructors, counselors and aides to observe entire area. Correctly rigged boards - done by instructors in beginning to facilitate lessons.

A sample two week beginning lesson sequence at camp presumes a master teacher and a counselor or experienced sailor for every 4-6 campers.

WEEK 1

SESSION 1	SESSION 2	SESSION 3	SESSION 4	SESSION 5
Land/Water Conditioning Exercises Simulator Demonstration Indoors - Mount Board without sail	Dry land-mount boards Put on PFD Mount Tethered boards in pool or open shallow water Paddle boards on short course	Simulator-Pull up sail Hand/Foot On water-Position Falling off Board Recovery to baord or land Pull up sail/ tethered boards	Rig/Derig Pull up sail Wind Direction Water currents	Mounting Pull up Sail Getting underway Pack it up/ Paddle in

WEEK 2

SESSION 1	SESSION 2	SESSION 3	SESSION 4	SESSION 5
Rigging the boards/knots Getting their own boards ready Launching	Tacking Jibing Directional Sailing Taking boards out Storage on dock/land	Campers Prepare boards Sailing to point & return in restricted area	Campers rig board Simulator/ Water practice Campers paired to get help from each other	Camp Regatta Simple point to point sailing

CHAPTER IX

EVALUATION

The boardsailing instructor will establish evaluation criteria based on the competencies important for the beginning boardsailor. Any type of testing technique should be given at a critical point of the course when the instructor wishes to assess present ability, chart progress on the presented material or to ascertain weak areas. The practical and theory parts of the test will determine if the pupil has mastered the basic elements to become a competent and safe boardsailor. A portable video camera with playback can be used to tape the students attempt on the water and later be reviewed to help the teachers evaluation and the students performance.

SAMPLE PRACTICAL TEST

1. Tying the following knots;
   a. Figure-Of-Eight Knot
   b. Prussic Hitch
   c. Clove Hitch
   d. Two Half Hitches
   e. Bowline
2. Giving the international distress/emergency hand signals. Student is asked to explain and demonstrate appropriate signals on command.
3. Naming the parts of the craft. (Instructor has parts scattered over testing areas and student identifies designated isolated part).
4. Rigging
   A. Rigging the sail assembly.
   B. Rigging the sailboard.
5. Getting underway and sailing a straight course from point "A" to "B" and return.
6. Sailing on all points of sail; close hauled, close reach, beam reach, broad reach and a run as well as tacking and jibing.
7. Stopping in an emergency situation.
8. Falling off and remounting the board in shallow and deep water.
9. Derigging and self rescuing on the water.
10. Derigging a sailboard and tying it on a car top carrier.

BRIEF ESSAY TEST:

1. What is the most important safety rule?
2. Describe sailing on a Starboard Tack.
3. Describe sailing on a Port Tack.
4. What is a tack?
5. What is a jibe?
6. How do you reach a point that is to windward?
7. How do you steer when on a run?
8. How do you reach the shore when the wind dies?
9. What can happen as you get further away from shore in an offshore wind?
10. What are indications of an approaching thunderstorm?

WRITTEN MATCHING TEST

1. Match the numbers on the diagram with the terms below:

_____ Sail
_____ Board or Hull
_____ Bow
_____ Uphaul
_____ Wishbone Booms
_____ Daggerboard
_____ Universal
_____ Stern
_____ Mast
_____ Skeg

2. Match the numbers on the diagram with the wind terms;

_____ True Wind
_____ Induced Wind
_____ Apparent Wind

3. Match the numbers on the diagram for the edges and corners of the sail;

_____ Luff
_____ Clew
_____ Leech
_____ Head
_____ Foot
_____ Tack

MULTIPLE CHOICE TEST;

1. Hypothermia is recognized by:
   a. Confusion.
   b. Numbing of extremities.
   c. Lack of coordination.
   d. All of the above.

2. The best way to prevent hypothermia is to:
   a. Wear a personal floatation device.
   b. Do not sail too far from shore.
   c. Wear a wetsuit.
   d. Move to Hawaii.

3. The emergency hand signal for , "I'm O.K." is:
   a. Waving arms like a bird.
   b. Clasping hands overhead to form an "O".
   c. Raising one arm overhead while keeping other at side.
   d. Raising one arm overhead, open handed and wave.

4. The international distress signal for "S.O.S.-HELP!" is:
   a. Waving arms like a bird.
   b. Raising one arm over head while keeping other at side.
   c. Clasping hands over head to form an "O".
   d. Screaming loudly.

5. The wind is blowing 8-12 knots and you continuously round up into the wind while trying the start sailing. What should you do?
   a. Tip the mast back while pulling in the back hand.
   b. Tip the mast forward while pulling in the back hand.
   c. Tip the mast forward and let go of the front hand.
   d. Tip the mast back and push out with the back hand.

6. You fall often or get pulled to leeward because the mast twists away from you and you are left holding the booms with your back hand. How do you avoid this situation?
   a. Hold on tight to the booms and bend at the waist to counteract the leeward pull.
   b. Tilt the mast forward and pull in with the back hand.
   c. Let go of the rig and start again.
   d. Release the back hand and not the front hand.

7. You frequently fall into the sail. What may be a probable cause of this?
   a. Putting too much weight on the windward rail.
   b. Leaning too far to windward.
   c. Letting the mast off the centerplane.
   d. The sail assembly is to heavy.

8. What is the best method for stopping in an emergency?
   a. Throw the anchor over.
   b. Drop the rig, jump into the water and grab the board.
   c. Lower the rig into the water.
   d. Drop the rig, lay flat on the board and hold on tight.

9. What does the daggerboard do?
   a. Helps when sailing off the wind in heavy air.
   b. Increases stability and prevents turning.
   c. Prevents turning and leeward drift.
   d. Increases stability and prevents leeward drift.

10. What does the skeg do?
   a. Provides directional stability.
   b. Prevents leeward drift.
   c. Speeds up turning.
   d. Stabilizes the hull and allows leeward drift.

An Open Class race

A Funboard race

CHAPTER X

RACING

Once you feel comfortable with the basic techniques of sailing from point A to B and have a working knowledge of tacking, jibing and sailing on the various points of sail, you ought to think about entering a race. Competition is fun and a great learning experience. It forces you to try those things that you might naturally avoid while sailing by yourself. The way a course is laid out forces you to sail both upwind and downwind to tack and jibe and learn to round marks. This practice coupled with watching the other competitors handle the various situations helps you to learn faster and get you past obstacles that may have been slowing your development. This should give you the drive and push to do even better. It is easy to be intimidated by the good sailors' abilities and knowledge of the rules, but in many parts of the country there are regattas for novice, intermediate or advanced sailors or else you may find different fleets for different ability levels at a particular regatta. Racing is probably the best way to quickly improve your skills and push you past the beginner stages. You will soon begin to learn new techniques, strategies and tricks. In addition to improving your skills, you will start to travel to new areas, since every regatta will not take place in your locale, and you will soon gain experience on ponds, rivers, lakes and maybe even oceans. Since you are at the mercy of the environment and the variables of the wind, water and other conditions. The challenges will always be there to prevent you from getting bored. Of course as you go to more regattas you will meet more fun people with a common love and your circle of friends will widen. Remember, if you're going to get into racing, take it seriously and be prepared. Learn some of the basic rules, get to the race site early, be at the skippers meeting, memorize the course and be on time for the start. Just as you prepare your board for the race, you should prepare yourself for the mental frustrations of racing. First, you probably won't win your first few times on the race course. Secondly, you may feel intimidated by other racers or feel you might get in the way of an expert going for a trophy. Too bad for the expert. He was a beginner once himself. If he's an expert he should be smart or good enough to avoid a confrontation. Besides, the more people he beats the more important he feels his victory is and without the other racers, there would be no race. If there is a novice fleet then start there, but just think, after a few races, you may become the expert and be the one encouraging new beginners to try racing. In the beginning you may lose every race, in time you may not lose every race and with a little practice, experience and effort you might start winning a few races.

THE OLYMPIC RACE COURSE

Regular triangle course racing is designed to test all of the sailors' skills by forcing him to sail upwind and downwind; tack and jibe and each and round marks. This is insured by the placement of the various marks in relation to the winds direction. The start and finish lines are usually imaginary lines drawn between a committee boat and a marker buoy which are laid perpendicular to the direction the wind is coming from. Starts are generally begun by the sound of a 10 minute warning gun which is accompanied by the raising of a white flag. 6 minutes before the start, the white flag is dropped. 5 minutes before the start, another

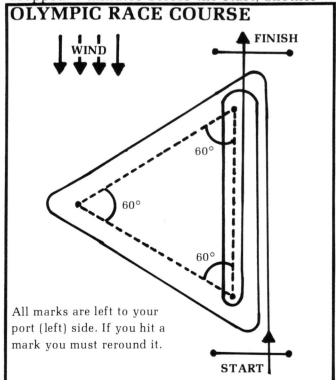

OLYMPIC RACE COURSE

WIND

FINISH

60°

60°

60°

All marks are left to your port (left) side. If you hit a mark you must reround it.

START

signal such as a gun shot is sounded which is accompanied by the raising of the prepatory blue flag. 1 minute before the start, the blue flag is dropped. At the start, another signal is sounded which is accompanied by the raising of a red flag and the race has begun. The winner is the first person who crosses the finish line after successfully completing the course. The race is over when the last boat crosses the finish line or when the time limit expires or when the race committee abandons the race. The above mentioned starting sequence is the type used at the Olympics and in most major regattas. However, at local regattas the race committee has the right to lay out any type or length of course they want and utilize any starting sequence they desire. The following diagram is what is known at the Olympic Course and consists of 6 legs; the start, windward, reach, reach, windward, downwind, windward, and finish. It is used at the Olympics and at most major regattas.

FUNBOARD RACE COURSE

Along with the more traditional racing, one cannot overlook the increasingly popular funboards and their addition to the boardsailing scene. However, these boards were designed for going fast off the wind and doing lots of reaching and jibing with minimal upwind sailing, so courses have been modified to allow funboard sailors to race competitively amongst themselves. The following diagram is an example of one such type of funboard race course.

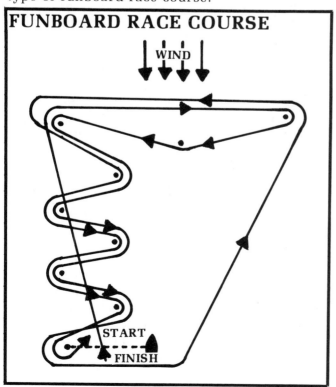

FUNBOARD RACE COURSE

FINDING OUT ABOUT REGATTAS

You've decided you want to race, but you don't know how to find out about local regattas. The best way is to go to a local sailboard dealer to find out about local regattas. He may have a calendar of events coming up or press releases and newsletters for future events. Additionally many of the boardsailing publications will have a list of upcoming major events, as well as some of the smaller popular events. If there is a local fleet in your area which has a mailing list for regattas, you may try to join the fleet and get on this list.

YACHT RACING RIGHT-OF-WAY RULES

Yacht racing right-of-way rules apply whenever you decide to enter the world of competitive yacht racing. Be it on sailboard or sailboats, and a brief knowledge of these rules is advisable. However, for the new racer, the following is a list of the more common right-of-way rules. This is not a complete list, nor are these legal interpretations of the official rules. They are merely guidelines to familiarize yourself with some words or phrases that you may hear shouted at you as you race around the buoys. Serious boardsailors should obtain and study a copy of the official rules;

YACHT RACING RIGHT-OF-WAY RULES

    1. Port - Starboard: When yachts are on opposite tacks (booms are on different sides) port tack (yacht with booms on the starboard side) keeps clear of starboard tack. Rule 36.

    2. Windward - Leeward: When yachts are on the same tack (booms on the same sides) the windward yacht keeps clear, or the yacht astern keeps clear. Rule 37.

    3. Changing Tack: When you are tacking or jibing, keep clear of the other yachts as you have no rights. Once you complete your tack or jibe and you now have right-of-way; give the other yachts room and time to keep clear. Rule 41.

    4. Luffing Before Starting: Before you start you may luff a yacht to windward, but you must do it slowly. Rule 40.

    5. Barging: At the start, don't "barge". That means don't try to squeeze between a yacht close to leeward of you and a starting line mark (which probably is a race committee boat). Rule 42.4.

6. Over Early: If you are over the line early at the start, keep clear of all yachts that started properly as you return to restart. Rule 44.

7. Buoy Room: When you are two boat lengths from a turning mark, an obstruction, or a finish line mark (which may be a race committee boat), give room to all yachts that have an inside overlap on you . Rule 42.

8. Luffing after the start: When another boat tries to pass you to windward, you may luff her until her skipper hails "mast abeam" (means her skipper is even with, or ahead of your mast). Then you must stop luffing and bear off to your proper course. Rule 38.

9. Touching A Mark: If you touch a mark, you may continue racing only after completely circling the mark.If you touch a starting line mark, you must wait until after you have started to circle it. While thus circling a mark, keep clear of other yachts. Rules 45 and 52.

10. Rule Infringement: If you infringe a rule while racing (you are racing from your preparatory signal until you clear the finish line), you are obligated to retire promptly. Sometimes the sailing instructions permit an alternative penalty, such as a 720° rule or a percentage scoring penalty clause. Rule 33 and appendix 3. Even when you have right-of-way it is your duty to avoid collisions. See Rule 32.

SCORING SYSTEMS

There are two types of scoring systems commonly used in competitions today to help determine the winner(s). The first is called the low point scoring system. Here the 1st place finisher receives 3/4 th's of a point, the second place finisher 2 points and all other finishers receive the same number of points as the place they finished in (3rd place gets 3 points, 4th place gets 4 points etc.). Each sailors results are added together and the sailor with the lowest cumulative point total is the winner.

The other common scoring system is called the Olympic scoring system. Here the 1st place finisher receives 0 points, 2nd place=3 points, 3rd place=5.7 points, 4th place=8 points, 5th place=10 points, 6th place=11.7 points and 7th place and thereafter receives the place that they finished in plus 6 points (therefore 7th place=13 points, 8th place=14 points etc.). Again the sailors results are added together and the sailor with the lowest cumulative point total is the winner.

Some regattas may have 5 or more races in a series. In many cases, the race committee may elect to allow a throwout race. Here the sailors worst result may be thrown out and not added into his final cumulative total. It is technically possible that when the throwout system is used, that you could be the overall winner before the throwout, but not be the winner after the throwout. It is up to the race committee to decide whether to have a throwout after 4, 5, 6 or 7 races or maybe not have one at all. Sometimes there may be a tie when all the results are added together between one or more sailors. The tie shall be broken in favor of the sailor with the most first places. If the tie still remains, then it will be in favor of the sailor with the most second places and so on. Sometimes, if this method still results in a tie, then the tying sailor with the best result in the last race wins the series.

FREESTYLE

For those who have mastered the basic boardsailing techniques, raced a few races and think they have learned all there is to learn on a stock sailboard prepare to explore the ever exciting world of Freestyle. While going from point A to point B you probably realized there are a number of ways to do this. You can go fast or slow on a reach, run or beat or by falling or not falling. But did you ever try doing these maneuvers while standing on the leeward side of the sail or on the windward side while inside the booms facing the sail or away from the sail or even on the windward side with your back to the sail and booms. Perhaps you tried it sitting or lying down. Maybe the hull was flipped up on either the windward or leeward rail with either the bow or the stern facing forward or better yet the hull was flipped upside down and you were standing on the bottom of the hull - Yes, all these ways of getting from point A to B are possible, and common, for a Freestylist. With a little practice, you too can open up and explore a new horizon in boardsailing and give yourself challenges to last a lifetime. Here are a few pointers which would help a beginner get started;

1. Watch others - Be able to see what you are going to try to accomplish before you try it.

2. Ask advice. If you see someone doing a trick you like, ask them to show you the basics and point out the risks.

3. Read books or articles on some of the more common basic maneuvers.

4. Start with the easy tricks first.

5. Check your equipment. Make sure your universal is securely attached to the hull and that your lines are securely fastened and not worn. When trying a railride, make sure the rails of your hull are not razor sharp and that you have a strong daggerboard that does not have a razor sharp leading or trailing edge.

6. Practice the tricks you want to learn under ideal conditions in order to master the basics as quickly as possible.

7. Wear a wetsuit if the water is cool as you may fall alot in the beginning. A wetsuit is also helpful in preventing bruised and scraped knees and legs when first trying a railride

8. Once you feel you've mastered all the tricks there are to learn, go try those same tricks in heavy winds and small waves and prepare yourself for a new challenge.

A forward railride

ENTERING A FREESTYLE COMPETITION

Once you feel you know enough tricks that could allow you to execute them over a 3 minute period, you are ready to enter a competition. In most competitions, sailors are given 3 minutes to perform a free exercise routine. They are judged by a panel of judges who score them based on the number of tricks they execute, the difficulty of the tricks and their execution and choreography of these tricks. Therefore, a person executing a group of difficult but unrelated and unconnected tricks might easily lose to a sailor who performs easier tricks that are all connected and interwined by a series of smooth flowing tacks and jibes. Watch your competitors while they are on the course. Listen to what the spectators cheer for and above all determine what made the winners win and learn from their performance. You do not have the luxury of choosing your conditions under which to compete - You go with what is at the time, so practice under all conditions. The more competitions you enter, the better you'll get because there is really no other way to simulate that tension and pressure of having to perform and remember a good routine. In time, and with a little practice you will be up there with the best of them.

FREESTYLE TRICKS

The following is a list of a few of the more popular and commonly executed freestyle tricks. This is just a small sample of the more than 150 freestyle tricks already identified in todays International Competitions.

1. **Head Dip** -Leaning over backward and dipping head in water while sailing

2. **Body Dip** - Dipping body in water while continuing sailing.

3. **Water Start** - Starting sailing from a dead stop with body immersed in water.

4. **Stern First**- Sailing stern first.

5. **Clew First** - Sailing with leech of sail forward.

6. **Inside Windward Booms** - Sailing with body between windward booms and sail.

7. **Inside Leeward Booms** - Sailing with body between leeward booms and sail.

8. **Back to Sail** - Holding booms by extending arms behind you with back to sail.

9. **Sitting (and variations)** - Sailing sitting down.

10. **Lying (and variations)** - Sailing lying down.

11. **Sail 360** - Turning sail through 360° with board staying in one direction.

12. **360°** - Turning hull through 360° on water.

13 **Forward Railride (and variations)** - Flipping hull - windward rail up, and continuing sailing on side.

14. **Forward Leeward Rail Ride** - Flipping hull - leeward rail up and continuing sailing on side.

15. **Reverse Railride (and variations)** - Flipping hull on side and sailing stern first.

16. **Pirouette** - A complete turn by sailor who releases booms, pirouettes, then grabs booms again.

17. **Duck Tack** - Tack by going under booms.

18. **Spin Tack** - A tack which includes a pirouette before filling sail on new tack.

19. **Foothold** - Sailing and steering with feet.

20. **Nose Dip** - Sailing with back to the sail and dipping nose into the water.

A forward double railride

TANDEM FREESTYLE

Combine two people with one sailboard, add a few ideas for some tricks and you have all the ingredients needed for tandem freestyle. It can be as basic as taking your boyfriend, girlfriend, dog or cat out for a ride to a dazzling display of spectacular tricks executed by seasoned veterans. It is another exciting dimension of boardsailing open to all those who have mastered the basics of going from point A to B and returning. For those who want to excel and compete in this field, tandem freestyle competitions are held at popular one design world championship events. A panel of judges watches each two person team perform a three minute routine. Points are awarded for the number of tricks performed, their difficulty and the execution and choreography of the free exercise.

When selecting a partner you should try to keep the combined body weight total to less than 300 pounds so you still have plenty of flotation. If you are going to attempt such tricks as shoulder stands, shoulder sits or railrides with one partner sitting on the others shoulders, then it is helpful if one member is stronger and larger than the other. If you plan to execute sail and body tricks then athletic skill and sailing expertise should be the primary considerations. Good communication is also important in discussing what you plan to try before you attempt the real event. Be prepared to get wet and fall a few times and just remember that it is all part of the game.

A good, buoyant, flat bottom Division I board is probably the best and easiest type of sailboard on which to practice. Make sure the universal is firmly positioned in the board and place some neoprene or rubber around any metal joints to protect the feet. If the air or water temperatures are less than 70° then be sure to wear wetsuits.

Tricks can be learned using either the enthusiastic, figure it out on the water approach or the discuss and plan it on the beach, try it on the water method. The latter has a much better success ratio although figuring it out on the water can also be lots of fun. The easiest way to learn tricks is as follows. Outline and discuss the maneuvers you plan to try so that both parties have a clear picture of the end result. Next, discuss the steps you will take to achieve this, including who will control the move and initiate the instructions. Now practice on dry land and see if any potential problems can be solved before you reach the water. Finally, go out on the water and try to pull it all together. Practice under good conditions. Find a large body of flat water without many waves or boat wakes and a steady light to moderate wind. When practicing, stay loose and don't be afraid to fall or get wet. Communicate with your partner and pretty soon you will have put together a graceful routine where each trick flows into the next creating a stylish production.

INTRODUCTORY TANDEM FREESTYLE TRICK LIST

1. Both on windward side of sail, one sailing normally, one standing inside the sailor's arms facing sail.
2. Both on windward side of the sail, one sailing normally, one inside the booms facing sailor and standing on sailor's knees.
3. One sailing normally, one on leeward side with back or front to the sail.
4. Both on windward side, one sailing normally with other sitting or standing on sailor's shoulders.
5. Double railride with both sailors on the rail with one facing the sail and the other with either back or front to the sail.

WAVE JUMPING AND SURFING

If you were to read any of the major boardsailing magazines, you might have the impression that 90% of all boardsailors lived in Hawaii, jumped and surfed waves. The reason is that magazines want to look attractive and exciting; wave jumpers and surfers contribute to some of the most beautiful, extraordinary and unusual photos one will find anywhere. In reality, this aspect of boardsailing accounts for less than 30% of the worldwide participants in the sport.

For the avid, dedicated boardsailor, nothing can compete with the thrill of sailing at top speeds into the face of an oncoming wave only to jump off its peak and soar 20' up in the air. You bring the board up over your body into an upside-down position before returning to the water and sailing off for the next wave. If surfing is your desire, then shooting down the face of a mast high wave and executing a bottom turn, cut back, or off the lip maneuver will certainly rank as one of the most breathtaking moments.

Wave jumping and wave surfing are practiced all over the world. From Hawaii to Florida or Europe to Australia, any type of wave is being challenged. Boardsailors are surfing huge ocean swells, cruising the ocean's shore breaks, jumping waves created by jutting points of land, flying across high wind chop and riding motorboat wakes. All are providing thrills and challenges to the dedicated enthusiast seeking to explore new dimensions.

Does this sound exciting to you? If so, your first step is to buy the right equipment. You need a board with footstraps that will fit your particular wind conditions. In lighter winds you will want a longer board and/or a bigger sail. Since most of these boards have no daggerboards, practice your jibes as well as sailing in a straight line. Remember that the board will turn in the direction you move your body weight. Pushing down on the leeward rail will force the board to head off.

When jumping waves, small choppy waves will be fine for learning and you can have lots of air if there is plenty of wind. To jump, speed off to the steepest part of the wave and sail over it before it starts to break. As the back end of the board leaves the water and wave and you become airborne, keep the sail sheeted in. Lean the sail slightly forward and pull the back end of the board upwind with your feet to counteract the nose of the boards tendency to head upwind. Practicing in small waves will make you feel alot more comfortable and let you become a little more radical before advancing to the bigger waves.

As with wave jumping, wave surfing should be first attempted in smaller waves. Begin by surfing down the faces and stay well out in front of the breaking wave and any whitewater that comes with it. Remember to keep your weight back to help prevent the nose of the board from pearling. As the wave flattens out, jibe and head back out to ride some more. As you begin to feel comfortable in the waves, try sailing in the critical section, just in front of the break and whitewater. In time, you will venture out into larger waves and will soon be carving deep bottom turns, executing cut backs and performing off the lip maneuvers.

In the proper conditions, wave jumping and wave surfing will provide the "go for it" boardsailor with all the thrills and excitement he could possibly desire.

Wave jumping

Wave surfing

SLALOM RACING

Slalom racing is a man against man competition where two sailors race around buoys on the same course in an effort to be the first over the finish line. There are no judges critiquing the event and the end result is an obvious winner. Courses can be set up near the beach and prove exciting for both the spectators and the racers alike. There are two types of slalom racing; long board and short board.

Long board slalom racing utilizes standard sailboards, as compared to funboards or short boards, with either stock or custom skegs and daggerboards to suit the days conditions. The course consists of 6 buoys set up in two rows of 3 buoys each on flat water. The buoys in each row are approximately 60-75' apart and the two rows are laid downwind and set parallel to each other about 75-100' apart. The sailors start on opposite sides of the course and after a one minute starting sequence, sail

around the course 3 times. Each leg is slightly different from the last one with the sailor finishing at the buoy he started from and the winner being the first to cross the line. This type of course tests your skills at sailing on all points of sail including fast tacking and jibing. The emphasis is of course on maintaining good steady speed through the course and at the turns. Practicing and competing on a long board slalom course will definately improve your long board sailing skills.

Short board slalom racing is for all those sailors who love the high wind, high speed thrills of funboard and short board sailing. Instead of testing the sailors upwind performance, each leg of the course is slightly off the wind with the buoys alternately placed inside and outside a line of breaking surf. A good course will consist of 6-8 legs ranging from 100-300 yards in length which

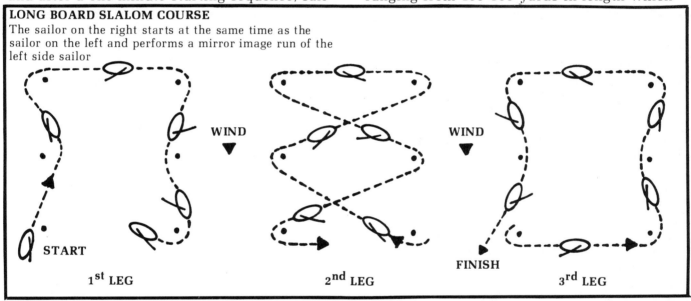

LONG BOARD SLALOM COURSE
The sailor on the right starts at the same time as the sailor on the left and performs a mirror image run of the left side sailor

WIND ▼   WIND ▼

START

1ˢᵗ LEG   2ⁿᵈ LEG   FINISH   3ʳᵈ LEG

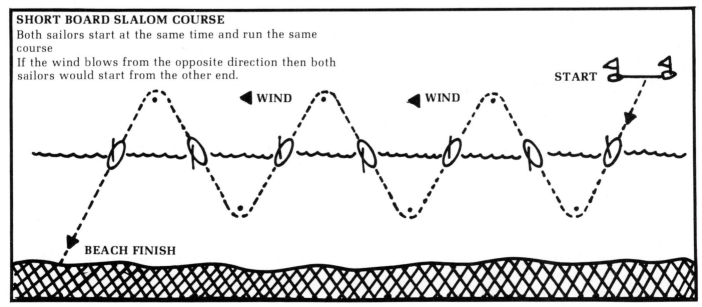

SHORT BOARD SLALOM COURSE
Both sailors start at the same time and run the same course
If the wind blows from the opposite direction then both sailors would start from the other end.

◀ WIND   ◀ WIND   START

BEACH FINISH

are set up to allow the sailor to sail on a beam to broad reach at all times. The sailor then tries to maintain maximum speed and control while maneuvering his short board around the course and through a series of fast, tight jibes at planing speeds. The layout of the course forces racers to jump the waves when going out and surf or outrun the waves when sailing in. When jumping, the emphasis should be on distance and not height. The starting line is usually set outside the surf and upwind of the first mark while the finish line is usually on the beach or between two marks after the last buoy. The best training is to go out and practice jibing on and in front of waves, both coming in and going out. If you don't have waves then zipping back and forth at full planing speeds and practicing fast, tight jibes while maintaining top speeds will improve your short board sailing skills.

LONG DISTANCE CRUISING

Long distance cruising, racing and ocean voyages have become quite popular in recent years. Today, boardsailors have sailed 100 miles in under 7 hours, crossed the Baltic Sea from Alaska to Russia and even sailed across the Atlantic from Africa to South America with a support vessel to carry food and supplies. No matter what the personal reasons are for attempting these feats, the personal satisfaction is truly rewarding and gratifying at the end of a successful voyage. However, these pinnacles of success are not achieved without much planning, practice and hard work.

When planning a long distance voyage, be sure to consider all the potential problems that could arise. Remeber you are dealing with an element over which you have no control, the weather, and it can increase or die down at any time. Be sure to ask yourself lots of questions. How long will you be gone? Will it include an overnight? Do you have water or food? Do you need a wetsuit? Do you have a PFD or other safety gear? Do you have the right sail for both heavy and light air? Do you have a compass if it is foggy? Does anyone know your itinerary or is someone waiting for you at your destination? What do you do if you have equipment failure? All these questions and more should be considered before you take off on a long distance voyage.

The next step is to prepare yourself physically. Building up both your strength and endurance are necessary to sail long distances. Ideally you want to sail daily for long periods of time. If this is impossible, you want to try to get the most out of the time you spend on the water. This means sailing without a harness and pushing yourself to the limits when you do sail. This sailing should also be supplemented with an overall physical fitness training program. In time, you will reach the level of fitness you desire.

Improved board control comes with increased strength. You will soon have the power to control and handle the board under any adverse sailing conditions. In time, the board will become an extension of your body.

Offshore there are no boardsailing shops to make repairs or to sell you spare parts so your equipment is particularly important. Choose products that are both comfortable, light and durable. These should include your harness, booms, mast and wetsuit. With practice and increased physical endurance, you should become a good long distance boardsailor.

TANDEM BOARDSAILING

Tandem boardsailing occurs when two sailors get together and sail on one board around 22' long which has two rigs, one placed behind the other, and share the wind, speed and steering. Although small in numbers, these boards are raced annually at both European and World Championship events. They go almost 30% faster than a standard sailboard in 10-15 knots of wind. They are used for racing, pleasure sailing and even for instructional purposes where the instructor has the luxury of demonstrating and then watching the student practice the techniques at close range.

Getting underway on a tandem board is similar to that of a stock sailboard. Both sailors begin together but the forward sailor must take care not to pull the sail in too far. The forward sail acts like a jib and should be raked aft with the foot close to the deck. It is kept slacker than the stern sail which should be pulled in tight and kept more upright. A space should be maintained between the two sails so the forward sail does not force wind into the leeward side of the aft sail. The stern sailor should be the lighter of the two so he may lean out to windward while the heavier person can hold the sail while standing upright and prevent the bow from lifting up.

Heading up is controlled by the aft sailor. The forward sailor sheets out while the aft one sheets in and rakes the mast back causing the board to head up. As the board heads up, the forward sailor may release the booms and as the bow passes through head to wind, he executes a tack. As the board starts to head off on the new tack, the aft sailor then executes his tack.

Heading off is controlled by the forward sailor who has the power to initiate the turning of the board off the wind. Once you are headed off, both sails should be kept at the same angle to the wind. When jibing, the aft sailor releases the booms and as the stern passes through head to wind, the forward sailor executes a jibe and the aft sailor does the same right after him. To head back up, the forward sailor keeps his sail sheeted out while the aft sailor heads up.

This type of boardsailing is fun whether you go out with a friend, student or business partner. However, tandem boardsailing is not the end of the line. A group of Europeans were recently photographed sailing a 63' sailboard which had 7 sailors and rigs. Either way, give it a try someday.

THE HARNESS

The harness is a safety aid as well as a tool for heavy air and long distance sailing. It allows you to maintain pressure on the rig while eliminating the constant strain on the arms, forearms and wrists. With a harness, the sailor may use the strong back, shoulder and leg muscles to counteract the forces that heavy air sailing imposes on the relatively weaker arms.

Most harnesses fit snugly over the shoulders and around the upper body from just above the waist and should provide good lower back support. A hook is attached to the front of the harness with webbing which pulls on both the lower and middle back for a good comfortable fit. Hooks come in a variety of shapes and sizes ranging from a small

single hook to the wider spreader bar designed to counteract the potential squeezing of the rib cage. Small hooks cause the pressure point to be centered over the breast bone whereas the wider spreader bar distributes the load over the sides of the rib cage. Two pronged V hooks are becoming popular on both small hooks and spreader bars as they automatically release the harness line if you rotate your body as in a fall. Hooks may be attached so that the opening faces either downward or upward. Deciding which way to face the hook is a combination of personal choice coupled with your skill level and the days activities; be it recreation, racing or wave riding and jumping.

The harness is hooked onto a set of lines which are attached, one on each side, to the booms. Each end of line should be tied off just inside of where your hands will be placed for the days sailing conditions leaving a loop of line hanging from the booms. The line should be just long enough to take the force of the rig off your arms. Lines that are too long will put excessive strain on the arms whereas lines that are too short will probably cause you to fall into the sail.

Hooking in with the hook down is achieved by pulling the rig towards you and then flipping the booms up so that the harness line swings up into the hook. If the hook is in the up position then pull the rig towards you, lower your body's center of gravity and let the harness line drop in on the hook. Once hooked in, simultaneously keep your hips in, lean your upper body back and extend your arms so that the strain of the rig is taken off your arms and put onto the harness line. If you start to feel overpowered, simultaneously pull the rig back towards you, sheet out and unhook. In time you may be able to repeat this procedure and regain control without unhooking.

There are many types of harnesses on the market. Some states require sailors to wear or carry PFD's (Personal Flotation Devices) so some harnesses have lots of flotation in them and serve the double purpose of a PFD and a harness. However, not all harnesses with lots of flotation are Coast Guard Approved PFD's, so check on this before purchasing. Cruising harnesses are large, well padded, comfortable and good for long distance races as well as heavy air racing and cruising. Surf harnesses are small and light without a backpack. They have very little padding or flotation and are easy to swim in. They are perfect for wave sailing, light recreational use and light air races that could turn into heavy air races before they finish. Recreational harnesses are the most common with moderate flotation, coverage and padding and they usually have a backpack. Backpacks can be used to carry most anything from keys and money to food, water, extra lines and even a wetsuit. One problem is that backpacks can drag in the water in heavy winds when you are hiked way out. They can also fill with water after a fall, making waterstarts harder and the harness heavier. However, a backpack made of mesh cloth or supplied with a drainhole should solve this problem.

When purchasing a harness, access your skill level and intended use and then look for a well designed and constructed harness to fit those purposes. The harness is an excellent energy saver and probably the best piece of equipment you can buy after a wetsuit as it will greatly increase the time you can spend out on the water.

REEFING SAILS

A valuable sail either for people who do a lot of offshore sailing and long voyages, or for beginners who only want to own one sail, is a reefing sail. Reefing as the name implies, means having one sail that can be enlarged or reduced in sail area without cutting it or taking it to a sail maker. Many of todays reefing sails are constructed fairly well and the reduced sail still has an efficient foil shape. The most common reefing methods incorporate one or two zippers.

METHOD 1:

A full sized pinhead sail may use one zipper to remove 10-15 square feet of sail cloth in the leech area and in effect come up with a high-wind sail. This extra piece of sail is either placed in one's harness or in a pocket that runs along the foot.

Hooked in

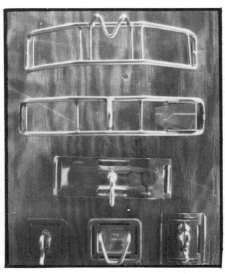

Variety of harness hooks

Hook down position

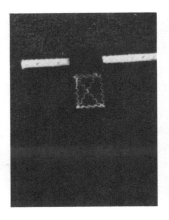 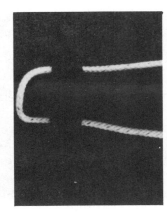  

One method of tying harness lines

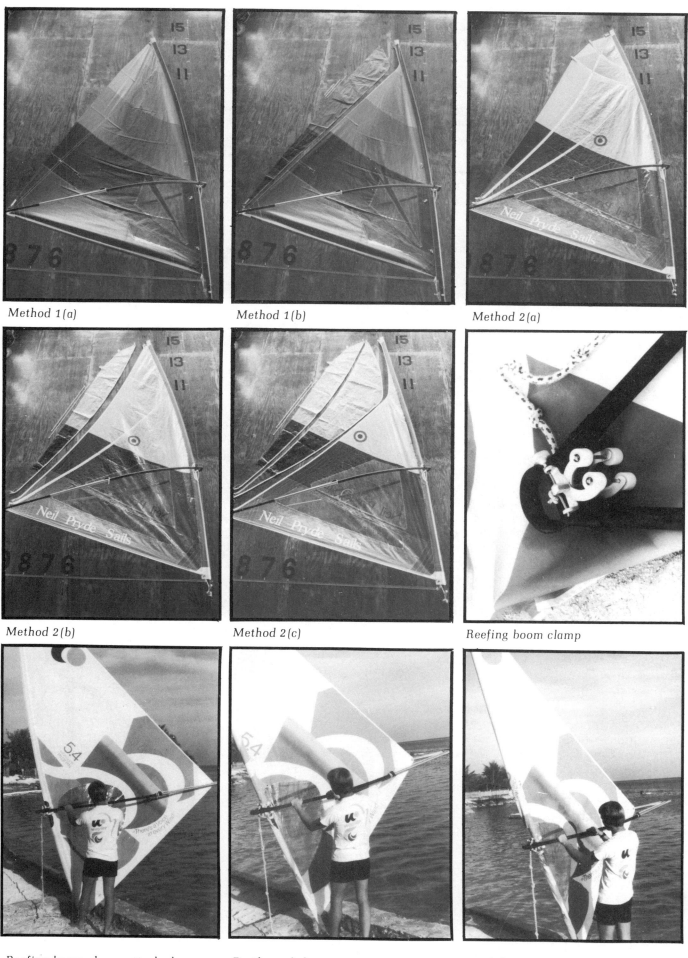

Method 1(a)

Method 1(b)

Method 2(a)

Method 2(b)

Method 2(c)

Reefing boom clamp

Reefing boom clamp attached

Partly reefed

Reefed even more

METHOD 2:

A fathead sail may use one zipper to take off the large roach area giving you a pinhead sail. The same fathead sail may have a second zipper in it which would further reduce this full sail to a high-wind sail as in Method 1.

While these methods involve zipping off outer sections of sail area, others may have the inner section of sail zip into itself. Still others incorporate lines to tie off sections of the sail, either upper or lower, that fold or roll up. The other major method of reefing sailboard sails does not use zippers. Here, reefing is achieved by rolling the sail on or around the mast to give the desired sail area. Be sure to remove any battens that would prevent a smooth roll up. Reefing may be carried out either onshore or offshore, even under severe wind conditions. Since rolling the sail around the mast will cover up the mast sleeve opening; inhaul lines and conventional boom-to-mast connections will not work. A variety of boom clamps are currently available which grip the mast and sail and prevent them from rotating which would cause the sail to unfurl. The boom height can still be adjusted to suit your preference and as the outhaul is tightened the clamp becomes tighter. A good reefing sail or reefing system can be a great help to a beginner because even as the wind speed increases you can still reef the sail to a manageable size. This will increase the safety factor of getting back to shore if you get caught offshore and the wind increases beyond your current capabilities. It can also serve as a good low-cost alternative to owning a complete quiver of sails in varying sizes.

HIGH PERFORMANCE SAILS

All the new developments, technology and changes that have taken place in the last few years have also revolutionized the way high-performance sails are shaped and constructed. It was mentioned earlier about sails that come with standard boards; now we will briefly discuss some of the high performance sails available. Nearly all the new designs incorporate a high-aspect cut on either a pinhead or a fathead sail. As we mentioned earlier, pinhead sails are ones where the head comes to a point. Fatheads or powerheads as they are sometimes referred to, have an extremely high roach area near the head that is supported by one or two large compression battens which run the width of the sail from the leech to the mast. Fathead sails were developed by and most commonly used by Hawaiian sailors for moderate winds and large waves. This large roach section high off the water allows the sailor to obtain as much power as possible when sailing through large waves and catch air that he would normally lose by being in the trough of the wave. This also allows him to carry more sail area for a given length of boom than a pinhead sail could provide.

Standard sails use booms almost 9 feet in length. Many of the Funboard hulls used today are this same length. Proportionately, it is easier to sail with booms between 6' and 7'6" on these shorter boards. The benefits of the fathead sail are that the sailor, using a fathead sail, short booms and possibly a mast extension can end up with the same size sail area that in a pinhead would require the standard 8'6" - 9' booms. Most of these sails carry a deep luff curve to help develop a built-in draft, and their full shapes and generally high clews make these sails ideal for reaching and offwind work. These sails are not legal for one-design or Open Class Racing, but if you sail in large waves or rough costal waters you may desire one. Similarly, if you live in an area that generally has very light winds then a large fathead sail on a set of standard length booms should give you the extra sail area to generate that go-fast power and help achieve planing speeds as quickly as possible.

Most of these sails incorporate a design called high-aspect ratio or cut. One of its advantages is that the clews are often cut high to keep the booms clear of the water when sailing in strong winds and large waves. The higher clew also results in the sail having a slightly higher center of effort than a low-aspect ratio sail of the same area. This gives the sailor more power which can help increase his stability and balance. When the sailor trims the sail by pulling in his back arm the center of effort travels forward from the leech (which fills first) to the position it would normally be in when fully trimmed. This higher center of effort also produces a shorter distance from the leech to the center of effort's normal position than on a conventional sail. The resulting advantage is easier sheeting in of the sail as well as easier and quicker sheeting out and depowering in heavy winds. Most of these sails will usually have what is called a leech line which gives you complete support and control of the leech stretch and provides the opportunity to adjust the load on the leech caused by different wind strengths. This adjustment will remove any flapping, fluttering or curl that appears on the leech. It is true that high performance sails are technologically advanced, but they are generally used with boards that are just as advanced. Don't get confused by all the choices. As a beginner, the basic sails that come with standard boards are really quite sufficient for you to get out there and go for it.

FABRIC:

Most sails are constructed out of dacron or some sort of mylar or mylar composite. Dacron is a woven fabric made up of individual threads which are intertwined to form a cloth grid. This woven property gives it excellent tear resistance and longevity and allows it to be folded, stuffed or crumpled in a bag without becoming seriously wrinkled. One of the major disadvantages of dacron is its elasticity. When load is applied in any direction other than along the threadlines, it tends to stretch out and the sail in time may become "blown out".

Mylar is a plastic film. It is rolled at high heat and pressure into various thicknesses. For its weight it is extremely strong and stretch-resistant, but does have a tendency to wear and tear easily. In order to get around this problem, manufacturers attach a paste on substrate or backing of light nylon or dacron to give the cloth better wear and tear strength. The end result is a mylar or mylar composite sailcloth which appears dull like regular sailcloth on one side and shiny on the other. It should not be crumpled up or folded in a lot of places as it may become seriously wrinkled, and although it may have a crinkly sound to it when it luffs, its weight hardly increases when wet as opposed to dacron. Mylar is quite commonly used on fathead and high-performance sails.

PANEL LAYOUT:

Until a few years ago all sails were laid out using the cross-cut or horizontal cut method of construction. Panels of sailcloth usually around 36" wide were sewn perpendicular to the leech and ran into the luff at roughly a 45° angle. The average full-sized or regatta sail normally has 5 panels. Today almost 70% of all board sails are still cut this way. Since mylar was developed, many sailmakers are now using a vertical panel layout instead of the horizontal one. Many surf sails are now vertical cut as they take the load of a breaking wave better than a horizontal cut. It can take two forms: the first is a vertical cut sail where the panels are laid parallel to the leech and run into the luff at an angle, and the second is the tri-panel vertical cut where the panels are laid out parallel to the leech and the luff. Many high-aspect sails like fatheads and full-luff marginals use vertical construction because of the stronger loads along the leech rather than in the sails' mid-sections. Many mylar fatheads are constructed like this because it can support the huge roach areas while producing a low-stretch, long-life sail. So how do you tell if you have or are getting a good sail? When purchasing a sail, check the stitching on the seams, corner patches and windows. It should be smooth and even with no pulled spots. The corner patches (head, tack and clew) should have plenty of patching and nylon webbing wherever chafing can occur. The tack and clew grommets should be sewn or pressed in and look like they'll last the life of the sail. The windows should be sewn flat and accurate. Softer sailcloth tends to break down sooner than stiffer cloth.

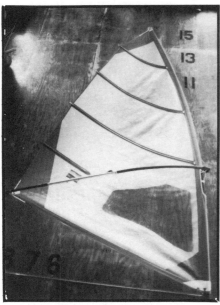

Freedom Sails Pan Am sail (80 sq. ft.) (numbers represent feet)

Freedom Sails tripanel wedge (62 sq. ft.) (numbers represent feet)

Freedom Sails leech cut (45 sq. ft.) (numbers represent feet)

A sail loft

FUTURE:

What does the future hold for sail designs? Basically, anything that the experts can dream up and the sailmakers can produce. The state of the art changes daily, both in types and combinations of sailcloth used as well as in the design and panel layout. New fabrics will supplement the current dacron and mylar.

You will find sailcloths given such names as Nijlam polyester scrim laminate, polyester mylar laminate, micron mylar, duo-film, Yarn temper and Lufflex. The panel layouts and construction techniques will include those we described earlier as well as new designs which may mix and match sailcloth panels like dacron and mylar in order to capitalize on the advantages of each. You may see horizontal head and foot panels connected by vertical corner panels, or maybe bi-radial construction using vertical panels above the booms and horizontal panels below. Some will use full-length battens extending from leech to luff while others may incorporate compression battens or others, none at all. Sails will soon be available in every color under the sun and in any combination imaginable.

A sail loft

SHORT BOARDS vs. FUNBOARDS

There is a difference between short boards and funboards. Short boards are basically surfboards with footstraps, mast tracks, and no daggerboards. They do not point upwind very well and are maneuvered upwind by leaning the windward rail into the water. Funboards incorporate the advantages of the short board with those of the long board by having a longer water line and using a centerboard to allow upwind pointing and speed. It will steer like a short board off the wind. The foot movements while steering short and funboards are different from a long board. Basically pushing down on the windward rail causes the hull to go to windward and pushing down on the leeward rail causes the hull to go to leeward on short and funboards. On long boards, pushing down on the windward rail causes the hull to go to leeward and pushing down on the leeward rail causes the hull to go to windward.

Footstraps are common on short boards and funboards and are a necessary and useful accessory. Many recreational production boards are also coming equipped with footstraps that can be removed easily since footstraps are presently illegal for Division I and II racing. Footstraps are most effective at planing speeds or in rough water. As a matter of fact in light winds you rarely need them and you will probably find yourself standing forward of the straps and not using them. Some boards may only have 3 footstraps while Pan Am type boards may have as many as 13 footstraps. This quantity of footstraps makes it easy to accommodate the various points of sail and different windspeeds that versatile boards are expected to perform in.

The bottoms of these boards appear generally flat and are designed for planing speeds, but if you look closely you will see such things as vees, channels, double concaves, tri-planes, and down wingers on the underside which turn these hulls into high performance machines. Some will use a single fin while others will use a thruster fin arrangement. The boards shapes will be given such names as pintails, swallowtails, acorn, teardrop, Pan Am (usually around 12'6" to 13'6") and tri-planes, or be called by their length in feet and inches such as 76 (seven, six), 811 (eight, eleven) or 911 (nine, eleven).

Adjustable or sliding mast tracks have recently become quite popular and what was once standard equipment only on Pan Am, short and funboards is now found on many recreational sailboards. Other boards may have 2 or more mast step inserts or a short track with a screwed in universal and these require you to drop the sail to make the necessary changes or adjustments. An adjustable or sliding mast track is basically a foot operated rachet system which allows a pivot point to be moved to 3 or more positions along the plane of the track much like a floating backstay on a larger sailboat. These have the advantages of a quick release and because they are foot operated they can be changed while sailing and will travel to the next point and relock. Most have the capablities of 3 or more positions. The proper positioning is determined by what point of sail you are on and the wind speed. The basic rule of thumb when sailing upwind is to put the mast forward and the daggerboard down to increase the wetted surface area and waterline. When heading off the wind, put the mast back and the daggerboard up to decrease the wetted surface area and maximize the planing potential. Beginners may find the mast forward postion the easiest to handle. It helps prevent the board from rounding up into the wind.

Basically, one could write an entire book just on the parts and varieties of short boards and funboards available, but this is a beginners book and to go into extensive detail on this subject may serve only to confuse you and discourage you from attempting the initial task of learning how to boardsail.

In short, there are many opinions as to which is the best board shape but in reality the main consideration is to analyze your performance requirements and find a board designed for those conditions.

WATER STARTS

As you advance into the area of high performance high wind sailing you will most likely be trying short boards and funboards. These boards will be classified as floaters, semi-floaters and sinkers. Floaters will totally support your body weight while keeping your feet dry and will allow you to uphaul your rig without much trouble. Sinkers on the other hand act somewhat like waterskis in the sense that when you aren't moving, the board sinks and will not support your body and rig weight. However, as the board starts to pick up speed, it rises to the surface and will support even a heavy person. This explains why short boards are not used in winds under 15-18 mph. They need the stronger winds so they can plane successfully. Pulling the rig out of the water by means of the uphaul and starting sailing using normal techniques are very difficult if not next to impossible on short boards.

This is when it becomes imperative to learn how to do a water start. Also as one ventures out in to the surf and big waves, water starts are the only quick way to recover from a fall unless you want to risk getting crushed by the next wave. Water starts can be executed by using any sized sail and booms provided there is enough wind to lift whatever sail size you are using. However, on short boards it will be easier to use and water start sails that use shorter booms (from 4' - 7'6"). The following technique for executing a water start works very well and with a little practice can be performed almost second nature.

A short board   *A thruster fin arrangement*

1. Once you fall or drop the sail first analyze your present situation. If you are on flat waters then go on to step 2. If you are in large waves, look and figure how long it will take before the next wave reaches you. If that is quicker than you can do a water start, then your first concern is to assure that the wave won't break your mast. The best security is to immediately grab your mast tip and swim with it into the face of the oncoming wave. Basically there should be a straight line from the wave, to you, down the mast and to the board. The purpose being that if you are down wave of the board, the wave could lift and drop the sailboard on top of you causing potential injury. Another danger if you don't get the board turned around is that the wave will lift up the hull due to its positive buoyancy and force the rig to be pushed down towards the seabed and possibly break a mast. Once the waves have passed you are ready to begin the water start.

2. Swim, holding the mast tip until you maneuver the mast so that it is resting perpendicular to the wind and the aft end of the booms (clew of the sail) are pointing downwind. The board should also be maneuvered into position so that the bow is pointing upwind. The exact point of sail is not important as long as it rests between a beam reach and upwind, pointing away from the rig.

3. While treading water, start at the mast tip and lift it out of the water allowing the wind to get underneath it.

4. While maintaining your grip on the mast and keeping the mast tip out of the water continue to work your way down along the mast towards the booms. Face the booms and board and as you move closer to the booms, the mast tip should be getting higher off the water and the wind should start to blow in under the sail and actually help lift it out of the water.

5. When you reach the booms, grip the mast with the windward hand about 1 to 2 feet above the booms and grip the booms about 3 feet back from the mast with the other hand. Don't put pressure on the boom hand at this point but be sure to keep the mast tip high out of the water with the windward hand.

6. With all the strength you can get treading water, lift the mast as high out of the water as you can. At this point, the forces of the wind should lift the aft (clew) end of the rig enough so that the aft end of the booms are actually lifted out of the water. The hand on the booms should not sheet in until the clew has broken the waters surface. Up until this point, the aft end of the booms being in the water has helped make it easy to keep the

mast up high. Once the booms clear the water, wind will start to pass under the sail and the mast will start to get heavy again and want to fall.

7. Once the aft end of the booms clear the waters surface, start to initiate pressure and sheet in with the back hand. Maintain pressure and keep the aft boom end a few inches off the water. This will keep wind in the sail and make it easier to push up.

8. Up until now you have been treading water and not worrying about the hull as it floats freely. Now you are ready to climb aboard. While maintaining the sail position in step 7 reach up with your back foot and feel for the hull. Once you find it, lift the back foot up onto the board and place it in a back footstrap. Move the back foot in or out until you feel the board is pointing on a beat.

9. The next step is to let the sail lift you out of the water and onto the board. While maintaining the position in step 8, wait for a strong gust of wind. Once you feel it, give a final push and lift up on the mast with the windward hand, sheet in with the back hand and tilt the whole rig slightly forward. As the rig starts to lift you out of the water, pull the back foot slightly towards you causing the board to head off and take the front foot and place it on the board close to the mast. Because it takes a few seconds to initiate planing, the front foot being forward will increase the wetted surface area initiating planing sooner. Too much weight aft will cause the stern to sink making it take longer to pick up speed.

10. Once the board starts to pick up speed and begins to plane, place the front foot in a front foot strap. Basically the stronger the winds, and the faster you go and the further aft you should place your feet. In lighter winds you may want to use the more forward footstraps.

11. On larger boards a majority of the steering is achieved by moving the rig fore and aft. While this principle works on short boards as well, additional steering is readily achieved by placing pressure on the windward or leeward rails. Pressure on the windward rail will help steer the board upwind. Pressure on the leeward rail will cause the board to head off.

12. Water starts may at first appear scary or difficult to execute. Don't be alarmed. After a little practice it will be easy. A good exercise is to attempt a water start anytime you fall or drop a sail in winds in excess of 15 mph. In time you may find yourself not even putting an uphaul on your booms when you rig up. When this happens you know you've mastered the water start.

CHAPTER XI

BOARD CONSTRUCTION

Most production hulls today are generally made out of polyethylene, ABS, fiberglass, epoxy, ASA or in the case of prototypes or Funboards, they might be made out of one or more of the high-tech materials on the market. Most hulls are built by forming the skin first and then injecting expanding foam. Polyethylene is a plastic synthetic (the same as your frisbee) which is resilient yet very puncture-proof and hard to damage. It may be straight polyethylene which is easily repaired by heating back in place, or it may be cross-linked polyethylene. The latter is more commonly used due to its interlocking molecular structure but is more difficult to repair, requiring more heat. It may be roto-molded or blow-molded. Each begins by heating the plastic to a liquid form. In roto-molding, a closed mold is rotated in a oven in all directions, spreading the melted material evenly over the mold. In blow-molding, air pressure forces the extruded polyethylene against the sides of the closed mold. It is here that straight polyethylene can get the molecules arranged linearly which can make it as strong as crossed-linked polyethylene. Each produces a hollow one piece skin which, after a short curing period, is then filled by injecting expanding urethane foam. Some polyethylene boards have aluminum stringers running down the inside length of the hull which provides additional strength.

ABS is a very hard plastic incorporating a rubber synthetic in the plastic. It is vacuum-formed in a two-part mold after which the two parts are welded together using heat and glue and later injected with expanding foam. ABS is slightly susceptible to ultraviolet sun rays, but is very easy to repair and can be manufactured to cosmetic perfection in most cases. Most fiberglass hulls are also made in two pieces and bonded together with fiberglass putty before injecting the foam. Fiberglass may come in polyester or epoxy,

with epoxy being the stronger. Epoxy fiberglass is an excellent material when making some of the "high-tech" hollow, Division II round-bottom boards with water-tight compartments and lighter weights, and is also currently being used in many of today's "production" Funboards.

Many epoxy boards utilize a styrofoam or styrene core. They start with a preformed core, lay the fiberglass (or other exotic material) over it and then saturate with epoxy resin. They can be made by hand or in a machine which heats, presses and cures the hull, which can allow for a stronger and thinner shell than its comparable polyester fiberglass partner. The epoxy or styrene process gives greater adhesion, strength and flexibility and the finished product will be 30% to 40% lighter than a fiberglass and urethane hull. Although most methods make the skin first and then inject the foam, some manufacturers preform a foam blank in a mold and form a skin around it.

ASA is a new plastic synthetic which, like ABS, must add a resiliency ingredient to make it manageable for the construction of sailboards. ASA adds acrylic to produce a plastic that is stiffer than ABS and resists ultraviolet rays. ASA is molded over a pre-shaped foam blank and is welded in the manufacturing process. It is easily repaired and has excellent longevity.

Performance boards and homemade Funboards are generally built by shaping blanks out of polyurethane foam, painting with an air brush, and then laminating with polyester resin and fiberglass cloth. If price is no object, it is possible to build extremely light high-speed boards which are very stiff using the latest technology and materials. One example might consist of a styrofoam or styrene core covered with Klegecell (a high-density foam) and then laminated with epoxy coated layers of uni-directional S-glass, E-glass, Kevlar or Carbon fiber.

SAILBOARD HULL REPAIRS

It is possible to dent, ding or even puncture the hull of a sailboard. If this happens, repair it as quickly as possible. Although 98% of the foams and cores found inside sailboard hulls are closed-celled and don't permit water absorption, water entering through the hull may spread between the foam and shell which may increase its weight or cause delamination of the hull.

Polyethylene:

Regular polyethylene can be repaired by simply heating and melting the two surfaces back together. If a hole exists, chips or small pieces of polyethylene may be placed in the hole and the whole group heated and melted together. It is the softest and most flexible material and the hardest to damage and usually has the best nonskid.

Cross Linked Polyethylene:

Requires much more heat to melt the plastic because of the molecular process which took place which results in the polyethylene becoming cross linked. There are some hot air tools on the market which permit you to weld polyethylene which basically heats both the area to be repaired and a welding rod simultaneously and allows you to lay a bead of plastic along the split or in the hole. Hot melt glue guns have been used extensively in the past and are fast and easy for filling holes and preventing water absorption but the bond is not a good as with welding and may have to be repeated in a couple of months to assure that it stays watertight. Epoxy resins have also been used in cases where the surface has been sanded or roughed up and where a hole in the hull would give the epoxy that little bite extra to bit onto and form a solid bond before it is finally sanded smooth. It is one of the more difficult materials to repair effectively but is also one of the most difficult materials to damage.

ASA and ABS:

Both materials are easy to repair. Quick repairs of small holes, cracks or dings can be carried out by taking small chips or pieces of the original material (ASA or ABS) and dropping them in the hole or crack. Then place a couple of drops of acetone on these pieces, wait a few seconds and repeat this procedure a few times until the pieces start to melt and get gummy. A cloth can then be used to press the pieces in place and once they dry, it can be sanded smooth. This same process also works well on polyester/fiberglass. Care should be taken not to use the acetone in sunlight but rather in a cool and damp place where it won't burn up and evaporate as fast.

A product that also works well for fixing and filling larger holes or areas on epoxy, ASA, ABS, or polyester boards is called Marine Tex. It is a salt resistant marine epoxy which comes in white or gray and although it works best when used on epoxy boards, it makes very good repairs on the other types. It can be sanded smooth and painted when dry. With the proper hot air tools, ABS can also be welded and is easier to weld than polyethylene.

Polyester/Fiberglass:

Repair techniques that can be used on boards made from polyester fiberglass are numerous and most are very easy. As a matter of fact it is probably one of the easiest materials to repair but due to its properties and characteristics it is also the one material that is most likely to need repairing. Any of the methods used for repairing ASA or ABS can be used on polyester. In addition to these, polyester resins and cloths are readily available. It is best to get polyester sanding resin since other types stay gummy even after they have set up and cured. Most of the resins are in a two part form consisting of the resin plus a hardener (catalyst which is added to a desired amount of resin). Once they're combined you should use the product immediately while it is in a workable state. Be sure to sand down and then clean the areas to be repaired with acetone before you apply the resin. In time (could be seconds, or minutes) a chemical reaction takes place, the product heats up and starts to harden or cure. Once cured, it can be sanded smooth and painted. In small holes, the resin may be used by itself. Larger holes or cracks may warrant using some fiberglass mat or woven cloth, which is placed in, around or over the area to be repaired and then saturated with the resin. This gives some structure to the resin and helps create a stronger repair. It can then be sanded smooth once it sets up and hardens.

Epoxy:

Boards can be repaired using any of the methods used for fixing ASA, ABS or polyester fiberglass with the exception being that epoxy resins should always be used on epoxy boards and not polyester resins since epoxy to epoxy bonds are superior to the other types and epoxy resins are stronger than polyester resins. If you are filling cracks or holes with epoxy you should look for a slow setting epoxy since the others generate a lot of heat and potentially boil up and out of the crack or hole and make a mess. Whenever you use resins, always read the labels and follow the instructions for intended use since many epoxy resins require a stricter temperature and mix control than polyester resins.

Urethane Repairs:

Most ASA, ABS, Polyester and Polyethylene boards are filled with some type of urethane foam (some may be denser, lighter or even stronger than others). Whereas epoxy boards usually contain a styrene core. Sometimes, the deck of the sailboard may become delaminated or mushy in the high traffic areas around the universal or in the common foot position areas. If you are not worried about the cosmetic beauty of your hull, these areas can be repaired by refoaming the delaminated area. Most marine hardware stores sell a 2 part urethane foam (commonly used in refridgeration units on ships). The 2 parts are mixed together and the mixture soon begins to foam up and expand (usually up to 5 times the original mixed volume) and then hardens as it sets. It can also be purchased premixed in a spray can that you just aim and squeeze although it is a little more expensive in this form.

Types of urethane foam

The first step is to drill two 3/8″ holes into the soft or mushy area and put them as far apart as possible. Next take a coat hanger and break up the bad foam inside and make sure there is a passage from one hole to the other. Now mix the foam and pour it in the lower of the two holes. Once the foam reaches the other hole stop and put some weights or planks over the mushy area being sure to leave the holes uncovered. The foam will expand and the excess hopefully will come out of both holes. Without the holes it would expand the hull from the inside, out, giving you a convex board instead of a concave one. The weights should help the board maintain its original shape. When it hardens the excess foam can be cut off and sanded and it is recommended that you seal the holes with a plug of epoxy resin to keep the water out. Some experts say that you should use epoxy resin around a wobbly mast stop or under a footstrap since it is stronger and has better compression strength than urethane which already failed once anyway. The method of repair is the same but the epoxy won't expand like the urethane foam. However, if large areas are to be filled, the epoxy will add more

weight to the board than the urethane would have. Urethane foam can also be used or sprayed inside booms both for flotation and as a sealant.

MAST REPAIRS

If a mast is going to break, it will usually do so in one of three distinct areas. These are at the base, the boom connection or near the upper tip. These areas may be strengthened by reinforcing them with epoxy resin and fiberglass cloth. However, if this is your racing mast check the class rules before doing so as reinforced masts may be illegal.

Boom connection and upper tip breaks can be repaired using an internal splint, epoxy resin, fiberglass cloth (tape) and some coarse (80 grit) sandpaper. The best internal splint is a 2 foot piece of mast with an outside diameter which is the same as the inside diameter where the break occured. This splint may be obtained from your local sailboard shop and will be cut from another broken mast. Sand smooth and clean the outside of the splint and the inside and outside of the mast about one foot on each side of the break. Mix the resin and coat the splint section before reinserting it. Push the two halves of the mast together. Saturate the cloth with resin and neatly wrap it around the mast for about one foot on each side of the break. Once dry, sand down the rough spots. Wait at least 24 hours before water testing and maybe land test it first to make sure its hard.

Mast bases may crack when sailing. You can jury rig your way home using an extra line that you may be carrying or the harness line opposite the one you need to sail to shore. Untie the downhaul. Tie a clove hitch with a stop knot in one end about a foot from the base of the mast. Make another hitch and tie it off with a stop knot. Slide the knot down the mast to within an inch of the mast base. The knot will tighten as the mast gets wider. If you can't pull it within one inch of the base then start again with a looser knot or tie it lower down the mast. Once tight and in the proper position, add another hitch and tie it off with a stop knot. Retie the downhaul, but do not overtighten. Return to shore. If possible, waterstart as it is easier on the mast than uphauling it.

Once you reach shore, repair the mast properly. Sand smooth and clean the base. Drill a small hole at the ends of any cracks before you repair them to prevent the crack from lengthening. Saturate the fiberglass cloth with epoxy resin and wrap it neatly around the cracked base. Let dry at least 24 hours and sand smooth before using it again.

OLYMPICS

In 1984, boardsailing was a scheduled event at the Summer Olympic Games in Los Angeles, California. The competition is held on one-design sailboards which are raced around an Olympic triangle course. Each country sends one individual to represent it in the Games. Each race is scored using the Olympic scoring system with the first place finisher receiving the lowest number of points and the sailor with the lowest cumulative total receiving the gold medal.

PROFESSIONAL BOARDSAILING

Professional boardsailing is fast becoming a viable lifestyle for the top boardsailors to pursue. Money and trophies are regularly being awarded at wave jumping competitions, World Cup races, speed crossings, Open Class races and a variety of other events. Prize money entices top sailors to attend the events, thereby promoting increased coverage by the media. In fact, many of the top boardsailors have been able to make a career out of the sport through the help of sponsors, business ventures and prize winnings.

Trophies

OTHER OPPORTUNITIES

Every dedicated boardsailor knows that the more you boardsail, the more you want to stay with the lifestyle. Around every major sport is an industry which offers many rewards and opportunities to its devotees both on the personal and professional levels. These areas can provide personal satisfaction and/or financial benefits for more than just the World Champion sailors. Top boardsailors may be awarded trophies and/or prize money at competitions when they are victorious over their competitors. They may also receive sponsorship in the form of products or services from companies that want to be

associated with them. Some sailors may choose to endorse particular products in return for a monetary consideration.

For the boardsailing enthusiast who may never become, or want to become, a World Champion, the industry offers many other commercial opportunities. Teaching or personal coaching either with a shop or on your own may be a rewarding way to spend time on the water. If you like building things you may find working for a board manufacturer or importer or for a custom sailboard builder constructive. If you have technical expertise, R & D work or new product testing could build new horizons. If you are handy with a sewing machine, working in a sail loft could appeal to you. A good salesman may find that marketing, selling or becoming a manufacturers representative might fulfill his work quota. You may even have that special look and enough boardsailing skills to be hired as a model for a commercial that uses boardsailing as a backdrop. Maybe someday, the right combination of distance, vacation time and finances may allow you to travel and boardsail in other parts of the world whether it is a journey to a competitive event or a vacation to a paradise in the sun.

CONCLUSIONS

How do you sum up an experience as fun, exciting, and addicting as boardsailing? My only suggestion is that you put down this book, pick up your board, and head for the water! As indicated in the previous chapter, boardsailing offers an unlimited potential for advancement, and the search for excellence need not end with the discovery of the perfect wave, or the thrill of a well executed maneuver. In fact, the sport of boardsailing offers a wide range of rewards and opportunities for the dedicated enthusiast to pursue, all of which can lead to a high level of personal satisfaction. In the final analysis, however, it depends on you. Are you challenged by the competition at the local level or do you have higher aspirations- which as of 1984 can lead you right up into the Olympics? Or perhaps you would prefer to be sailing off into the sunset- just you, the wind, and the water? Whatever your choice, boardsailing is an experience that will provide lingering memories of time well spent. I have been involved in the sport since the early days and I can not overemphasize its universal appeal. Welcome to a wonderful new horizon!

CHAPTER XII

GLOSSARY

ABAFT: 45° off the daggerboard; towards the rear of the board.

ABEAM: at right angles to the centerline of the board.

ACROSS THE WIND: perpendicular to the direction of the wind.

AFT: towards or near the stern or back of the board.

AIMING: art of positioning the board for an intended course.

ALL AROUND SAIL: a sail for recreational sailing generally between 50 sq. ft. (4.7 sq.m.) and 60 sq.ft. (5.5 sq.m.).

ANCHOR EFFECT: the ability of the rig to keep the sailboard from moving when the sail is in the water.

AREA: measured in square feet (sq.ft.) or square meters (sq.m.). There is more than one way of measuring area. Square feet divided by 10.76 gives you square meters.

ASYMMETRICAL BOARD: a description given to a board whose stern section is not symetrical. For example one side of the stern (your turning side) may have a pintail while the other side (your cut back side) may have a shorter rail line.

ATTITUDE: is the boards position relative to its horizontal, vertical and longitudinal axes.

BACK: when the wind shifts to come more from the right.

BACK: towards the back of the board.

BACK FOOT: the foot closest to the back of the board.

BACK HAND: the hand closest to the back of the board; the sheet hand; the hand that pulls in to fill the sail with wind and lets out to spill the wind from the sail.

BACKING THE SAIL: holding the sail pressed back against the wind in the direction in which the board is moving.

BATTENS: used to keep the leech/roach extended and to hold the leech area of the sail flat. Battens may range anywhere from a short one to full length ones extending from the luff to the leech.

BEAM REACH: sailing with the wind abeam at approximately 90° to the course and centerline.

BEAR OFF: (head off or bear away) to alter course away from the wind more downwind (opp. - head up).

BEAT: (v) sailing on a tack upwind; (n) an upwind or windward leg of a course.

BEATING: sailing a zig-zag course to windward close hauled on alternate tacks. Also called beating to windward or beating to weather.

BLANKET: to sail upwind of another sailcraft so that its sail lies in the wind shadow of your craft.

BOARDSAILING: the generic name for the sport we are participating in. Also called sailboarding. Commonly called windsurfing which is incorrect and should be only used when one is sailing a sailboard manufactured by Windsurfing International.

BOARDSAILOR: the generic term for the person that sails a sailboard; sometimes called sailboarder.

BOOMS: the wishbone assembly that attaches to the mast and clew of the sail. The sailor holds on to the wishbone to support and control the sail.

BOOM LENGTH: different lengths are suited to different sails and purposes. Generally open class, one design and funboard racing sailboards use the longest booms (7'6" to 9' or 230 cm to 270 cm). Funboard cruising and semi-sinkers utilize medium length booms (6' to 7'6" or 180cm to 230cm) and sinker boards use the shortest booms (5' to 6'6" or 150cm to 200cm). Feet multiplied by 30 gives you centimeters.

BOOM OPENING: the opening in the mast sleeve where the booms are attached.

BOW: the front end of the board.

BROAD REACH: sailing with the wind abaft of the beam at an angle of between 110 and 170° to the centerline.

CENTERBOARD: a wing like foil that increases the sailboards lateral resistance to sideways slippage through the water. It is inserted into and through an opening in the board which lies along the centerline. It can pivot around an axle, is multi-positional and can recess totally up into the hull.

CENTERLINE: an imaginary line running down the center of the hull from the bow to the stern dividing it into two equal halves. Used as a guideline to help direct students feet into proper position.

CENTER OF EFFORT: (CE) the total aerodynamic force that results from the varying pressures to windward and leeward of the sail is said to act through the center of effort of the sail.

CENTER OF LATERAL RESISTANCE: (CR) the imaginary point in the under-water body through which the forces of lateral resistance act. The center is on the axis about which the board pivots.

CENTERPLANE: an imaginary plane that extends upwards from the centerline. The mast should be tipped foreward and back along the centerplane while steering.

CLEW: rear most and outer corner of the sail. Point at which the outhaul is attached.

CLEW HANDLE: a narrow strip of nylon webbing sewn onto the clew area to help adjust outhaul tension.

CLOSED HAULED: sailing as close as possible to the wind. The wind is coming from ahead at an angle of about 45° to the centerline.

CLOSE REACH: point of sail between beam reach and close hauled.

COMING ABOUT: turning the front of the board into and through the wind so that the wind now comes from the other side.

CRINGLE: also called a grommet. A term used for the eyes at the tack and clew.

DACRON: a brand name for a commonly used type of woven polyester sailcloth.

DAGGERBOARD: serves the same purpose as the centerboard. Regular daggerboards slip straight through the well and have only oneposition while kick back daggerboards can rotate around an axle and are multi-positional but they don't recess into the hull like a centerboard.

DAGGERBOARD TRUNK: also called daggerboard well. An opening along the centerline of the hull that goes completely through the board and is where the centerboard or daggerboard is inserted.

DECKING: is the non-skid surface of the board. It may be molded in or applied separately.

DISPLACEMENT BOARD: a sailboard hull that usually has a pointed vee shaped bow and rounded bottom much line a conventional sailboat. They push through the water, displacing it as they move forward.

DOWNHAUL: a line which attaches the sail to the universal joint. It is tied between the tack of the sail and the universal.

DRIFT: movement over the ground due to currents or tidal streams, also movement through the water when an object is blown to leeward by the wind.

EASE: easing wind pressure on the sail by letting out on the sail or sheet hand to let the sail out further. Easing the sail is sheeting out.

EYE OF THE WIND: the direction from which the true wind is blowing.

FALLING OFF: turning away from the wind. Also the act of leaving the board and entering the water.

FAST TACK: coming about by stepping quickly around the front without using the uphaul.

FAT HEAD SAIL: term used to describe a sail which has one or more full length battens to support an enlarged head and increased roacharea.

FLAT BOTTOM BOARD: a sailboard hull that generally has a flat bottom all the way from the bow to the stern. In heavier air, these boards plane and usually ride on top of or skim over the waters surface.

FLOATER: a type of short board. They are usually the longest of the short boards and have maximum floatation for their size.

FOOT: (of sail) the bottom edge or base of the sail.

FOOT: to sail faster upwind by heading off slightly to obtain more speed rather than pointing closer to the wind.

FORE: at, toward or near the bow or front end of the board.

FORWARD: towards the bow (front end) of the board.

FREE SAIL SYSTEM: a type of sail system incorporating an articulated mast foot which allows the sail assembly (rig) the freedom of movement to turn or rotate in any direction. It is what distinguishes sailboards from other sailcraft.

FREESTYLE: the name given to the hot-dogging maneuvers executed by a boardsailor. It includes everything from graceful body turns to the more advanced sail and board tricks.

FRONT FOOT: the foot closest to the front of the board.

FRONT HAND: the hand closest to the front of the board; the mast hand; the hand that holds the mast on the centerplane.

FUNBOARD: a loose term given to sailboards that are designed to produce maximum speeds with the minimum of effort. Most have footstraps, the capabilities for up to three skegs, an adjustable mast track and a fully retractable centerboard which differentiates them from the short boards. (By the way, all sailboards are fun, not just funboards).

GROMMET: the eyelet usually found at the tack and clew of a sail.

HARDEN: bring the sail closer to the body with the sail hand. Hardening the sail is sheeting in.

HARNESS: a devise used to aid sailing by attaching the body trunk directly to the booms permitting the sailor to take much of the strain and load off the arms.

HEAD: the top area of a sail.

HEADER: a windshift which causes you to turn away from your chosen destination.

HEAD OFF: (bear off) to turn or steer away from the wind (opp.-head up).

HEAD TO WIND: headed directly into the wind.

HEAD UP: to turn or steer towards the wind. (opp. - head off).

H.E.L.P.: Heat Escape Loss Position, used for hypothermia.

HIGH ASPECT RATIO: (HAR) usually used to describe surf sails. Generally they have longer head to tack and/or shortened mast to clew lengths. The higher the aspect, the shorter the booms and the higher and further forward the center of effort. They may be either Flathead, Plump Head or Pin Head designs.

HIGH CLEW: a sail which has a clew which is set higher than normal.

HIGH WIND DAGGERBOARD: a fixed daggerboard of reduced dimensions which is designed to move the boards center of lateral resistance further aft.

HIGH WIND SAIL: generally for windy days with winds Beaufort Force 4-6 (11 to 27 knots). Sail area is generally between 43 and 53 sq. ft. (4.0 and 5.0 sq.m.) Low aspect ratio high wind sails also make good training sails for beginners and students.

HIKING OUT: leaning to windward to counteract the pull of the sail.

HORIZONTAL CUT: description given to the horizontal panel layout for conventional sails.

HYPOTHERMIA: a state of reduced mobility caused by excessive loss of body heat through exposure to cold; can be fatal. Hypothermia refers to lowered body temperature and loss of heat from the body core, which includes the head, neck, chest and groin area.

IN: when the back arm pulls in towards the center of the board to fill the sail with wind.

INHAUL: a line attaching the booms to the mast.

IRONS: head to wind and dead in the water with no steerage.

JIBE: to change the direction of the board by turning the front of the board away from the wind and stepping around the back of the board to the other side. To change the side of which the booms are held while the stern passes through the eye of the wind.

JIBING: turning the board and changing the sail and sailors position from one tack or side to the other with the stern passing through the wind while the bow passes away from the wind.

LEECH: the back edge or outhaul side of the sail running from the head to the clew.

LEECH CUT: also known as vertical cut. A more recent form of sail cutting achieved by laying out the sail panels so that they radiate from the head and are parallel to the leech. Commonly used on surf sails because in theory they better accomodate the stresses imposed on a sail by stronger winds and crashing waves.

LEE SHORE: the shore that is downwind of your present position.

LEEWARD: the term used to refer to the downwind side of something. (opp. - windward).

LEEWAY: sideways movement through the water. The leeway angle is the angle between the direction in which the board is pointing and the course which it sails through the water.

LIFT: a windshift which helps take you towards your chosen destination.

LIGHT WIND SAIL: a sail used in light winds with an area usually in excess of 75 sq.ft. (7.0 sq.m.).

LINE: what a rope is called when it is on a sailcraft.

LUFF: (n) the front, leading or mast edge of the sail from the head to the tack.

LUFFING: (also the verb to luff) anytime the sail is not completely filled with wind. When the sailor allows the sail to flutter with the mast facing the wind and the clew pointing in the direction of the wind.

LUFF UP: to change direction and sail a course closer to the wind.

MAST: the long, cylindrical piece that fits into the sail and provides vertical support for the sail.

MAST BASE: the top part of the universal which fits into the mast.

MAST BEND: a method of bending the mast to evaluate precise characteristics for cutting a sail.

MAST FOOT: the bottom part of the universal which fits into the mast step.

MAST HAND: the forward hand; the hand holding the booms that is closest to the mast. (opp. - sheethand)

MAST SLEEVE: also called luff sleeve. It is the tubular leading edge of the sail into which the mast is placed.

MAST STEP: a slot or hole in the board which the universal plugs into to hold the sail to the board.

MINI SAIL: the smallest of sails. They are generally for children and beginners and range from 20 to 40 sq. ft. (1.8 to 3.7 sq. m.).

MYLAR: used in the manufacturing of sails. Mylar (a polyester film) is laminated or bonded together with polyester yarn to come up with what is commonly called mylar sailcloth.

OFFSHORE BREEZE: a breeze that blows from the land to the water.

OFF THE WIND: any course other than close hauled.

OLYMPIC COURSE: commonly used in triangle racing consisting of 6 legs in the following order: beat, reach, reach, beat, run, beat.

ONSHORE BREEZE: a breeze that blows from the water to the land.

ON THE WIND: close hauled.OUT: the back arm extends out, away from the center of the board and body to spill wind out of the sail.

OUTHAUL: line at the end of the booms that holds the clew of the sail in place. Controls the amount of curvature in sail.

OVERLAP: in racing, boats are overlapped if an imaginary line drawn perpendicular to the centerline of one boat crosses any part of another boat.

OVERSTAND: (said of marks in racing) to sail more upwind of a mark than is necessary to get around it.

PAN AM BOARD: is a state of the art racing funboard which is usually 12'6" to 13'6" long (375cm to 405cm) and extremely light for its length at around 30 to 35 pounds (13.5-16 kilos). It usually has many footstraps (normally between 8 and 13), a fully retractable centerboard, an adjustable mast track and a narrow pintail stern.

PEARL: a board pearls when the nose drops enough to dig in and slow or stop the board.

PIN HEAD SAIL: normal shaped sail with a pointed head. Opposite to a fat head sail, it may or may not have battens and either a straight or hollow leech.

PITCH: is the boards rotation about the horizontal axis.

PITCHING: is when a sailor runs fore and aft on the board causing the bow and stern to go up and down.

PLANING: is when the board is riding on top of or skimming over the waters surface.

PLUMPHEAD SAIL: has a built up roach area but not as large as a fathead sail. It is an intermediate shape between a pinhead and a fathead sail.

POINT UP: to turn more upwind.

POLYESTER: material used to produce a variety of sailcloths.

POLYURETHANE FOAM: a common core material in sailboard hulls.

PORT: left side of the board when looking forward. (opp.-starboard).

PORT TACK: sailing course in which the booms are to starboard, with the wind coming over the port side of the booms. If your left hand is forward you are on a port tack.

POWERHEAD SAIL: see Plumphead sail.

PROFILE: also called chord. This is the maximum draft position. It is located about 35% to 45% from the luff when measured over its length between the mast sleeve and leech.

RADIAL CUT: the many varieties and cuts of sails where the panels radiate from a central point.

RAILS: the edges that run the length of the port and starboard sides of the board. They can be hard or soft depending on the angle formed when the top and bottom meet.

RAKING THE MAST: term used to describe the tipping of the mast fore or aft and/or windward or leeward. Used when changing directions.

REACH: sailing with the wind from the side.

REGATTA SAIL: generally used for open class and one design racing. Sizes vary from manufacturer to manufacturer but the maximum limit has recently been 72 sq. ft. (6.8 sq.m).

RIG: the complete sail assembly including the mast, booms, sail, battens and universal.

ROACH: area of sailcloth built up beyond the straight line between the clew and head and supported by battens. Any twist is created by the roach which must be even to avoid stress on the battens.

ROCKER: is the vertical deviation on the underside of the after section of a hull.

ROLL: is the boards rotation about the longitudinal axis.

ROLLING: is when the board tips from side to side.

ROPE TACK: to come about grabbing hold of the uphaul as you step around to the other side.

RULES OF THE ROAD: standardized means of deciding who has the "right-of-way" in situations where yachts meet.

RUN: sailing with the wind from astern.

RUNNING: sailing before the wind when the wind blows from astern.

SAIL AREA: see Area.

SAILBOARD: the generic term for what you sail on when you are boardsailing.

SAILBOARDER: see Boardsailor.

SAILBOARDING: see Boardsailing.

SAIL CLOTH WEIGHT: is usually weighed in U.S. ounces or grams per square meter (g/m²). U.S. ounces multiplied by 42 gives you grams per square meter.

SAIL EMBLEM: a design on a sail used to designate a particular brand of board or weight group.

SAIL CLOCK: a reference used to teach the basics of sailing in relation to wind direction and sometimes easier to explain to a beginner than the nautical terms for points of sail.

SAIL NUMBER: a personal number used for identification purposes when racing or for identifying your property.

SAIL TUNING: adjusting the sail camber to match the wind strength.

SCOOP: is the vertical deviation of the underside of the forward section of the board.

SEMI DISPLACEMENT BOARD: a sailboard hull that incorporates a pointed vee shaped bow section up front and a flat bottom from the mid-section aft.

SEMI FLOATER: (also called semi-sinker) a type of short board which may either be water started or uphauled depending on the sailors weight.

SEMI SINKER: see Semi-Floater.

SHEETHAND: the aft hand; the hand holding the booms that is farthest from the mast. (opp.- mast hand)

SHEETING IN: pulling in with the back hand so as to harden the sail and fill it completely with wind. (opp. - sheeting out).

SHEETING OUT: letting out with the back hand so as to ease the sail and let the wind spill from the sail. (opp. - sheeting in).

SHORT BOARD: a type of board which is small and maneuverable with footstraps, many with the capabilities of up to three skegs and most with an adjustable mast track. Most do not have centerboards or daggerboards which differentiates them from funboards.

SIMULATOR: a dry land teaching aid that simulates the feel of boardsailing and is helpful in the initial stages of instruction.

SINKER: a type of short board. Usually the shortest of the short boards with minimal floatation. The total volume will not support the sailor and rig unless planing. It must be waterstarted.

SKEG: the fin underneath the back end of the board. Aids in directional stability.

SPIN OUT: is when the skeg looses its traction in the water. It is caused by a combination of air being forced down the sides of the skeg and too much sideways foot pressure.

SPREADER BAR: a base plate for a harness hook that is extended laterally over the ribs to eliminate the crushing effect of a conventional harness.

STARBOARD: right side of the board when looking forward. (opp.-port).

STARBOARD TACK: sailing course in which the booms are to port with the wind coming over the starboard side of the booms. If your right hand is forward then you are on a starboard tack.

STERN: aft (rear) end of the board.

STORM SAIL: a sail designed for very windy days in excess of Beaufort Force 6 (27 knots). Sail area is generally between 30 and 48 sq. ft. (2.8 and 4.5 sq.m.).

TACK: (of sail) the inside bottom corner of the sail near the mast base.

TACK: (v)
1. to change direction of the board by turning the front of the board through the eye of the wind and stepping around the front of the board to the opposite side. To change the side of which the booms are held by steering the front through the eye of the wind. (opp.-jibe).

2. the tack you are on is generally designated by the side of the board (starboard or port) that the wind is blowing over.

3. to work to windward by sailing on alternate courses, so the wind is first on one side of the board and then the other.

TAIL: the aftermost part of the board.

TANDEM: a lengthened board designed for two sails and two sailors.

TANDEM FREESTYLE: when two sailors sail together on a standard board (one sail) and perform and execute tricks and freestyle maneuvers.

TEAM RACING: a contest in which the individual boardsailors overall position counts towards the total points of his team. It is therefore possible to win the race as an individual but to have your team lose.

TELL TALE: small pieces of light material (such as wool or audio tape) that are positioned on the sail to indicate the air flow over the sail.

TOWING EYE: a hole or attachment on the bow of many sailboards where line may be passed or tied off through.

TRAPEZE: a harness system that attaches to the mast above the booms height. Commonly used with the Wing Mast.

TRIANGLE RACING: racing over a course that consists of at least a beat, reach and run.

TRIM: to pull the sail in using the back (sheet or sail) hand until the sail rides more towards the centerline.

TRI-RADIAL: a sail in which three sail panels radiate from the head.

TWIST: is the result of wind pressure on the sail which causes the leech to twist or open. When the leech is twisting off it means that the twist is so extreme as to distort the aerodynamic shape of the sail.

TWIST POINT: the point of the leech of the sail between the clew and the luff where the sail opens to depower the rig. The twist point is not a stationary point.

UNDERLAY: used when your final approach tack to an upwind mark still leaves the mark to windward.

UNIVERSAL: the design or joint at the base of the mast which allows the rig the freedom of movement to turn in any direction by the articulation of the mast foot while connecting it to the board. It is this joint that makes a sailboard a freesail system and unique from other sailcraft.

UPHAUL: the line used to pull the rig from the water.

UPWIND: between you and the direction the wind is coming from.

VEER: the action the wind is said to do when it shifts to come more from the left.

VERTICAL CUT: see Leech Cut.

VISUAL REFERENCE POINTS: beginners may not be able to readily determine the wind direction. Visual reference points such as trees or buildings may help beginners to get their bearings.

WATER: the actions and movements of water may be broken down into several groups;
1. Breaking Surf; waves which break on approaching the shore or shallow water.
2. Breaking Waves; the crests of the waves curl over and break.
3. Choppy Seas; short steep seas which do not all move in the same direction.
4. Cross Seas; waves which approach the board from abeam.
5. Currents and Tidal Streams; horizontal movement of water. Currents often flow in only one direction, or may alter direction due to natural causes such as wind; tidal streams change direction regularly in response to the rise and fall of the tide.
6. Following Seas; seas overtaking the board from astern.
7. Head Sea; waves which approach the board from ahead.
8. Swell; long seas which are not due to the wind of the moment.

WATERSTART: a freestyle trick that developed into a necessity for starting on sinkers and semi-sinkers. Basically the sailor lies in the water out to windward of the board and holds the sail out of the water and lets the sail pull him up onto the board.

WEATHER: The general atmospheric condition as regards to temperature, moistures, winds etc.

WEATHER: windward.

WETSUIT: a garment made of neoprene and worn to retain body heat in or on the water.

WIND: the actions and movements of wind may be broken down into several groups;
1. True Wind; the actual wind that strikes a sailboard which is not moving.
2. Induced Wind; the speed of the board through the water gives rise to the induced wind. Also called a head wind.
3. Apparent Wind; the wind which arises when the true wind is combined with the induced wind. The apparent wind is used to sail the board, and is the wind felt when the boardsailor sails through the water.
4. Calm; no wind or very light wind.
5. Freshening Wind; a wind increasing in strength.
6. Gust; a sudden increase in wind speed.
7. Backing Wind; when the wind direction changes in an anti-clockwise direction.
8. Veering Wind; when the wind direction changes in a clockwise direction.
9. Heading Wind; when the wind direction changes and comes from further forward at a more acute angle to the course being sailed.

10. Freeing Wind; when the wind direction changes and comes from further aft.

11. Fluky Wind; when the direction of the wind alters continuously.

12. Offshore Wind; wind which blows from the land to the water.

13. Onshore Wind; wind which blows from the water to the land.

14. Fresh Wind; force 5, 17-21 knots.

15. Strong Wind; force 6, 22-27 knots.

WINDOW: panels of transparent plastic sewn into sails to allow you to see to leeward.

WINDWARD: the side which is closest to the wind. The upwind side of something. Toward the direction from which the wind is coming. (opp. - leeward).

WINDWARD SHORE: the shore that is upwind of your present position.

WING: is found on the rail of a board and is produced by reducing the beam or altering the plan form within a small distance.

WING MAST: a mast with an oval, streamlined shape in a fore and aft plane. It is designed to reduce drag on the rig.

YACHT: a general term for a water vessel used exclusively for pleasure.

YAW: the rotation of the board about the vertical axis.

YAW: the difference between the direction of motion and the direction the board is pointed.

CHAPTER XIII

ANSWERS TO TEST QUESTIONS;

BRIEF ESSAY TEST:
1. Never leave the board.
2. Sailing with the wind coming over the right side of the board pushing the rig out over the left side of the board.
3. Sailing with the wind coming over the left side of the board pushing the rig out over the right side of the board.
4. A course change where the bow passes through the eye of the wind.
5. A course change where the stern passes through the eye of the wind.
6. By tacking or beating to windward.
7. Stand with the feet straddling the centerline and move the sail side to side.
8. By executing one of the many self rescue techniques.
9. The wind may get stronger, the waves may get higher, you may get overpowered and risk fatigue and hypothermia.
10. Dark, towering cumulus clouds and muggy windless weather.

MULTIPLE CHOICE TEST:
1. D.
2. C.
3. B.
4. A.
5. B.
6. D.
7. C.
8. B
9. D
10. A

WRITTEN MATCHING TEST:
1. 3 - Sail
    6 - Board or Hull
    10 - Bow
    8 - Uphaul
    1 - Wishbone Booms
    4 - Daggerboard
    5 - Universal
    7 - Stern
    2 - Mast
    9 - Skeg
2. 1 - True Wind
    3 - Induced Wind
    2 - Apparent Wind
3. 1 - Luff
    2 - Clew
    5 - Leech
    3 - Head
    4 - Foot
    6 - Tack

CHAPTER XIV

INDEX